W9-BZB-317

We Lived the Game:

Legends of Indiana

Women's Basketball

Dick Denny

Blue River F
Indianapolis, I

WHITE RIVER BRANCH
1664 LIBRARY BLVD.
GREENWOOD, IN 46142

We Lived the Game: Legends of Indiana Women's Basketball
Copyright © 2011 by Dick Denny

All rights reserved under International and Pan-American
Copyright Conventions

No part of this book may be reproduced, stored in a database or
other retrieval system, or transmitted in any form, by any means,
including mechanical, photocopy, recording or otherwise, without
the prior written permission of the publisher.

ISBN-13: 978-1-935628-07-1

Cover Design: Phil Velikan
Cover Photos (L-R): Katie Douglas, Lin Dunn, Stephanie White
(courtesy of the Indiana Fever); Bria Goss (courtesy of Ben Davis
High School); Jennifer Jacoby (courtesy of Jennifer Jacoby);
1976 Indiana State Champions, Warsaw High School (courtesy
of Judi Warren).

Layout: MaryKay Hruskocy Scott
Proofreading and Editing: MaryKay Hruskocy Scott

Printed in the United States of America
10 9 8 7 6 5 4 3 2 1

Blue River Press
Distributed by Cardinal Publishers Group
Tom Doherty Company, Inc.
www.cardinalpub.com

To my daughter, Shannon Thompson, who introduced me to the pleasure of high school girls' basketball when she played varsity competition three years for Coach Chuck Boehlke at Indianapolis North Central from 1989 to 1992.

About the Author

On April 16, 2011, Dick Denny was inducted into the Indiana Sportswriters & Sportscaster Association Hall of Fame.

The honor culminated a 55-year journalism career that included stints at the *Muncie Star*, *Fort Wayne Journal-Gazette*, *Chicago Tribune*, *Bowlers Journal Magazine* and *The Indianapolis News* and *The Indianapolis Star*.

Since retiring from Indianapolis Newspapers Inc. in 1997, Denny has written four sports books about Mike Aulby, former Professional Bowlers Association stand out from Carmel; *Glory Days: Legends of Indiana High School Basketball*; *Coach: Reflections of Indiana Football Legend Dick Dullaghan*; and We Played The Game: Legends of Indiana Women's Basketball.

About the Book

One of my first assignments as a member of *The Indianapolis News* sports department was to cover the Western Tennis Tournament at Woodstock.

Title IX was about to be introduced and Billie Jean King, whom I had first watched play tennis at River Forest, Illinois, while a member of the *Chicago Tribune* sports staff, would spend long stretches of her off-time at Woodstock telling the late Bob Williams of *The Star* and me what the virtues of Title IX would be for the female gender.

I was reminded of Billie Jean's passion for gender equity when I interviewed the players, coaches and administrators featured in *We Lived the Game: Legends of Indiana Women's Basketball.* These people illustrate how far girls' high school basketball has come since the Indiana High School Athletic Association (IHSAA) sanctioned a state tournament for females in 1976, just four years after Title IX was approved on June 23, 1972.

Eleven of the players I selected to write about became Indiana Miss Basketballs—Judi Warren (1976), Chanda Kline (1978), LaTaunya Pollard-Romanazzi (1979), Maria Stack (1980), Cheryl Cook (1981), Sharon Versyp (1984), Vicki Hall (1988), Jennifer Jacoby (1991), Stephanie White (1995), Lisa Shepherd-Stidham (1997) and April McDivitt-Foster (1999).

White and two other players featured in the book—Katie Douglas and Kelly Faris—have won NCAA Division I championships, Douglas and White at Purdue in 1999 and Faris as a freshman with the University of Connecticut in 2010. Faris has become a perennial champion, winning a Class 2A state championship all four years at Heritage Christian High School.

ACKNOWLEDGEMENTS

Spend a little time at the Indiana High School Athletic Association headquarters in Indianapolis or the Indiana Basketball Hall of Fame in New Castle and your appreciation of the Hoosier state's unique sport will soar.

When I set out to chronicle the history of the female gender in Indiana basketball, I sought the assistance of the IHSAA and Hall of Fame staffs. I was rewarded immensely.

Chris Kaufman, IHSAA communications director, and Jason Wille, sports information director, were unstinting in their efforts to answer every question—and there were many—I threw at them. We had many completions.

Chris May, executive director at the Hall of Fame, and his two aides, Sharon Roberts, assistant director, and Becky Beavers, publications manager, welcomed me at every turn, either seeking facts or photos.

After almost a year of writing, my editor, MaryKay Hruskocy Scott, whom I got to know and respect when she worked for Dale Ratermann in media relations for the Indiana Pacers, put her fine touch to my project. She now does work for Tom Doherty at Cardinal Publishers Group.

With the help of the above professionals, I hope you enjoy *We Lived the Game: Legends of Indiana Women's Basketball*.

—Dick Denny

FOREWORD

No one in the Indiana media has more knowledge about high school girls' basketball in the Hoosier state than former *Indianapolis Star* prep writer Pat McKee, who is now girls' basketball coach at Columbus North High School.

McKee was a women's basketball assistant coach for four years at Butler University and for 16 more years was head coach at Mount Vernon and Indiana's First club teams.

Pat and I have had a long-time relationship since I wrote about sports down the hall from *The Star* while at *The Indianapolis News*. He graciously agreed to put his expertise to work in writing the following forward for my book about many of the luminaries—players, coaches, referees and administrators—that I selected to feature in this female version of *Hoosier Hysteria*.

—Dick Denny

From Warsaw in 1976 to Jeffersonville in 2011 and 76 champions that have been crowned between them.

From Judi Warren to Bria Goss and 34 Miss Basketballs in between.

From Janice Soyez to Bobbi DeKemper, Tom May, Pete Pritchett, Donna Sullivan, Mike McCroskey, Jan Conner, Cinda Brown, Dave Riley, Donna Cheatham, Mike Armstrong, Alan Vickrey, Stan Benge and hundreds of coaches who have inspired thousands of young women to excel on the basketball court and off it.

All of those mentioned and many more have etched their names into the history of Indiana high school girls' basketball, a game that has improved immensely since the Indiana High School Athletic Association sanctioned the first formal state tournament at the conclusion of the 1975-76 season.

Warren was the star player, and Soyez the coach, for Warsaw's first state championship, but they would be the first to tell you that the seed for Indiana girls' basketball had been planted much earlier—that they just happened to be at the right place at the right time to receive state-wide recognition in the sport.

Decades earlier, there was girls' basketball in Indiana with players such as Huntingburg's Ruth Heitman and Wakarusa's Lenore Doering starring for teams in the 1920s and 1930s, respectively. Somewhere along the way, however, it became considered "unladylike" for girls to participate in basketball. Thus, while boys' basketball was growing hugely popular with players and fans throughout the 1940s, '50s and '60s, girls' basketball essentially disappeared from the state's consciousness.

Although there was some girls' basketball offered through the Girls Athletic Association (GAA) in the 1960s, the sport's profile didn't rise again in the land of Hoosier Hysteria until the IHSAA—at the urging of Patricia Roy, Conner, Sullivan, Margaret Kelly, Florida Lowry, Bernita Adkins and others—agreed to oversee girls' sports and offered its first girls' basketball state tournament in 1975-76.

Roy and then-IHSAA commissioner Phil Eskew had a steak-dinner wager over how many fans would attend the first girls' state finals.

Roy was thrilled when Warsaw, led by the charismatic Warren, along with Bloomfield, East Chicago Roosevelt and Indianapolis Tech, brought more than 13,000 fans to two sessions at Indianapolis' Hinkle Fieldhouse. There Warsaw capped an unbeaten season with a 57-52 victory over Bloomfield for the championship.

That season was a jump-start as East Chicago Roosevelt, featuring superstar LaTaunya Pollard, captured the 1977 title. Warsaw, this time led by Chanda Kline and Anita Folk, won another crown in 1978 and Pollard-led Roosevelt claimed its second title in 1979.

The 1980s was a decade of phenomenal growth with players such as Indianapolis Washington's Cheryl Cook, Heritage's Jody Beerman, Mishawaka's Sharon Versyp, Crown Point's Nancy Cowan and Anne Kvachkoff, Austin's Jodie Whitaker, Indianapolis Warren Central's Linda Godby, Anderson's Dana Wilkerson, Indianapolis Brebeuf Jesuit's Vicki Hall, DeKalb's MaChelle Joseph, Scottsburg's Renee Westmoreland and Noblesville's Courtney Cox raising individual skills to a new level.

At the same time, teams from Crown Point, Warren Central, Fort Wayne Northrop, Noblesville, Scottsburg, Rushville and Benton Central (Oxford) were becoming well-known regulars at the state level and crowds mushroomed—more than 31,000 attended the two-session state finals in 1989.

The early-to-mid '90s brought more of the same with players such as Jennifer Jacoby of Rossville, Cindy Lamping of Batesville, Abby Conklin and Kristin Mattox of Charlestown, Tiffany Longworth and Debbie Benziger of Kokomo and Carrie Mount, Amy Walker and Marlo Inman of Bedford North Lawrence becoming well-known names.

Then came Stephanie White, the Seeger superstar who set the then-state scoring record, drew crowds to girls' games unlike ever before and sometimes was described as a female Damon Bailey, the boys' all-time leading scorer from Bedford who had been a similar phenom just five years before.

By the end of the decade, Perry Meridian's Katie Douglas, Richmond's Lisa Shepherd, Lake Central's Kelly Komara and Kristina

Divjak, Martinsville's April Traylor and Kristen Bodine, North Central's Kyle Black, Connersville's April McDivitt and New Albany's Kennitra Johnson were leaving their mark. And others such as Ben Davis' Shyra Ely and Ashley Allen as well as Wawasee's Shanna Zolman and Beech Grove's Katie Gearlds were beginning to be heard.

Simultaneous to the rise of those players was Bedford North Lawrence's three consecutive state finals appearances that included the 1991 title, Kokomo's back-to-back championships and Lake Central stopping the Lady 'Kats one game short of a three-peat in 1994. Huntington North and Center Grove (Greenwood) followed with outstanding groups. Then there was Martinsville, led by Traylor and Bodine, which won the final non-class tournament in 1997 and the first Class 4A in 1998.

The '97 semi-state with defending champ Center Grove, Douglas-led Perry Meridian and Martinsville saw an overflow crowd at Southport Fieldhouse. That environment was matched two years later when Johnson-led New Albany outlasted McDivitt-led Connersville en route to the '99 Class 4A title and four years after that when Gearlds-led Beech Grove edged North Harrison in overtime on the way to the 2003 Class 3A crown.

Over the last decade Ben Davis has claimed four 4A state titles, North Central two others and South Bend Washington captured one with three additional runner-up finishes. There also were memorable runs by Terry Haute South, Castle and Carmel. Fort Wayne Bishop Luers won five titles, including four in a row at one point in Class 2A and 3A, while Heritage Christian captured four consecutive crowns in Class 2A and Tri-Central took three straight in Class A.

Ely and Allen were Ben Davis' early-decade leaders, while Alex Bentley and Goss are more recent Giant headliners. South Ben Washington's Skylar Diggins was a national player of the year in 2009, while Zollman (now the all-time leading scorer with 3,085 career points), Gearlds, Heritage Christian's Kelly Faris, North Central's Amber Harris, Brebeuf Jesuit's Ta'Shia Phillips and Oak Hill's Courtney Moses were among other big names. Harris became a WNBA champion when the Minnesota Lynx won the

2011 title. Ruth Riley also is an Indiana prepster who has been a WNBA champion.

Thanks to Dick Denny and his research. I look forward to learning more about the remarkable people he chose to write about. I also look forward to seeing the teams and players of the future who will write their names in what has become the fabulous history of Indiana girls' basketball.

—Pat McKee

CHAMPIONSHIP TEAMS

HINKLE FIELDHOUSE, INDIANAPOLIS

YEAR	CHAMPION	COACH	RECORD
1976	Warsaw Tigers	Janice Soyez	22-0
1977	East Chicago Roosevelt Rough Riders	Roberta DeKemper	24-0
1978	Warsaw Tigers	Janice Soyez	22-0
1979	East Chicago Roosevelt Rough Riders	Roberta DeKemper	23-0

MARKET SQUARE ARENA, INDIANAPOLIS

YEAR	CHAMPION	COACH	RECORD
1980	Indianapolis Southport Cardinals	Marilyn Ramsey	25-2
1981	Evansville Reitz Panthers	Louise Owen	26-1
1982	Monroeville Heritage Patriots	Cheri Gilbert	24-2
1983	Bedford North Lawrence Stars	Pete Pritchett	26-1
1984	Crown Point Bulldogs	Tom May	26-0
1985	Crown Point Bulldogs	Tom May	25-4
1986	Fort Wayne Northrop Bruins	Dave Riley	29-0
1987	Noblesville Millers	Ray Lyttle	27-0
1988	Fort Wayne Snider Panthers	Lamar Kilmer	27-1
1989	Scottsburg Warriors	Donna Cheatham	26-1
1990	Huntington North Vikings	Fred Fields	26-4
1991	Bedford North Lawrence Stars	Pete Pritchett	29-0
1992	Kokomo Wildkats	Mike McCroskey	29-1
1993	Kokomo Wildkats	Mike McCroskey	27-1
1994	St. John Lake Central Indians	Tom Megyesi	25-1
1995	Huntington North Vikings	Fred Fields	26-1
1996	Center Grove Trojans	Joe Lentz	25-2
1997	Martinsville Artesians	Jan Conner	26-1
1998	Class 4A: Martinsville Artesians	Jan Conner	29-0
	Class 3A: West Lafayette Red Devils	Steve Dietrich	23-5
	Class 2A: Huntingburg Southridge Raiders	Stan Roesner	22-6
	Class A: Bloomfield Cardinals	Paula Fettig	26-2

YEAR	CHAMPION	COACH	RECORD
1999	Class 4A: New Albany Bulldogs	Angie Hinton	26-0
	Class 3A: Nappanee NorthWood Panthers	Steve Neff	24-3
	Class 2A: Fort Wayne Bishop Luers Knights	Gary Andrews	27-1
	Class A: Frankfort Clinton Prairie Gophers	Connie Garrett	25-2

HINKLE FIELDHOUSE, INDIANAPOLIS

YEAR	CHAMPION	COACH	RECORD
2000	Class 4A: Indianapolis Ben Davis Giants	Stan Benge	28-0
	Class 3A: Indianapolis Cathedral Irish	Linda Bamrick	27-1
	Class 2A: Fort Wayne Bishop Luers Knights	Gary Andrews	28-0
	Class A: Bourbon Triton Trojans	Mark Heeter	20-7

CONSECO FIELDHOUSE, INDIANAPOLIS

YEAR	CHAMPION	COACH	RECORD
2001	Class 4A: Indianapolis Ben Davis Giants	Stan Benge	27-2
	Class 3A: Indianapolis Cathedral Irish	Linda Bamrick	29-1
	Class 2A: Fort Wayne Bishop Luers Knights	Gary Andrews	28-0
	Class A: Bourbon Triton Trojans	Mark Heeter	23-3
2002	Class 4A: Terre Haute South Braves	Alan Maroska	25-2
	Class 3A: Fort Wayne Bishop Luers Knights	Teri Rosinski	21-5
	Class 2A: Hanover Southwestern Rebels	Donna Cheatham	25-2
	Class A: Cayuga North Vermillion Falcons	Ken Gentrup	25-1
2003	Class 4A: Kokomo Wildkats	Charlie Hall	26-0
	Class 3A: Indianapolis Beech Grove Hornets	Dawn McNew	28-1
	Class 2A: Middletown Shenandoah Raiders	Todd Salkoski	24-5
	Class A: Fairland Triton Central Tigers	Kathie Layden	23-4
2004	Class 4A: Indianapolis North Central Panthers	Alan Vickrey	23-3
	Class 3A: Indianapolis Brebeuf Braves	Kendall Kreinhagen	26-3
	Class 2A: Rochester Zebras	Tony Stesiak	25-2
	Class A: Fairland Triton Central Tigers	Kathie Layden	21-6
2005	Class 4A: Indianapolis North Central Panthers	Alan Vickrey	20-7
	Class 3A: South Bend St. Joseph's Indians	Mike Megyese	25-1
	Class 2A: Middletown Shenandoah Raiders	Todd Salkoski	22-5
	Class A: Fairland Triton Central Tigers	Kathie Layden	19-7

YEAR	CHAMPION	COACH	RECORD
2006	Class 4A: Newburgh Castle Knights	Wayne Allen	25-3
	Class 3A: Fort Wayne Bishop Luers Knights	Teri Rosinski	24-4
	Class 2A: Indianapolis Heritage Christian Eagles	Rick Risinger	25-3
	Class A: Lafayette Central Catholic Knights	Geoff Salmon	18-10
2007	Class 4A: South Bend Washington Panthers	Marilyn Coddens	28-1
	Class 3A: Indianapolis Brebeuf Braves	Kendall Kreinhagen	23-6
	Class 2A: Indianapolis Heritage Christian Eagles	Rick Risinger	26-3
	Class A: Hamlet Oregon-Davis Bobcats	Terry Minix	25-3
2008	Class 4A: Carmel Greyhounds	Scott Bowen	23-4
	Class 3A: Plymouth Rockies	Dave Cox	22-4
	Class 2A: Indianapolis Heritage Christian Eagles	Rick Risinger	27-1
	Class A: Fort Wayne Canterbury Cavaliers	Scott Kreiger	21-5

LUCAS OIL STADIUM, INDIANAPOLIS

YEAR	CHAMPION	COACH	RECORD
2009	Class 4A: Indianapolis Ben Davis Giants	Stan Benge	30-0
	Class 3A: Fort Wayne Elmhurst Trojans	Mark Redding	25-2
	Class 2A: Indianapolis Heritage Christian Eagles	Rick Risinger	26-1
	Class A: Fort Wayne Canterbury Cavaliers	Scott Kreiger	23-4

ALLEN COUNTY WAR MEMORIAL COLISEUM, FORT WAYNE

YEAR	CHAMPION	COACH	RECORD
2010	Class 4A: Indianapolis Ben Davis Giants	Stan Benge	28-0
	Class 3A: Fort Wayne Concordia Cadets	Dave Miller	24-3
	Class 2A: Austin Eagles	Jared Petersen	26-2
	Class A: Fort Wayne Canterbury Cavaliers	Scott Kreiger	25-2
2011	Class 4A: Jeffersonville	Chad Gilbert	28-2
	Class 3A: Evansville Memorial	Bruce Dockery	28-1
	Class 2A: Fort Wayne Bishop Luers	Denny Renier	24-2
	Class A: Vincennes Rivet	Tim Young	28-0

TABLE OF CONTENTS

STAND UP AND CHEER

JUDI WARREN

Homer Stonebraker (Wingate, 1914 graduate), Robert "Fuzzy" Vandivier (Franklin, 1922) and John Wooden (Martinsville, 1928) were three pioneers of the Indiana state high school boys' basketball tournament which began in 1911 and is now considered one of the premier sporting events in the United States.

They all won state championships and are now in the Indiana Basketball Hall of Fame at New Castle.

Judi Warren has joined the above renowned trio in the pioneer class of Indiana high school basketball, having led Warsaw to the first girls' state tournament title in 1976, even though the first Indiana Miss Basketball and first recipient of the Pat Roy Mental Attitude Award humbly downplays those distinctions.

"I guess I have received the title of pioneer," said Warren, who was inducted into the Indiana Hall of Fame in 2002, two years after ending a 19-year coaching career at South Dearborn in Aurora, Maconaquah in Bunker Hill and Carmel. She is in her 22nd year teaching physical education to kindergartners through fifth graders in Carmel.

"I don't really consider myself that (a pioneer). I was just doing what I loved to do. Fortunately for me the Indiana High School Athletic Association came on with the state tournament at the right time. It became a hit and I became a success. But I was just doing what I normally would have done."

Judi was born in Warsaw, because there

was no hospital in nearby Claypool, where she grew up with her parents, Layne and Janet, and two older siblings, John and Jill.

"Claypool has around 350 people," she said. "It's pretty much a farming community. I went to elementary school there up to the seventh grade. That's when we consolidated and I went to Warsaw."

John is seven years older than Judi, Jill three years older.

"I was the baby and I was always the tomboy from the get-go," stated the 5-foot-1 Judi, who learned the joy of basketball at an early age being a ball chaser for John and his buddies playing on the family driveway.

"After a couple of years they allowed me to kinda play with 'em and teach me a few things. Most of them were nice to me, but I think that's how I got my competitiveness, because I didn't want 'em to be nice to me. I wanted 'em to play me a little tougher."

Judi was quite successful at ball-chasing for John and his buddies.

"What else do you do when there's nothing around but get a ball and make believe and play?" she said. "I had to do a lot of that, because after my brother graduated from high school he went away to the service. I was still in elementary school and I think there were 15 kids in my sixth-grade class.

"There were only four of us that lived in town. I'd get out there on the driveway and there was a bush right next to the chimney. I'd throw the ball against the chimney and receive the pass. Then I'd give a little fake to that bush and try to shoot over it."

One of the things Judi is most proud is that she helped make girls' basketball in Indiana viable and increasingly equitable with the boys' game.

"As a youngster there were no girls to emulate," she recalled. "Back in the 1960s when I was in elementary school, the high school boys' teams were really good. They had big bonfires before county tourneys and cakewalks at the ball games and penny pitches.

"A little kid remembers those things and gets excited about that kind of stuff. I was a jock from the get-go and outside from the time the sun came up until we'd get grounded a couple of times when we'd come home with the street lights on. My mom was always calling me in to practice the piano, bake cookies and do my 4-H stuff. I just wanted to be outside and play."

Judi shot well enough over that bush to be a four-year starter at point guard for Coach Janice Soyez's Warsaw Lady Tigers. The first three years were under sanctioning of the Girls Athletic Association.

"GAA was an opportunity to play," Judi said. "If you won, great; if you lost, no big deal. It wasn't like it was on the announcements the next day at school. And it wasn't that anybody read it in the newspaper or really cared too much. When it became sanctioned by the IHSAA and there was going to be a tournament like the boys, it really meant something.

"We didn't have any idea what people in Indianapolis were doing. We didn't play any teams down south. But in our own little area we would be very successful. We thought we were all-world and we could go out and win the state. We had been watching the boys' tournament for years and knew a little about what the tournament was going to be like."

Warsaw's Judi Warren (13) drives straight ahead in 1976 state championship game en route to victory and Miss Basketball status. (Photo courtesy of Judi Warren)

Judi wore No. 22 at Warsaw as a freshman.

"That's another thing," she remembered. "They didn't make girls' uniforms then. We just wore T-shirts and a pair of shorts. They just had iron-on numbers when we played in GAA. I believe in our junior year there was a company in Goshen that started making uniforms for girls. So we got new uniforms, but all the 20s were bigger sizes. All the teens were the smaller sizes, so I had to change numbers and I decided to go with No. 13. I was gonna make it lucky, and it worked."

In bringing Warsaw its first state basketball championship, Coach Soyez's team was 22-0.

"We were playing for the fun of the game," Warren said. "We had no idea where we were going, what we were doing. We would just show up and play.

"As far as scouting reports, coaches didn't go out and watch other teams play or trade game films. If you played a morning game, you'd see a little of what the other team was doing and maybe that would help you a little bit in the night game.

"It was such a neat experience with a group of girls that played together from junior high to our senior year, and we truly became family. To this day we're all really close and even though we don't get to see each other very often, when we do we pick right up just like old times."

Warsaw played in the 1976 Tippecanoe Valley sectional at Akron. The Lady Tigers defeated Plymouth, 52-38, in the championship game after seeing a 32-point lead slip to 11 in the closing minutes on Feb. 10, 1976, a Monday night.

"As sectionals seem to always do, we had a terrible snow storm," Judi said. "We could get to Tippecanoe Valley, but once we got there the snow kept coming and coming and coming. They had people that spent the night in the gym. I didn't ride the bus back to Warsaw, because Claypool was a little bit closer, so I got to go home with my parents. We were able to make it, but it was a nasty night."

Six days later Warsaw beat Wawasee, 50-36, for a regional title. That victory advanced the Lady Tigers to the semi-state where they defeated Norwell of Ossian, 63-56, and Wes Del of Gaston, 57-44, at Fort Wayne Northrop High School.

So it was on to the state finals in Indianapolis. What was that week like?

"From what I remember, it was supposed to be like a normal week," Judi said. "But that wasn't going to happen. We went down (to Indianapolis) on Friday and had the opportunity to go to the Final Four banquet. We also had practice at Hinkle Fieldhouse. That was awesome. I had never been to Hinkle before. We had never been to Indianapolis all that much, and staying in a hotel was a lot of fun."

As game time approached, Judi thought of "all those great guys that had the opportunity to play in Hinkle Fieldhouse. And you see all the birds flying around up there."

5

She also had to pinch herself thinking about the thousands of fans who would see the girls play in a first IHSAA state finals.

"When we started the season there were maybe 50 people at a game," Judi stated. "That was parents and close friends. By the time we were in the sectional, we maybe had 200, 300 people there.

"Each week it started to get bigger and bigger. By the time we got to Hinkle and went runnin' out there, there's almost 10,000 fans. When we saw all those black and orange hankies waving and heard the fans screaming, it was really exciting."

In the semifinals on March 1, 1976, Warsaw defeated East Chicago Roosevelt, 62-44, and Bloomfield beat Indianapolis Tech, 47-45. That paired Warsaw against Bloomfield in the title game that Judi says was "kind of scary" before she made five free throws in the final 64 seconds to ice a 57-52 victory.

Chanda Kline, a sophomore, was Warsaw's leading scorer with 19 points. Judi was next with 17.

"Bloomfield had the Miles twins who were pretty good," Judi said. "One played the post, the other guard, and they were used to playing with each other all their lives. We were not playing well and came up against a team that could run with us. It did come down to the final seconds.

"Our other guard, Lisa Vandermark, kept bringing the ball up, because Bloomfield kept trying to deny it to me. She kept turning the ball over. Finally she said, 'You've gotta take it.' "

With the score tied, 52-52, a Bloomfield player started grabbing Judi's jersey as she dribbled across court and a referee finally called a foul. Judi sank both free throws on her one-and-one opportunity.

Bloomfield then missed a shot and Warsaw got the rebound. As Judi dribbled down the left sideline, her leg started to cramp.

"My leg was dragging along beside me, and there was a girl standing there in front of me," Judi said. "She got called for a reach-in foul, but it probably could have easily been called a charge. I went to the line and made two more (one-and-one) free throws and we're up four points."

In the final seconds, Judi was fouled again. She made the first to put Warsaw ahead five points.

"I went wild," Judi exclaimed. "I was pulling my hair and it looks funny on the video."

Judi missed the second free throw, but a Bloomfield player had gone into the lane too soon.

"I got another chance and I missed that one, too," she said. "Bloomfield got the rebound, but time expired and the game was over. We were running around the court and hugging each other. It was true exuberance."

"Hoosier Hysteria" became a reality for Judi and her teammates that March night as they continued to celebrate and be celebrated on their return to Warsaw.

"Probably the best part of all was it was around 9:30 at night when the game got over and we headed back to Warsaw," Warren said. "And we didn't even take a school bus. We had an optometrist in Warsaw who had a motorhome.

"We had a restroom on there and we had it all decorated. Before we left for the state finals we had a big sendoff in Warsaw with a pep session. That was pretty amazing, because we had never had any kind of recognition throughout our years of

Hoosier Hysteria gripped the female side of Indiana high school basketball in 1976 when the Warsaw team traveled to and from Indianapolis for the state championship the Tigers won—in a motor home owned by an optometrist in the Kosciusko County city. (Photo courtesy of Judi Warren)

high school. We got back to town, it's midnight and the streets are lined up. Kids were in their pajamas, they're on top of cars, they're honking the horns. It's early March and it's cold."

That celebration in the Warsaw gym had special meaning for Judi and her teammates.

"I don't know if you remember a guy by the name of Ike Tallman (he coached Muncie Central to the 1963 boys' state championship)," Judi said. "He was the boys' coach at Warsaw at the time. We had talked to him about getting equal practice time.

"We had practiced every night from 7 to 9 after the boys' varsity, Jayvee's and freshmen practiced. We thought this wasn't right, that we should at least have one or two times to practice right after school."

Instead of going by bus to Claypool after school and then have her parents drive her back to Warsaw for the night practices, Judi would stay after school almost every day, do her homework and then walk to a nearby dairy barn to have a light meal.

"I'd watch the boys practice and then we'd practice," she said. "Then I'd go home, take a shower, have some left-over dinner

Judi Warren (13) and Chanda Kline (14), both Miss Basketballs, help celebrate Warsaw's 1976 state championship. (Photo courtesy of Judi Warren)

and go to bed. We thought there had to be a better way. Well, Ike Tallman said, 'When you girls can fill the gym and bring in the money like the boys have, then we'll sit down and talk about it.' "

Before an SRO gym that historic night in Warsaw, Tallman got on the microphone and said, "Girls, I see that now you can pack the gym. We're going to have to sit down and talk about equal practice time."

The next year the girls had Monday, Wednesday practice after school, the boys had Tuesday and Thursday, and they would flip-flop on Fridays.

"That probably meant almost as much as winning the state championship, to know that we were able to get some equal rights," Judi said. She added that the Warsaw boys got rings for winning a state championship, but the girls did not.

"We got medals," she said. "But because we didn't get state rings, one of the clubs in Warsaw—I think it was the Optimist Club—provided the opportunity for us to design our own rings. The ring is real cool. It's got a tiger on it, an orange amethyst stone and it's gold."

Judi does not wear the ring, which she keeps at home.

"My finger has gotten a little bit fatter," she said, smiling. "It doesn't fit quite as well."

College recruiting for girls was all but unheard of in 1976 when Warsaw was making basketball history.

"I didn't know anything about recruiting," Judi said. "In junior high I had an excellent P.E. teacher who was also the GAA sponsor, Vivian Eidemiller. She was incredible. She would do anything and everything to help you out.

"Vivian coached all of the sports we were playing. I wanted to be like Coach Eidemiller. I knew I wanted to go to college and I wanted to become a P.E. teacher. That was my focus through junior high and high school, and I idolized Coach Soyez."

Ball State was a teacher's college and Judi had the idea that was where she would enroll, until shortly after the state finals her senior year.

"I was fortunate enough that Ruth Callon, the coach at Franklin College, saw the state tournament finals and called me up afterwards," Judi said. "Indiana State and Franklin were the only schools in Indiana that gave female athletic scholarships at that time.

"You had to be 5-foot-8 to play at Indiana State. (The coach) had a pencil mark on her door, meaning you had to be above that mark or you weren't considered. We got the opportunity to play Indiana State when I was at Franklin and I went over to her office and sure enough, there was that mark. I didn't reach it. We did beat Indiana State at their place."

Judi started four years as the Franklin point guard and had "a great experience. The first year we won the small college state championship. That was the first time Franklin had ever done that. They hadn't paid the fee for us to continue on in the tournament. Again another road blocked. But the next year after that they paid the fee. We did win the small college state championship three years I was there."

Judi Warren, No. 13, shows her magical presence in 1976 state championship game. (Photo courtesy of Judi Warren)

Warren got to meet two of the male pioneers mentioned in the first part of this narrative.

"While at Franklin I went to Mr. Vandivier's house a couple of times," she said. "I got a chance to talk to him and look at his memorabilia. It was really neat, kinda like meeting John Wooden. I was kinda in a group, so I didn't get too much time to talk with Coach Wooden, but it also was a neat experience."

Before graduating from Franklin, Judi got another fortuitous phone call, this time from officials at South Dearborn High School. She went for an interview and was offered a job as basketball coach and P.E. teacher.

"It was southern Indiana and that was kinda hard," she said. "I'm pretty close with my family and that was a 4-hour trip. I had great kids to work with and good facilities."

She also learned a valuable coaching lesson in the sectional. South Dearborn was ahead by one point and a Knights player was shooting a free throw.

"I should have pulled the girls off the line, but I didn't," she recalled. "The girl shot the free throw and a girl went over another girl's back and got called for a foul. The other team went down and made both free throws and we got beat by one. It was one of those learning experiences. I was a young coach and should have known the game."

Judi spent one year at South Dearborn before moving on to Maconaquah, where she coached seven years.

"We did really well," she said. "We had a couple of undefeated regular seasons and won five or six sectionals. I'd have to look through all that stuff. Those things aren't important to me. What is important to me is helping kids understand the game of basketball. It's not different than the game of life. You have your ups and downs, your wins and losses. It's what you do sometimes with those losses. It makes you a better person."

Maconaquah would have to go to Huntington North for the regional.

"We would either go against Kokomo or Huntington North," Judi stated. "We were a smaller school, but competitive. I loved the opportunity to go against those bigger schools. I don't think I would have liked to have won the state tournament with a small school (under the current class system) and not having had the opportunity to beat the best."

In 1988 Judi went to Carmel, where she coached until retiring in 2000. The Lady Greyhounds were runners-up to Huntington North in the 1995 state finals, losing, 43--39, after coming back from a third-quarter 19-point deficit to beat Washington, 75-74, in the semifinal game that day.

"We did not play our best in the championship game," Judi said. "The Warsaw team that won the first girls' tournament was to be honored at halftime of the championship game, a 20th anniversary honor.

"I never knew it, but my Carmel team that year wanted us to get to state so I could be there when the Warsaw team was being honored. It was kinda tough. I wanted to be there with my Warsaw teammates, but I needed to be in there with my Carmel team. I did my normal halftime stuff, and when I came out, they were already doing the honoring for Warsaw and kinda had me at the end of it."

Judi has been a player, a coach and a hall of fame board member, and now she relishes her new role of fan. Her 29-year-old son Andy played basketball at Carmel, Mt. St. Clair in Clinton, Iowa; and Anderson University. He is now an assistant coach at Guerin Catholic High School in Noblesville. Andy also sells insurance for Dave Shepherd Insurance in Carmel (David Shepherd was Indiana Mr. Basketball in 1970).

Warren was not married when Andy was born in Warsaw right after her one year of coaching at South Dearborn.

"That was one of those low-point disappointments," she admits. "It didn't really tarnish my name, but I hadn't lived up to the expectations that everybody had. It was tough and it was the reason I left South Dearborn."

Judi returned to Warsaw and did

Judi Warren, holding her Pat Roy Mental Attitude Award and wearing her victory medal, poses with her family after Warsaw won first girls' state championship. (Photo courtesy of Judi Warren)

filing in the personnel office at the Warsaw hospital for a year. She yearned to get back into coaching, but it wasn't easy to find someone who would give her a second chance.

"I went on several interviews," Judi said. "As soon as they found out I had Andy, the door was kinda closed behind me. When I went to Maconaquah, the superintendent was Ray Geyer. He sat down with me and said, 'I know everybody makes mistakes. You learned your lesson, hopefully. I'm willing to give you a chance, but don't prove me wrong.'

"I learned from that mistake and I was gonna make sure I could do a good job for him and take care of my son."

She passed both aims with flying colors.

"Fortunately Andy loves the game of basketball," Judi said. "He went everywhere with me. He'd go scouting. He had his own little court with a little chalk tray, and it had a little box underneath where he could hold all of his little cars.

"I was fortunate to have a very good baby sitter for him when I was at Maconaquah. They're like grandparents to him now. I also was working on my master's at the time. I look back on that time and I don't know how I did it. But Andy was very easy to raise."

When Andy enrolled at Mt. St. Clair, Judi said it was getting to the point where 19 years of coaching basketball was starting to wear on her and she wanted to see her son play as a collegian.

"So I said I've had enough. It's been a great ride, but it's time to move on," she said. "Life is good for me and Andy. By the time I go and watch the Carmel girls play and watch Andy's teams play on the weekend it's very fulfilling.

"And I'm still involved with the hall of fame. Up until 2009 I served on the board. I've got to take a year off. You can only serve like eight consecutive years. Then you can get back into it."

Indiana is lucky to have had a basketball pioneer as dedicated and proficient as Judi Warren.

Chanda Kline

Bob and Joyce Kline used to take their two kids, Barry and Chanda, to watch the Warsaw High School boys' basketball team play when they were in grade school in the 1960s. It struck a chord with Chanda.

"I had my official scoring book that my grandma, Winifred Metzger, had bought for me, where I kept track of the points, etc.," recalled Chanda, who helped the Lady Tigers win the first Indiana girls' state championship in 1976 and the third state tournament in 1978 before becoming Indiana Miss Basketball.

"My mom tells the story where one night she found me in my bed, under the covers, with a flashlight tallying up the points for that night's game. I was six years old."

From that humble beginning, Chanda went on to earn 13 varsity letters at Warsaw High: four in basketball, three in volleyball and two each in badminton, track and tennis. She was state singles champion in badminton two years.

"I enjoyed all the sports and as one season ended I would gear up for the next sport season," Chanda said. "I loved the competition."

It was as a 6-year-old that Chanda began to develop a passion for basketball—outside the covers of her bed.

"I started shooting baskets when I was six years old," said Chanda, who is now a jack-of-all-trades at the Lake City Animal Clinic in Warsaw, where she has been working since 2002 (she had worked at another clinic for 16 years before joining the Lake City clinic).

"We had a regulation-size basketball goal in the driveway. I also learned with a men's basketball, not the smaller-size basketball they have these days. I was bound and determined to get the ball in the hoop. Once I accomplished that, there was no looking back. I was hooked."

Chanda Kline, No. 14, maneuvers for Warsaw in 1976 state championship game. (Photo courtesy of Chanda Kline)

Like so many Indiana kids, the Kline siblings learned much of their basketball prowess at night under the spotlight off of the garage.

"We had neighborhood games and also played h-o-r-s-e," Chanda said. "Of course, the games were rough, so that's where I learned to take an elbow here or there without a problem."

Chanda's dad and brother were very good basketball players, she said, and that quickened her development.

"Barry was an excellent shooter and defender and was also good at stealing passes," she said. "I would watch how he would anticipate the opponents' next move. He had quick feet and was always between the opponent and the basket."

Chanda could always score. She led the Lady Tigers with 19 points in their 57-52 victory over Bloomfield in the 1976 state championship game at Hinkle Fieldhouse and again was Warsaw's high scorer in the 1978 title game—a 75-60 triumph over Jac-Cen-Del of Osgood—with 29 points on 11-of-16 from the field and 7-of-8 from the foul line.

She had 11 rebounds in that game, a testament to her dad's training.

"I took great pride in trying to be a good defensive player and my dad taught me to believe that every rebound was mine for the taking, not to wait for the ball, but go after it," she said.

"I liked it when we would press full court and I would be in a position to steal the pass and then pass off to a teammate for an easy two points. I actually got more joy out of giving a good pass for an assist than I did scoring."

How good was Chanda?

"She was very good," her coach, Janice Soyez, said. "Maybe it's because she practiced with her brother Barry, who was a good basketball player. She had a pure shot. When we played East Chicago Roosevelt in the 1978 semi-state at Benton Central, somebody sat on her head and we thought she had a concussion.

"My assistant coach, Mary Hurley, took her into the locker room and they checked her out. They said she could come back in. But we were not to give her the ball in the backcourt, just wait 'til we got up there in the front court.

"She was kinda dazed, but she could turn and shoot it. Later it was diagnosed as a concussion. But in that dazed condition she had that pure shot."

As a senior, Chanda averaged 19 points and 11 rebounds per game. The Lady Tigers were 68-5 in her varsity career and she had 1,113 career points while shooting 53.2 percent from the field and having two steals per game and three assists. Chanda was inducted into the Indiana Basketball Hall of Fame in 2004, joining her teammate, Judi Warren, and coach, Soyez.

Hearing that the IHSAA was going to hold a girls' state championship for the first time in 1976 was incredible news, according to Chanda.

"Our main goal was to win the first state championship," she said. "We had to practice at odd hours at the high school along with practicing in elementary and junior high gyms. We just went out and played when it came game time.

"We were a fast break team and ran a freelance offense. Coach Soyez was good about just letting us play. We would come up with our own plays and try them out. I could just give a look to Judi Warren and she knew where I was going to be and then would zip the ball to me for an easy two points."

Being a sophomore on the senior-dominated 1976 team was no problem, Chanda says.

"I was never treated any different being the only sophomore in the starting lineup. I let my play do the talking and was eager to contribute in any way to meet our goal, win that first state championship. The seniors had a sense of urgency where I knew that there was an outside chance I could be a part of three state titles.

"Running onto the Hinkle Fieldhouse floor for warm-ups, with the Warsaw fans cheering our every move, was such a high. The crowd is yelling, 'We're No. 1,' as the team gets presented the trophy. As I put my hand on the state trophy, that is when I knew we had accomplished something special and I wanted to have that feeling again."

She did two years later, when she capped her outstanding high school journey by being named Indiana's third Miss Basketball prior to the Indiana-Kentucky All-Star series. Indiana lost twice to Kentucky in the

Chanda Kline, Warsaw's Miss Basketball in 1978, goes up for a classic jump shot. (Photo courtesy of Chanda Kline)

17

Warsaw celebrates its 1978 state championship triumph.
(Photo courtesy of Chanda Kline)

All-Star series that year (1978). Kentucky led the series, 13-3, before Indiana became dominate.

Chanda will never forget how Warsaw fell in love with its girls' team during the 1976 and '78 tournaments.

"I remember the lines of people in the school hallway to get tickets," she said. "The further we went in the tournament the longer the line would be the next week. We had great fans and community support. My senior year, the athletic director made the comment to my mom that he didn't realize I had such a big family when she asked for 25 tickets."

Chanda keeps her two state championship rings in a safe place.

"The last time I wore one of them is when the Warsaw girls went to the state finals and our state championship was recognized at the tournament," she said.

In 1978 Chanda enrolled at Indiana State, where she played basketball for two seasons before a knee injury ended her career. That was the season Larry Bird and teammates almost completed a perfect season, before losing for the only time in the NCAA tournament championship game to Magic Johnson and Michigan State.

"I did not know Larry Bird," Chanda stated. "I know Steve Reed, former Warsaw player who played guard with Bird. Steve provided Larry with many good assists. Campus was an exciting place to be during the 1979 NCAA tournament.

"Larry Bird had a lot of help. There were other people around him who played key roles. I was a role player at ISU."

As a freshman Chanda averaged 5.5 points and three rebounds a game for the Lady Sycamores, who were 14-10.

"I had mono my freshman year," she said. The next year Chanda averaged 4.4 points and three rebounds a game as ISU went 19-13. But Chanda tore an ACL before New Year's.

Even though Chanda's basketball career was cut short by injury, she insists that her competitive side "is still alive and well." That's evident in a part of her email address: thundercat14.

"I like to play golf as often as I can," Chanda said. "I hit a long drive and once a fellow golfer yelled, 'Go thundercat.' So I use that in my email address. The 14 part of the email address comes from one of my basketball uniform numbers when I was in high school."

Chanda not only is a long hitter in golf, she also hits for distance in her job.

"My duties include meeting with pharmaceutical representatives to ensure we are aware of the most up-to-date products available," she said.

"I also order supplies, track and update inventory, pricing, customer service and assist with after-hours emergencies."

Warsaw's Lake City Animal Clinic has a winner in Chanda Kline, just as she was a winner in basketball.

LaTaunya Pollard

Bobbi DeKemper had not been girls' basketball coach at East Chicago Roosevelt High School very long in the early 1970s when she saw a young gal in the physical education class she was teaching holding a basketball.

"Bobbi asked me to take a shot, a very long one, and it went in," said LaTaunya Pollard-Romanazzi, who now lives in Montgomery, Tex., near Houston with her Italian husband, Mario Romanazzi, and their two kids.

"The rest is history," LaTaunya added with obvious pride over her many accomplishments at the high school, collegiate and professional level.

And what history! The 5-foot-9 shooting guard led Roosevelt to two state championships, in 1977 and 1979, and was named Miss Basketball in '79. Roosevelt was undefeated in both title years, 25-0 in '77 and 23-0 in '79. In the '77 championship game LaTaunya outscored the entire Mount Vernon (of Fortville) team, 36-35. Roosevelt won, 66-35.

LaTaunya lost only twice in 94 games in high school, both times to eventual state champion Warsaw—62-44 in the semifinals of the 1976 state finals and 46-45 in the semi-state in '78.

In four years at Long Beach State University in California, LaTaunya scored a school-record 3,001 points and lost only 26 times in 128 games while averaging 23.5 points per game. Among her many school scoring records was her 48 points for a single game.

She was a three-time Kodak All-American—1981, '82 and '83—and as a senior was awarded the Wade Trophy as the best college player in the nation. The number 15 she wore as a 49er (15 also was her number in high school) has been retired and hangs in the rafters at The Pyramid.

Because there was no women's professional basketball in the United States when LaTaunya graduated in 1983, she went to Italy to play professional basketball. She logged eight consecutive seasons, averaging 39.5 points per game in 1983, which is still the all-time record in Italy.

LaTaunya set a single-game scoring record of 99 points in the Italian Championship League. She laughed while recounting that accomplishment.

"I had to soak my arm after that game," she related. "I had 45 points in the first half and 54 in the second half. We played the last-place team. We were second-to-last. If I hadn't missed so many shots, I might have had 150 points."

That LaTaunya became the first superstar of Indiana high school girls' basketball in the modern era is not surprising to Patty Broderick of Indianapolis, who refereed one of her Roosevelt games (LaTaunya and Patty are the only two people from Indiana in the Women's Basketball Hall of Fame in Knoxville, Tenn.).

"LaTaunya had the body, she had the height, she had the razzle-dazzle moves, she had quickness, she had speed, she could put the ball behind her back, she would take it off the board and she was a physical player, an outstanding player," Patty said.

"I would give her the title of the female Oscar Robertson in Indiana high school basketball."

When LaTaunya heard that appraisal, she said, "That's awesome to be mentioned in the same breath with Oscar Robertson (who led Indianapolis Crispus Attucks to successive boys' state high school championships in 1955 and '56). I never won a championship in college or professionally, but I still consider myself a great player.

I've never seen another female play basketball the way I did, and I don't say that cockily. My talent was a gift from God."

LaTaunya honed that talent in the alley behind her East Chicago home, where she lived with five brothers and six sisters. She was the seventh oldest child.

"We didn't have a lot as a family, but we had each other," she said. "My mom is alive and well in East Chicago. My dad passed away seven years ago. I would shoot in the back alley, get my rebound, then wait until a car went by, and shoot again. I never got hit by a car."

LaTaunya and Normella Upshaw, who went on to play with Pollard-Romanazzi at Long Beach State, saw a tryout flyer and made DeKemper's Lady Rough Riders team as eighth graders. When the coaching staff found out they weren't old enough for the varsity, the two were told to come back a year later.

"I played with boys and I got better," LaTaunya said. "I knew my time would come."

From the time she became a starter as a freshman, LaTaunya says, "It wasn't about me. We were a team. Normella Upshaw was a power forward and really good at her position. Pinky McClain was a forward and Dana Cook was a forward-center. Vernell Jackson was the playmaker and very, very good."

The Roosevelt players bonded well. According to a northwest Indiana newspaper story in 2007 that recognized East Chicago's rich high school tradition, male and female, the Rough Rider girls rode their bikes through town together, played cards together and shot baskets in the Pollard backyard together. They even dressed alike in their three-piece 1970s suits.

"We looked like the Jackson 5." LaTaunya said with a laugh.

DeKemper was inducted into the Indiana Basketball Hall of Fame with the first class of women in 2002. Three of her players followed: Carmella Lynn Martin Dunn, a senior on the 1976 team, in 2003 and Pollard-Romanazzi and Upshaw in 2005.

"Bobbi DeKemper is a friend, first," LaTaunya said. "She is probably the best coach I ever had, and I've had some good coaches. She was very patient with me and very caring. She was a disciplinarian but fair. I just love Bobbi DeKemper."

And what about Judi Warren, the first Indiana Miss Basketball who led Warsaw to a 62-44 victory over Roosevelt in the semifinals of the 1976 state finals?

"Warsaw was very well prepared and they were the better team," LaTaunya said. "I commend Judi Warren. She was a very special player."

Of the more than 150 scholarship offers LaTaunya received, how was it that she decided to travel all the way to California to play college basketball?

"I probably didn't open half of the letters I received," she said. "My family was struggling financially and I didn't want to go (to college). But Bobbi DeKemper called me in and said, 'You have to try. If you don't like it, come home.' "

LaTaunya made visits to the University of Nevada Las Vegas (UNLV) and Long Beach State.

"I was going to go to UNLV," she said.

But LaTaunya flew to California to visit Long Beach State.

California learned about the prestige of Indiana basketball when LaTaunya Pollard-Romanazzi left East Chicago to play at Long Beach State where she had a brilliant career. (Photo courtesy of Long Beach State)

One knowledgeable person called LaTaunya Pollard-Romanazzi, who led East Chicago Roosevelt High School to two state championships in the late '70s, the Oscar Robertson of Indiana women's basketball. (Photo courtesy of Long Beach State)

On her flight home to East Chicago, Joan Bonvicini, the Long Beach coach, was on the flight. She and LaTaunya chatted and LaTaunya was impressed with her honesty.

"To be honest, that is the reason I signed at Long Beach," she said.

LaTaunya stayed all four years at Long Beach State and made Bobbi DeKemper proud.

While at Long Beach State, Pollard-Romanazzi met a fellow who played basketball at Bakersfield Community College in California and they were married in 1984. The marriage lasted only four years, but it produced a baby girl. Thiara Ott is 23 now and married

Since there was no women's professional basketball in the United States at that time, LaTaunya headed to Europe to continue her career. It was at Bari in southern Italy later that she met Mario Romanazzi through a mutual friend of a teammate.

"He spoke a little English and we hit it right off," she said. "And we had pizza." When in Italy, do as the locals do—eat pizza.

LaTaunya and Mario have been married 17 years and have two children—Erica, 15, and Kevin, 13. LaTaunya is now a basketball mom.

"Erica wasn't blessed with her mother's talent, but is working very hard," LaTaunya said. "I am so proud of her. Kevin has good skills and he can be a shooter like his mom."

Pollard-Romanazzi was only 31 at the end of the 1991-92 season in Italy when she decided to retire and return to East Chicago.

"I was burned out," she said. "It got to be about money, money, money. My life wasn't right after I retired and my older sister Diane, who was living in Texas, encouraged me to come down to Texas."

Mario is manager of a warehouse and LaTaunya is working at a day-care center teaching 3-year-olds. She was a stay-at-home mother eight years before returning to work at the day-care center in 2010.

"Before I had been at home those eight years, I was in the school system working with special-needs kids, and I drove a school bus," she said.

Pollard-Romanazzi turned 50 on July 26, 2010, and she again chuckled, saying, "I'm kinda old. I do have some regrets. I didn't take care of my finances as I should have and not being able to play in the 1980 Olympics (she qualified for the U.S. team, but then-President Jimmy Carter decided his country would boycott the Games in the Soviet Union) was a big disappointment. It was a once-in-a-lifetime opportunity taken away because of politics."

LaTaunya firmly believes the good in her life far outweighs the bad, and that basketball has been a blessing.

"Basketball enabled me to help my family financially and I was able to travel," she said. "I think I left a mark on basketball that will always be there (she and Stephanie White were two of the 50 finest high school players—male and female—in the state chosen to commemorate the opening of Conseco Fieldhouse in Indianapolis in 1999).

"I had fun in Europe and met a lot of nice people. I just wish I could have competed professionally before the American people. My family is together and I'm living my life for God. I give all the glory to Him."

Has Pollard-Romanazzi become a Texan? Nay, she says.

"I'm a Hoosier," said LaTaunya, smiling hugely. "East Chicago will always be my home."

MARIA STACK

What do Maria Stack and Blair Kiel have in common? Believe it or not they were on a Columbus Little League baseball All-Star team together.

Stack, of course, scored a record 42 points and grabbed 22 rebounds, also a record for an Indiana girls' state high school basketball tournament championship game, as Columbus East lost to Indianapolis Southport, 67-63, in overtime in 1980 when Maria became Miss Basketball.

Kiel was rated the third-best quarterback in the U.S. as a senior at Columbus East in 1979, then started four years at the University of Notre Dame before playing for the Indianapolis Colts in a 10-year pro football career.

Columbus is less than 100 miles from Cincinnati, where the Big Red Machine of manager Sparky Anderson fascinated Maria in the mid-1970s.

"I loved watching the Reds and I loved Johnny Bench," said Maria, who is a supervisor at the Johnson County Juvenile Detention Center. "I idolized him and I wanted to be a catcher like him. The Little League coach said I had to try out, and once I did, he said, 'Oh, yes, you can catch.' I pitched and played shortstop, too."

"I was the first female in Columbus to play Little League. I batted third and I just tried to get on base. I had a really good arm. I made the All-Star team with Blair Kiel. He was great. We had great sports teams when I was in high school. Blair was good at basketball, football and baseball. I played anything and everything that had a ball—baseball, football, basketball, volleyball, softball and even track."

As a high school senior Maria had a softball throw of 254 feet in track, which was third-best in the nation at that time (she finished third in the state meet).

Football? "I was really good in football," she said. "I was really quick. Plus I was a girl and nobody would get on me. Oh yeah, I got tackled. We learned when they kicked off and I saw somebody big coming at me, I'd get down. My oldest brother Mike played guard on the Columbus East football team and I would go with him.

"We didn't specialize then, they let you play everything. Right now coaches want you to play their sport all year round. I'm glad I didn't have to experience that, because I probably would have had to choose."

Maria's grandparents lived in Brown County and her family would go there every weekend. That's where Maria learned to love basketball.

She has a nice basketball goal on the driveway at her home in Franklin, but it was primitive at her grandparents' home in Brown County.

"We had dirt at the grandparents' home, so we just nailed our goal to a tree. We didn't have anything fancy like we do now. We just played."

It was while in the fifth grade that Maria's basketball career took a positive turn that at first was quite negative.

"I wanted to try out for the boys' basketball team, because they didn't have a girls' team," she declared. "My brother Ed tried out for the team, but they wouldn't let me try out. That's when my mom (Nancy) got an attorney. She sued the school corporation. It made national news."

Mrs. Stack's mission prevailed.

"The following year they allowed girls to play sixth grade, seventh, eighth and ninth," Maria said. "It takes people to step forward to fight for what's right and that's what she did."

Girls' basketball at Columbus East got a sensational start when Maria's sixth-grade team went undefeated. By the time she was a high school senior the Lady Olympians were really good.

Athletics always put Maria in a better mood if things weren't going well.

"If I was down, I knew I could always go out and shoot," she said. "We lived real close to the high school and there was a coach that gave me a key to the gym. And there was a janitor that showed me how to turn the lights on and off.

"I could pretty much go into the gym whenever I wanted. Everybody was always wondering, 'How did you get into the gym?' I would say, 'There was a door open.' That really helped me, because I spent a lot of time in that gym."

Columbus East lost only three games when 5-foot-5 Maria was a senior. Two of them were to Southport.

Southport defeated Columbus East during the season, 57-55, then got a second victory in the state championship contest. In the semi-state the Lady Olympians defeated Loogootee, 46-42, and Boonville, 66-43.

In the first games of the state finals at Market Square Arena, Southport beat Marion, 73-55, and Columbus East downed Twin Lakes, 50-41.

A crowd of 8,629 witnessed a championship game that ended sensationally.

"The game was tied (55-55)," Maria recalled. "I remember taking the ball down the court, then pulling up for a 7-, 8-foot shot and it going in with about four seconds left. Then Southport called a timeout. We put on a full-court press and knocked the ball away. The ball was in the corner and the girl (Laura Krieger) hit that miraculous shot that sent the game into overtime."

Southport outscored Columbus East, 10-6, in overtime to claim the title. There was no shot clock then and no three-point line.

"We played with a men's ball," Maria said. "Now the girls' ball is smaller. For myself the competition was good and I thought everybody had good sportsmanship. There was a lot of hustle and it was physical. I remember going on the floor a lot and getting tangled up with Amy (Metheny, who had 28 points for Southport) for a loose ball. I also remember going for a ball and coming down on the scorer's table. What I remember most was that I've gotta get two points, I've gotta get two points."

Maria was 14-of-35 from the field and 14-of-20 from the free-throw line.

"I always called myself a scorer, not a shooter," she said. "I was a streaky shooter. Sometimes when I would shoot in the final game it seemed like the basket had a lid on it. A lot of balls were in-and-outers. I wasn't particularly impressed with my shooting statistics, because my goal always was to shoot over 50 percent (she was just 40 percent from the field that night).

"When I think of the pressure of the game and that I played almost the entire game except when I got hurt on the scorer's table (and was out for less than a minute), and we had already played one game that day and your legs get tired, you have to take all that into account."

Maria Stack of Columbus East was Miss Basketball in 1980. (Photo courtesy of Maria Stack)

Of her extraordinary rebounding performance, Maria smiled and said, "Either you're aggressive or you're not. I was aggressive. Yes, I'm proud of those records I have for the championship game. They've sustained over the years: 1980, that's a long time."

After the title game Maria remembers being exhausted and facing a media mob.

"I also remember my coach, Jackie Burton (who is in the Indiana Basketball Hall of Fame), coming and getting me and taking me back to the locker room. The outcome wasn't what we wanted, but we could hold our heads up high. There were lots of teams that would have loved to be where we were at."

Maria's collegiate basketball career didn't get started until 1981-82, when she was invited to enroll at Otero Junior College in La Junta, Colo., by Coach Bill Barnett. She sat out a year after graduating from Columbus East because of some family issues and because she had few basketball offers.

"In volleyball I did," she said. "But I didn't think I wanted to play volleyball. Bill Barnett watched me play in high school. We got all the paper work together and off I went. I loved my two years in junior college playing for Coach Barnett. He was in a unique situation. He coached the men and women in basketball and he also coached baseball."

Did Maria tell him that she had been a catcher? She laughed and said, "No, I didn't try to dish that. But I had an excellent career at Otero. I played shooting guard. We had really good teams. I think we only lost five games in the two years I was there.

"Both years I got injured in the tournament. One year I tore an ACL in my right knee, then the next year I sprained my ankle really, really bad (the Lady Rattlers didn't win a national title either year)."

Maria still has several records at Otero. She holds three individual records, all against McCook, Neb., on Feb. 16, 1983: points, 49; free throws made, 17; and free throws attempted, 21. She has two season records: 623 points in 1982-83 and points per game average, 29.5, that year. She has two career (1981-83) records: points, 1,199, and points per game average, 27.2.

Those records enabled Maria to receive a scholarship offer to San Diego State. She told herself that "I'm gonna go out there and see how good I really am. They had the best conference at the time, with Cheryl Miller at Southern California plus UCLA and Arizona State.

"We had a young team and a new coach had just come in. I just stayed there a year because of some of the illegal activity that was going on. A lot of girls flunked off the team."

Maria played point guard and averaged around 14 points playing 38 minutes a game. At the end of the season she contacted Gonzaga coach Bill Evans in an effort to transfer to the NAIA school in Spokane, Wash. (Gonzaga became NCAA Division I for women in 1986-87).

"They gave me a full-ride scholarship and I did phenomenal," she said.

Maria set three one-season records that still stand: 707 points, 179 free throws and 264 field goals. She also is second in steals with 96 and third in assists with 207. In addition Maria was named All-American and received the Frances Pomeroy Naismith Award in 1985 as the nation's top player shorter than 5-foot-8.

After her one season at Gonzaga, Maria could have gone overseas to play professionally, because at the time there were no pro leagues in the U.S.

"I wasn't interested in that," she stated. "I had been playing for a long time and I wanted to get into my career and get settled in. Back in '84, '85 the economy was kinda like it is now. Jobs were tough to find.

"I ended up getting a full-time job running a printing press for making bags. I did that for a while. For the past 17 years I've been working at the Johnson County Juvenile Detention Center. I didn't want to be a teacher. I'm really fortunate that I found my niche. I love going to work every day and working with the kids."

Like her good friend Amy Metheny, Maria has had to overcome obstacles.

"Basketball has been really good to me," she said. "It taught me a lot about life and dedication and hard work. We were really poor.

Nobody in my family (brothers Mike, Bob and Ed, who is deceased, and sister Julie) had gone to college, so there wasn't a lot of preparation. I knew I wanted to go to college and that was a goal of mine. But not having anybody that had ever been there to impress you or have the knowledge is different."

Of her work at the juvenile center, Maria says, "The kids can be anywhere from 10 to 18 (years of age). They can come from wealthy families, poor families. They will sometimes take kids away from families. It's sad, but sometimes it's for the better, especially if their parents have addictions or they abuse them."

It is Maria's aim not to judge the kids. "I just try to be respectful and try to tell 'em there are people that do care out there and that they can make it."

To the young people of today Maria stresses this message: "Whatever your passion, go with it. Any kind of sports or ballet or piano or whatever you're good at, you should stay dedicated, you should work hard and you should keep your goals in line and long-term.

"I think that's what sports and especially basketball have done for me."

Amy Metheny

Once an Indiana basketball all-star always an Indiana basketball all-star.

That's the feel-good story of Dr. Amy Metheny, who in 1980 led Indianapolis Southport to the state high school girls' tournament championship in a 67-63 overtime victory over Columbus East that helped her become the Pat Roy Mental Attitude Award recipient and claim membership on the Indiana All-Star team that split with Kentucky.

Twenty-nine years later Amy's remarkable accomplishments of overcoming huge obstacles at Indiana University, where she helped the Hoosiers win the 1983 Big Ten championship, and later a debilitating disease—dysautonomia. -- were chronicled in the 2009 book *Chicken Soup for the Soul: Inside Basketball* by her I.U. coach, Dr. Maryalyce Jeremiah, who now coaches at Cal-State Fullerton.

Pat Williams, senior vice president for the Orlando Magic of the NBA who earned a master's degree from Indiana University, organized the 101 stories in the book for which Coach Mike Krzyzewski, whose Duke Blue Devils beat Butler, 61-59, in Indianapolis' Lucas Oil Stadium for the 2010 NCAA title, wrote the forward.

"In seeking contributions for this book, over 15,000 individuals in the NBA, collegiate and high school ranks have been contacted, and you now hold in your hands 'the All-Star team' of those submissions,"

MENTAL ATTITUDE AWARD '80

Amy Metheny receives the Pat Roy Mental Attitude Award after helping Southport win the 1980 state championship. (Photo courtesy of Amy Metheny)

Williams wrote in the introduction.

"The responses have served as an affirmation of my love affair and involvement in Dr. Naismith's wonderful game."

"Persevering Amy" is the name of Dr. Jeremiah's piece that tells about the new Hoosiers' coach—Jeremiah—prior to the 1980-81 season saying that Metheny was "awful short" at 5-foot-4 when she introduced herself in the summer of '80.

But Amy was determined to play for the Hoosiers as a walk-on (in those days high school players had to try out before being put on a college roster), even though she faced road blocks her freshman, sophomore and junior years that might have turned off less determined student-athletes.

"I've been watching Indiana basketball ever since Steve Green days," Amy said. "I was in grade school when my dad and I used to watch it on black-and-white TV in the kitchen on Channel 4 WTTV.

"I always said if I couldn't play on the I.U. men's team, which I would have done for Coach Bob Knight if I could have, then I wanted to play for the I.U. women's team, which was the next best thing."

Metheny contracted a case of strep throat shortly before tryouts as an I.U. freshman, but pressed on before being cut at the end of the first week. Rather than pout, Amy told Jeremiah she would try out again the next year.

Being cut was devastating, according to Amy.

"I had just come off one of the greatest high school years ever, but Maryalyce Jeremiah had no idea who I was. She was from the University of Dayton (where she won an NCAA Division II national championship).

"I knew I wanted to stay close to home and my parents (Harold and Diane) could come to my games. And I knew I wanted to go to medical school. After I got cut, my parents called. My mom said, 'We'll come and pick you up. You go wherever else you want to go.'

"I said, 'I'm trying again next year.' My mom said, 'Have you lost your mind?' My mom would say she's the realist, but I would say the pessimist. My dad's the opposite. He sees the glass always half full and I'm just like my dad."

Amy went to Coach Jeremiah's office and thanked her for the tryout, and added that if there was anything she could do to help that year to let her know. "I don't think the coach could believe this. Almost everybody else who got cut wasn't real happy. I came in and just said, 'I'll be back next year.' "

To prepare for a second tryout, Amy rounded up some Bloomington area players and they went to the AAU national finals. Jeremiah asked Amy to work her camp in the summer of 1981 and that helped Amy to be invited to participate in Maryalyce's second season.

"I started my first game and tore all the ligaments in my ankle against Toledo," Amy said. "I go driving down the middle two minutes into the game, go up in the air and come down on somebody's foot. I ripped my shoe and tore my ankle. That was a rough year."

How rough? Amy spent a long time with her ankle in a cast.

"When you come back and you can't cut, and you're a 5-4 point guard, it shakes your confidence," she said. "But I worked really hard that summer (1982) and my roommate, Nikki Lucky from Saginaw, Mich., said we were going to come in and win.

"But eight games into the (1982-83) season we had won only twice. I hadn't got to play much. They had brought in some other players. I met with Coach Jeremiah and I told her I wasn't going to play the next year without a scholarship."

That struck a chord with Jeremiah.

"What do you think is wrong with the team?" she asked Amy.

"We don't play defense," Amy offered. "We score 80 points a game and we're not winning."

Metheny's blunt observation triggered a huge change by Jeremiah. Amy and Nikki became starters and the Hoosiers won 17 of their next 18 games on the way to the Big Ten title and a spot in the NCAA tournament. Indiana lost to Georgia in the Mideast Regional. Georgia lost in the national championship game.

Of that turnaround by the Hoosiers that was spurred by Metheny, who led the Big Ten in assists during that amazing run by I.U., and Lucky, Jeremiah wrote in *Persevering Amy*: "I remember thinking that this young, persistent and hard-working "pint" of an athlete with the engaging smile had taught us all an important lesson: it is not the size of the dreamer but rather the size of the dream that feeds our perseverance."

Amy was offered a scholarship for the 1983-84 season, but it wasn't enough to entice her to continue to wear Cream and Crimson.

"I knew when we played Georgia and lost, that was my last college game," she said. "Although I had two years of eligibility left, one thing I learned about the college game is that I had gotten injured, which slowed my progress a little bit.

"We had a great team coming back, but I had prayed long and hard and I feel like God was calling me to be a doctor, and I had a chance to go to the mission field. There wasn't anything I loved more than basketball.

"There is a big difference between the guys and the girls in college basketball. My grades were definitely affected by our travel schedule. I knew I had to make my grades a priority in getting into medical school. I would say the toughest decision I ever made in my life was hanging up my shoes. I knew there wasn't professional women's basketball at the time. I don't regret that I quit the college game, because it was the right thing to do for me."

Amy's senior year at I.U. was filled with study and keeping the 30-second clock at home basketball games. She couldn't turn her back on her beloved I.U. But she didn't get into med school the year after she got her undergraduate degree.

"By the time they picked the candidates they hadn't gotten all my senior-year grades," she said. "I was told it was closed."

Amy Metheny, No. 10, poses with Indiana University 1983 Big Ten championship teammates (above) and with her cello (below). (Photos courtesy of Amy Metheny)

Never one to procrastinate, Amy became an assistant to the late Chuck Mallender, the women's basketball coach at the University of Indianapolis. He was Amy's first coach and was the father of Linda Mallender, who was a year younger and on Southport's championship team in '80.

Amy took a full load of classes at U of I and worked in the biology lab. She also was the head softball coach for a year. The following year Amy received a yes on her medical school application.

In the first two years of med school, Amy spent the summers playing basketball with Athletes in Action and experienced for the first time working in the third-world mission fields.

"It was like playing basketball, where you're good at something, you love it and I felt like that was something I could do well," she said.

In an *Indianapolis Woman* magazine story, author Ann Ryder wrote that Metheny was on a third-world mission to Pakistan in 1989 as a senior in medical school when she experienced a life-changing situation. Amy helped deliver a premature baby who died in the primitive conditions of an outdoor hospital.

While sitting on the roof of a walled mission compound and seeing some poor families she had served all day traveling on a dirt road, Amy turned to God and wrote a personal prayer: "Do whatever you have to do, Lord, to make me the person I have to be."

Amy returned home with new inspiration. She did her pediatrician residency at Methodist Hospital in Indianapolis, then began a practice in Santa Clarita, Calif., a suburb of Los Angeles, where there were lots of kids, "perfect for a pediatrician," she said.

Ever since her sophomore year at I.U., Amy expressed a desire to move to California because of the weather.

"We went to California to play Irvine in a Christmas tournament when I was at I.U. and it was 70 degrees," she said. "We left a snowstorm in Indiana. They took us to the beach and we all thought we had died and gone to heaven."

In her first year of work Amy was diagnosed with a condition called dysautonomia.

"It's funny," she recalled. "I think the first four years I had it my parents would call and say, 'Now what do you have again, so and so asked us?' My mom would have to write it down. It's a dysfunction of the autonomic nervous system and they think the problem is in my brain stem, maybe a childhood viral attack to the brain stem. They don't really know what causes it."

Looking back, Amy says she began suffering sick spells as early as her first year of college.

"I had these episodes where I got light-headed, felt nauseous and like I was going to pass out," she said. "My sophomore year at I.U., right after my injury, I remember on a road trip to Texas I was real sick and had lost about 10 pounds during the season. Everybody else was in trouble for gaining weight and I got yelled at for losing weight.

"I didn't think anything of the episodes. They would come and go. You're trained as an athlete not to listen to your body, to push through pain. I had that same mentality when it came to my illness, just ignore it. But that didn't work."

Early in her California practice, Amy ended up in a hospital.

"They brought every specialist they could basically bring and they ran every test imaginable," she stated. "They thought I had a tumor in my pancreas. They put me on a three-day fast, no food, no sugar water, nothing. They drew my blood every hour for three days.

"Finally, a neurologist diagnosed that it was dysautonomia. A year and a half later I went on permanent disability."

The date was Oct. 24, 1995.

"I remember that day well," she said wryly.

Going on disability was a big change in Amy's life.

"The first two years after quitting work I was almost bed-ridden," she said. "I had to rely on my roommates and went to the hospital a lot. I got to know the paramedics at the local fire station well."

Amy was advised to go to the Mayo Clinic It was quite beneficial as she got better physically and mentally. She also got involved in The Vineyard Christian Fellowship Church.

More than 1,000 people stood and applauded as former Indiana University basketball coach Bob Knight walked to the microphone to begin a typically candid and humorous talk at an Indiana Basketball Hall of Fame fundraiser Dec. 17, 2009 at Primo's South.

None among the throng was any more enthusiastic than Amy Metheny, who helped Indianapolis Southport win the 1980 girls' high school basketball championship and later was a big part of Indiana University's 1983 women's Big Ten title team.

After Knight finished speaking, he signed autographs and greeted many of the attendees. Metheny was one of them.

"I reminded him that I always wanted to go to Indiana and if I could have, I would have played for him," Amy said with a big grin.

"But I wasn't a boy and I had to play for the I.U. women's team. Coach Knight just smiled. That was really a great night. It was so much fun."

"It started in California when the surfers would put their surf boards up in the back of the church after surfing on Sunday mornings," she related. "All the pastors would wear aloha shirts. I liked that casual attitude.

"I went to the Vineyard seminary two years through correspondence. Our pastor went back to the military after 9/11. He was a Navy reserve pilot and went back fulltime. When that church kind of disbanded, I decided it was time to come back to the Midwest.

"I was in California for the weather; you're in Indiana because of the people. Sports is so much a part of our culture. There is such a camaraderie that comes with that. Being back involved with that and I.U. and the Indiana Basketball Hall of Fame brought back so many great memories."

In the mid-2000s, Amy was asked to be on the Hall of Fame Advisory Board. In 2008 she was asked to be on the Hall of Fame Executive Board.

There was no gender inequity in the Metheny household. Harold and Diane raised three daughters who all played varsity basketball at Southport. Amy is the oldest, Krista is the second oldest and Rachel is the youngest. She got a scholarship to play basketball at St. Joseph's College in Rensselaer.

Harold was a great dad for girls, Amy stated proudly.

"He didn't make us feel like we needed to be boys, but anytime we'd say, 'Dad, would you come and play ball with us?' he was always out there," she added. "My dad played at Shelbourne High School and won a sectional, which was a really big deal in those days for such a small town. He went on to play semi-pro ball and probably would have been a great college player. But he was too poor to leave his family without any help.

Amy Metheny shows off the Tamika Catchings USA 10 jersey she purchased at a Catch the Stars Foundation fund-raiser by one of her favorite players. (Photo courtesy of Amy Metheny)

"My dad coached all our summer teams. My mom and dad were at every game we ever played. They were both school teachers."

When Amy was in grade school, the boys wouldn't let her play because they said she double dribbled. "I didn't know what a double dribble meant," she said. "Nobody told me the rules. So I went to the library and took out a book about the rules of basketball so I could play with the boys.

"When I got inducted into the Hall of Fame (2008), I heard from some of those boys. They like to think they're responsible for me being inducted into the Hall of Fame, and you know what? They're absolutely right, because they let me play with them. That made you better."

Metheny's basketball dreams began growing immensely in March of 1976 when her dad and Chuck Mallender took Amy and Chuck's daughter Linda to the first Indiana girls' state championship in Hinkle Fieldhouse.

"Linda was in seventh grade and I was in eighth grade," Amy said. "We were looking ahead. We were going to win the high school championship, we were going to go to college, we were going to be on the Olympic team. We had dreams.

"Our fathers had the same dreams. I remember sitting in the stands watching Judi Warren as a point guard. Being a point guard myself, I related to her leading her team to victory and their whole community going crazy, watching Judi being lifted up as the mental attitude winner. I remember saying, 'I want that my senior year.' "

Amy says there could be no greater role model for the first Indiana Miss Basketball than Judi Warren.

"Judi set the stage. She may not be the best player that's ever played in the state of Indiana, but she was the best leader that ever led her team, and if you watched that 1976 state championship game, she did."

Amy helped learn leadership qualities while competing on a Nerf goal in her family's kitchen.

"We used to shove the kitchen table aside and we'd play on that Nerf goal: three girls and our neighbor boy, Bobby Hawkins, who played on the Southport team. I would visualize winning the state championship."

Going into the 1980 state tournament Southport had lost only twice. Coach Marilyn Ramsey's Cardinals defeated Greencastle, 68-52, and Indianapolis North Central, 70-67, in the semi-state to earn a spot in the Final Four at Market Square Arena in Indianapolis.

"A week before the state finals my aunt sent me a newspaper article she had been saving for four years," Amy said. "It was about Judi Warren and Warsaw winning the state finals. My aunt wrote at the top, 'Now it's your turn,' and sent it to me."

Southport beat Marion, 73-55, and Columbus East downed Twin Lakes, 50-41, in the early games of the state finals. That set the stage for one of the most memorable girls' state championship games ever. In the first overtime game in the event, Amy scored 28 points in leading the Cardinals to a 67-63 triumph that gave Southport a 25-2 record.

But it was Maria Stack of the Olympians who was the individual star. She scored 42 points—still a championship-game record—and grabbed 22 rebounds.

Amy laughed and said, "Did I guard Maria Stack? Thankfully we played a zone defense and I was not responsible for her 42 points. I remember a newspaper reporter asked me, 'What was the plan against Maria?' I said, 'I don't know, but whatever it was it didn't work.' Maria clearly had one of the greatest single games of all time.

"Maria was inducted into the Hall of Fame in 2007, a year before I went in. We saw each other and we laughed. That game has connected us forever."

What made that game so memorable, besides Maria's record 42 points, was how it ended, Amy says.

"If we had blown out Columbus East, nobody would ever talk about it again. But because it was such a great battle and it was so exciting with Laura Krieger hitting an amazing shot to send it into overtime, it made the game one of the greatest state championship contests ever."

Southport led the whole game until the final seconds of regulation when Stack hit a shot to put Columbus East ahead by two points.

"We call time out," Amy recalled. "The thing is for me to bring the ball up the court, take a shot, pass it off or whatever I could do. I drove down the left side of the lane and three players came in on me. Out of my peripheral vision I see Linda Mallender, my teammate forever.

"I contend even today that Linda would have caught that pass had she been healthy. She had torn her ACL on Thursday before the game on Saturday. She was literally playing with a dragging leg. Linda was wide open on the opposite side of the basket and I dished it off.

"The minute I dished off the ball, I looked and saw Linda standing under the basket, waiting for me to shoot. The ball bounces off Linda's elbow. It could have gone out of bounds. The ball starts rolling toward our bench. I couldn't believe this was how it was going to end."

Instead, Laura Krieger jumped over one of her teammates who almost tripped her, picked up the ball and heaved it two-handed while falling down. With no time on the clock, the ball went in, tying the score at 57-57 and sending the game into overtime.

During the game, Amy, a 70 percent free throw shooter normally, missed seven of nine free throws. Southport pressed both games that day and Amy believes the reason the team was only 13-of-23 from the foul line in the title game was because the players were exhausted.

"But this is what is great," Amy said. "I missed the free throws, so Laura Krieger gets to hit a shot that is remembered forever. That would have been a three-pointer today. After she made that shot, I walked over to the bench very calmly and in the huddle said, 'We've won the game. It's ours now.'

"After the game I saw Laura sitting there with about every reporter in the state of Indiana interviewing her and she's spinning the ball, leaning back and holding court. You know what? Good for her.

"We had a reunion of our high school team at my house in the summer of 2009 and Laura was there with her husband and parents. We watched the game and to see Laura relive that shot was unbelievable."

Amy Metheny always has been the consummate team player. In 2007 she organized a 25-year reunion of I.U.'s Big Ten women's basketball championship.

"That's the point guard's job," she said with a chuckle. "We were motivated by Debra McClurg, one of our teammates. She was being inducted into the Indiana Basketball Hall of Fame that year. We wanted to go and support her. I called everybody on the team, 11 people, and do you know, 11 of 11 came back for that event."

Amy hadn't seen some of her teammates for 10 or 15 years.

"They came from Florida, Georgia, Connecticut, Ohio, Michigan. We got together for a whole weekend. We sat round Friday night in my living room and reminisced and laughed and laughed and laughed. Sports bond you.

"We came from all walks of life. Yet we had to figure out how to be a team. We had girls from the inner city, African Americans. We had girls from southern Indiana that liked country music. We had the most diverse warm-up tape you've ever heard. We let everybody pick two songs. I had the Christian Lock. They thought I was nutty. And I like the instrumental orchestra, because I played the cello.

"We could tease each other about our differences, but we also realized we're sisters for what we went through in college, the ups and downs."

What lies ahead for Amy?

"That's a great question," she said. "I've learned with my illness to take life a little more day-by-day. When I got sick, I sort of realized I couldn't will everything to happen.

"But I was always a big dreamer. Most of the things that I had dreamed about came true. And even if all of your dreams don't come true, you are better for having the dreams."

Amy Metheny remains a dreamer who will always believe that her cup is half full, not half empty.

CHERYL COOK

From her native Haughville on the west side of Indianapolis to the Great Wall of China and many other countries throughout the world, with stops in between at Washington High School and the University of Cincinnati where she became known as the Cookie Monster: That is the remarkable basketball journey of Cheryl Cook.

"I wouldn't trade my life for the world," said the 1981 Indiana Miss Basketball. "If I had to start over, I would want my whole story to play out like it has. I came from the Haughville area and no one thought I would go this far with the game of basketball.

"A lot of women said they didn't play basketball in their lifetime, but I just had that vision and drive and work ethic. I've walked the Great Wall of China and not a lot of people can say that. That made such an impact in my life, being able to travel and play the game that I love."

When Cheryl was inducted into the Indiana Basketball Hall of Fame on April 24, 2010, her acceptance speech was short and emotional.

"First of all, it was a great honor bestowed upon me," she said. "I just lost my mother, Tama Cook, four years ago, so when I got to her and to say what she did for me in regard to my basketball career and supporting me in anything I did, I lost my train of thought.

"Everything I said came from the heart. I wish I could have drug it out and thanked people. There was nothing meant by me losing my train of thought. I still miss my mother as if it were only yesterday. Hopefully everyone knows that. Indiana basketball is in my blood and always has been."

Cheryl is the third oldest of four boys and four girls. Her father was in the military for 33 years and received two Purple Hearts. But he was absent from the family a lot.

"Obviously he sent checks home, but that wasn't enough," Cheryl said. "We needed him. Once he went to war, he'd come back, but my mother had to fend for herself. I think she did a heckuva job raising eight kids by herself.

"Mother was very watchful. She made sure that we didn't hang out in the streets. She made sure that we attended church. None of us have criminal histories and we've all been to school. We never had a hungry day or a dirty day. I owe it all to her."

While the mother was working three jobs—the primary one being as a nurse—the kids would have to entertain themselves at home.

Cheryl and her siblings began to play basketball very primitively.

"It stared out with a pair of socks rolled up," she said. "We made our own baskets in the crevice of the door at 1122 Belmont and we shot our socks at the baskets. I picked the game up from there and I ran with it because I loved it."

Cheryl described herself as a tomboy as a youth and she used to watch her brothers play basketball at a park across the street from the family home. She was too young to see some of the Washington High male greats play—Billy Keller, Ralph Taylor, Eddie Bopp, George McGinnis and Steve Downing.

"I'm a basketball fanatic," she said. "I got the opportunity to talk to those great players when I got older. I loved the tradition at Washington and I just wanted to be a part of it."

As a junior at Washington High, Cheryl says she learned a valuable life lesson. Her coach, Charles Payne, kicked his star player out of practice for zipping passes to teammates he thought were too hard to catch.

"I wasn't doing it to be vindictive," she said. "I'd grown up with four brothers. But he (Payne) said if I couldn't learn to adjust and not pass the ball so hard, then I could just go home.

"He said, 'Guess what, there's no I in team and you need to go home and come back with a better attitude.' And most definitely I did. I've never been kicked out of anything associated with basketball again."

Cheryl's respect for Payne remains vivid.

"Not only was he a coach, he was a father figure," she said. "He was a role model, he was a mentor. I owe a lot to him, because without him I don't know where my career would have gone."

She also praised her AAU coach, Lyman Battles.

"He was a police officer and I played for him at the PAL (Police Athletic League) Club," she offered. "He took me on college trips when my mom had to work. He bought me things so I would look nice and be able to present myself well when I went on college visits. He did it all. I owe a lot to him as well."

One game at Washington High remains special for Cheryl.

"Perry Meridian (on the south side of Indianapolis) was supposed to win the state championship and people thought there was no possible way we could beat them (in the sectional final)," she said. "My team wasn't that strong, but we had a lot of determination and we felt we could beat anyone if we played as a team.

"We shocked everybody and ended up knocking them out of the tournament. That was my biggest feat in high school."

The most points Cheryl scored in one game at Washington was 51 and she had 1,428 career points. As a senior she averaged 29.7 and the honors came fast and furious—McDonald's High School All-American, Converse All-American and the most treasured of all, Miss Basketball.

"My coach came and got me out of class and said I had been named Indiana Miss Basketball," she said. "I was like, 'Wow.' I didn't know the magnitude of that. I was humbled and I was proud for my family, my high school and the Haughville area."

Then it was on to college. Cheryl took official visits to such schools as Cincinnati, Louisville, Kentucky, Southern California and Hawaii. Why did she pick Cincinnati?

"Everyone wants to know that," she said. "But Cincinnati was the only one that stressed academics. That was important for my mother and myself. I also chose Cincinnati because I had a supportive family and they always liked to see me play. Cincinnati was close to Indianapolis and they stressed academics."

Cheryl, who was a communications major at Cincinnati, was the second Indianapolis basketball superstar to attend the Ohio school. The first was Oscar Robertson, who led Crispus Attucks to successive boys' state championships in 1955 and '56. He had a fabled career for the Bearcats.

"Robertson did not help recruit me, but I have met him," Cheryl said. "He's an over-all champion and also a great role model. When you step on the campus at the University of Cincinnati, the first person they talk about is Oscar Robertson and his legacy.

"I had an awesome career at Cincinnati. When I go to the Olympic Training Center (in Colorado Springs), everyone says, 'Why did you choose Cincinnati? It's a small school.' I didn't want to be that big fish in a small pond. I just wanted to fit in somewhere. I wanted to be comfortable, I wanted to control my own destiny and make my own legacy. I think I left a good one."

Cheryl scored 2,367 career points, the high-mark for women at Cincinnati to this day. She was named Metro Conference Player of the Year three times and became a Kodak All-American. In 1983 she won a Pan-American Games gold medal in Caracas, Venezuela, and three years later she earned a World Championship gold medal in Madrid, Spain, as the U.S. defeated Russia, 108-88, in the championship game.

While at the University of Cincinnati, Cheryl Cook met the Cookie Monster when Sesame Street played in the city. (Photo courtesy of University of Cincinnati)

Indianapolis Washington High School's Cheryl Cook played all around the world, from her home-base Haughville to the Great Wall in China. (Photo courtesy of University of Cincinnati)

Both of Cheryl's numbers, No. 12 at Washington High and No. 24 at Cincinnati, have been retired.

"A senior had 12 once I arrived on the Cincinnati campus," she said. "So I doubled it and 24 has been my number ever since."

Cheryl, who was inducted into the University of Cincinnati Athletic Hall of Fame in 1995, was always known as Cookie to her family and friends. One day, however, she took on a new nickname, Cookie Monster. She was practicing with the Bearcats at Riverfront Coliseum. *Sesame Street* was playing there that night. It was suggested that Cheryl have her picture taken with the Cookie Monster.

"I love that nickname," she said, smiling. "Whenever I step on the University of Cincinnati campus, they say the Cookie Monster is back. I loved playing on the big stage at Riverfront Coliseum. People in the Cincinnati area supported us and that's why we had to move from the fieldhouse on the Cincinnati campus to Riverfront Coliseum."

After graduating from Cincinnati in 1985, Cheryl played six years professionally in Spain and Italy. There was no WNBA at that time.

"There's no question I would have played in the WNBA if there had been that opportunity for us back then," she said. "I can honestly say that we have arrived as women in sports. I think everyone around the nation is starting to take women's basketball seriously. It is an awesome thing to see and be a part of."

Cheryl played in Madrid, Spain, her first season as a pro.

"It was great," she stated. "I played for a team called British Petroleum. I didn't know the language or the currency when I first arrived, but I took a crash course at the University of Madrid, 'cause I kept running out of money.

"I was making $10,000 a month. I called my agent and said, 'They're not paying me all my money.' He said, 'Yes they are.' I would go to the grocery and I was just showing them my money. They were taking it. The second year I took a Spanish class and they couldn't get anything over me after that."

The 5-foot-10 Cook led the league in Spain in scoring her first two years at 37.6. Her highest overseas contract was for $100,000.

"I could make $100,000 go a long way," she said. "I'm doing excellent financially."

It was late in Cheryl's professional career that she was invited to a 10-player tryout in North Carolina to select a female player for the Harlem Globetrotters.

"They tried to turn me into a dribbler," she said, laughing. "I didn't care whether I made it or not, but the experience was good for me. I used to watch those guys on

Basketball bonding can be a beautiful thing.

Take Cheryl Cook, Amy Metheny and Linda Mallender for example. All three are in the Indiana Basketball Hall of Fame. Metheny entered in 2008, Cook and Mallender in 2010.

Cook, who was named Indiana Miss Basketball in 1981 after an outstanding career at Indianapolis Washington High School, competed often against Metheny and Mallender, who helped Indianapolis Southport win the 1980 state girls' championship, in AAU basketball.

Metheny and Mallender would often drive to Haughville on the west side of Indianapolis to pick up Cook, because Cheryl's mother would be working to support eight kids.

"We competed against each other so much, they said the heck with having us on opposite teams," Cheryl said. "Linda's dad Chuck was the coach and I ended up going on their team and playing with them.

"We became friends. They were like my sisters. They are awesome people and I'll never forget 'em. I love 'em for what they did for me. We were always friends and family first."

television when I was a young girl. Just to be on the same court with them was an amazing time."

Cheryl made it to a five-player veterans camp. Lynette Woodard, a teammate of Cook's on the gold-medal winning Pan-American Games team, was selected.

"We were happy for her," Cheryl said. "It was a humbling experience to be asked and make it to the veterans camp."

Cheryl lives in Bedford, Ohio, a Cleveland suburb. She is a unit administrator at the Cuyahoga Hills Juvenile Correctional Facility in Highland Hills, Ohio.

"It's a men's prison," she said. "I've been there 10 years now. I've been coaching there for the last four years and three years in a row we won a state championship. I'm the only female coach ever and I love it."

Cheryl is able to communicate well with the young men because she has been through tough times, too.

"They don't have people that support 'em," she said. "They make mistakes. I don't judge 'em. What I can do is get 'em back on the right track. I was fortunate enough to have a mother that was strong-willed. I had neighbors that looked after us to make sure we didn't get into mischief. Mother worked hard and we knew what was right and what was wrong. I try to do the same for these young men."

Cheryl would like to be superintendent someday at a correctional facility. It could be anywhere.

"You know what they say, your career comes full circle," she said. "I might end up in Indiana. You never know."

In July, 2010, Cheryl held her first basketball camp in Atlanta with 40 kids on a military base.

"I met a young lady and her husband in Spain," she said. "I just happened to go to a bowling alley and I met her and her husband. We've been friends for 15 years. She's from England and her husband is an American.

"We lost contact, but she looked me up on the University of Cincinnati Web site. She was not a basketball player. They were military and they invited me to the military base. I saw all these Americans and I said, 'This is great.' "

The English woman, who wrote contracts for entertainers, got Cheryl's number and called her.

"She said, 'I've got an idea. Why don't we start a basketball camp?' " Cheryl said. And the idea has become a reality, just like so many other endeavors by one of Haughville's finest.

COMING OF AGE

SHARON VERSYP

On April 16, 2010, Purdue University officials announced that women's basketball coach Sharon Versyp had been given a two-year contract extension that guaranteed the 1984 Indiana Miss Basketball compensation of $358,000 per year and an additional $325,000 annually tied to academic, athletic and paid attendance performance.

"In my wildest dreams I never thought I'd ever make that kind of money for being involved in a game I've loved ever since I watched Judi Warren lead Warsaw to the first girls' state championship in 1976 and I became the first Indiana Miss Basketball to play for Purdue," Sharon said.

Eight days after she received the contract extension, the former Mishawaka High School standout was inducted into the Indiana Basketball Hall of Fame.

"I was really humbled by this honor and so appreciative of all of the friends and family that were there to support me," Sharon said.

"Basketball and this state are such a big part of my life and have given me many blessings, so to be inducted into the Indiana Hall of Fame is a real honor. As they say at the Hall of Fame (in New Castle), 'In 49 states it's just basketball—this is Indiana.' "

Sharon went into the hall the first year she was eligible. She likes to tell the story about how competitive she was as a youth.

"My Mishawaka neighbors were mostly

guys," she said. "They were like, 'Oh, girls can't play basketball' when I'd shoot baskets. They'd challenge me: 'If you make it from here, I'll give you $2. If you make it back here, I'll give you $5.' Back then I thought this is a great way to make some money if you were a girl that could actually play the game."

She added that college athletics for women has come a long way, but it has a lot further to go.

"Men's basketball has been around over 100 years and women's basketball has been around about half that," Sharon went on. "To be able to have my life come full circle and be at a university where I graduated and helped build a foundation and obviously have a great contract and a contract extension, it's come a long way.

"You look at these numbers, but then you look at others (men with even higher salaries). It's all relative of how long you've been in the game. I didn't know how quickly this could occur in my life, being able to do what I love, to be able to give back to the sport and obviously making an amazing career. Financially it's obviously beneficial."

And very stressful, Sharon added with a laugh.

"Be careful what you wish for," she said. "Women coaches, they want to be paid the money, they want the extensions. But you need to make sure you do all the right things, because if you don't win, they'll get rid of you.

"You're seeing that in the women's game. In the men's game it's been that way for a while, because the money's way up there. Women are following in the men's footsteps. You're getting the pressure that if you don't win, then you're gonna be fired."

Despite these thoughts, Sharon is not intimidated by the stress big money brings.

"You keep grinding it out and doing what you love to do," she said. "I'm all about character of kids. My philosophy is teaching life skills through sport, and I do things the right way. If I have to do things the wrong way, I'll get out."

Sharon is the baby of the three children of Robert and Kathleen Versyp.

Purdue women's coach Sharon Versyp was a recruiting whiz long before she reached the collegiate coaching level as an assistant at the University of Louisville in 1996.

Believe it or not, as a junior at Mishawaka High School Sharon talked Marvin Wood into coaching the school's girls' team nearly 30 years after he and his miracle Milan team defeated mighty Muncie Central, 32-30, in 1954 to win the Indiana boys' high school tournament in one of this state's most memorable sports achievements.

It happened this way. During the 1982-83 season, the Mishawaka girls' coach, John Taylor, suffered a massive heart attack and had to undergo surgery. Wood had coached the school's boys' team and at the time was a counselor at Mishawaka High.

"I knew Coach Wood and I went to see him after coach Taylor had a heart attack," Sharon said. "He was a legend in his own right, having coached Milan and Bobby Plump (whose last-second field goal beat Muncie Central and inspired the movie *Hoosiers*).

" 'You don't have to do it forever and it would be a great opportunity,' I said. Marvin went home to talk with his wife Mary Lou about it. He wound up coaching us for a year and a half."

Mishawaka lost to Heritage of Monroeville, 48-42, in the first game of the Fort Wayne Semi-State in 1983. The next year Wood's team went into the Fort Wayne Semi-State against

"They passed away early in my life, when I was 24 (Robert) and 34 (Kathleen)," she stated. "It was kinda like when you lose your parents at an early age, you feel like an orphan a little bit. But what they instilled in me, my passion, my drive, my intensity, all those things I credit to them. They really prepared me for life. Everything I am is because of them."

Name the sport, and Sharon was most likely involved as a youth.

"I grew up being a gymnast first," she said. "Being a gymnast you have to be mentally, physically and emotionally tough. You had coaches so disciplined, so structured, I think that set the foundation, besides my parents' foundation. Gymnastics was a big key for me."

She did everything in gymnastics that pertained to strength—uneven bars, vault, tumbling.

"The ballet, the finesse, the shaky smiles. I was not good at that. And I played baseball and basketball. I could hit, steal all the bases, steal home. I hit some home runs, but mainly I just placed the ball, and I was really, really fast."

Through middle school Sharon was a three-sport athlete.

"I played volleyball and basketball, and I ran track," she observed. But when she got to high school she played softball, which was easier on the legs than track. In the summers Sharon played volleyball and basketball.

Sharon not only loved volleyball, it brought her a state championship in her senior year at Mishawaka.

"We won state against the No. 1 team in the country, Muncie Burris," she said matter-of-factly.

"You beat Muncie Burris?" I said quizzically, the perennial power of girls' volleyball in Indiana.

"Yes, sir, 1983," Sharon replied emphatically. "It was the best game ever in the history of volleyball back in the day. It was unbelievable. It kept going back and forth in the third match. I blocked the last hit to win the game.

"We won in three matches. Back then you didn't do rally scoring, so it took forever. I think the finals were at Ben Davis in Indianapolis. The place was standing-room-only.

Eastbrook of Marion unbeaten at 24-0.

"I had never heard of Eastbrook," Sharon said. "We had to run into Jana Bragg and Dawn Davenport and lost, 60-58. Dawn Davenport was like 6-foot-4 and going to Texas to play volleyball. Jana Bragg, I think, was going out west to play basketball. They beat us, but we had an incredible run."

Wood, who died of cancer in 1999, had a profound influence on Sharon's life and basketball career.

"Marvin taught me so much about the game," she said. "He would always say, 'Quick, but do not hurry.' I always remembered that and I use that terminology today."

Wood was never known as a yeller, but Sharon says she finally got him to yell one time, because she got him mad enough to let out a yell.

"He never raised his voice too much," she went on. "He just had that passion. It was awesome. And he coached our AAU team. Karen Phelps, Digger Phelps' daughter, played AAU with us. She was at South Bend St. Joe, but she played with our AAU team.

"Marvin coached AAU for two or three years. It was just kind of a chain of events and he wound up coaching at St. Mary's, an all-women's college (at Notre Dame, Ind.). Mary Lou and I are very close. We touched each other's life and brought a different identity to him and to me. He made a huge impact on my life."

That was one of my best memories. I never won a championship in basketball."

Sharon did have an outstanding basketball career under coaches John Taylor and Marvin Wood for the Cavemen. Taylor suffered a heart attack in her junior season. Sharon then talked Wood, who coached Milan to its historic boys' state championship in 1954, into taking over for Taylor. He had coached the Mishawaka boys' team and was a counselor at the school at the time.

Wood coached the Mishawaka girls' team for a year and a half. The team lost in the first game of the Fort Wayne Semi-State in 1983 and '84. Mishawaka's 60-58 loss to Eastbrook of Marion was its only setback in 25 games in the '83-84 season.

As a senior Sharon, a 5-foot-9 point guard, averaged 23.8 points, 4.3 rebounds and 3.8 assists per game and became Miss Basketball, helping Indiana sweep Kentucky in the All-Star rivalry. She scored 1,189 career points and Mishawaka was 58-9 in her three varsity seasons.

Sharon was good enough to play volleyball or basketball at any school in the country.

"I could have played volleyball at Texas, which was the No. 1 team in the country at the time (1984)," she said. "Back then Louisiana Tech was so great in basketball. My biggest thing was deciding what I wanted to play. I thought basketball was more challenging.

"You had to be skilled in so many different areas. Academics is very important, first and foremost, and I did want my family to see me play, so I chose Purdue for basketball. I wanted to go to a program to help build it."

Sharon, one of only seven four-year starters in Purdue women's basketball history, did that. She led the team to three consecutive winning seasons at a time when the program had enjoyed only one winning campaign in the previous 10 years.

"I'm still in the top 10 in 10 statistical categories (10th in career points with 1,565)," she said. "That's amazing with all the outstanding people who have played here and the championships they've won."

Sharon was named all-Big Ten in 1988, which was a feather in her cap after playing for three different coaches at Purdue.

"Dr. Ruth Jones, who recruited me, died of cancer between my sophomore and junior years," Sharon said. "They hired Marcia Reel. She was only here one year, then I played for Lin Dunn my senior year.

"Those three years were difficult. You're a young kid, you're trying to find your way. Our team stuck together, which I thought was great. Mentally, emotionally and physically it was a tough experience having three coaches and one who died.

"But overall the journey, the things that happened while I was there, those four years were instrumental in building who I am, being able to handle adversity. When you're going through it, you don't realize it because you're 18 to 22, and you're like, 'How can this be happening?' The academic experience, the basketball, the whole journey was really special."

Rather than heading to Australia to play professionally for $20,000 to $30,000 a year following graduation from Purdue, Sharon opted to begin a coaching career in 1989 as the girls' basketball coach at Lawrence North High School in Indianapolis, coaching alongside Lawrence North boys' coach Jack Keefer until 1993.

"He was a tough one, but he actually had a lot of respect for me," Sharon said. "We had a really good working relationship."

Lawrence North was 0-36 (0-18 and 0-18) the two seasons before Sharon arrived.

"The only way to go was up," she explained. "You win one game and you're awesome. But we were successful. We got the team to winning and started challenging for the conference."

Sharon credits the year she spent assisting head coach Jan Conner at Benton Central High in Oxford with preparing her well for the Lawrence North assignment.

"When I was a fifth-year senor at Purdue I helped Jan Conner," she said. "I was student teaching at Lafayette Jeff High School, but going over and coaching with Jan. That year we were state runner-up (Benton Central lost to Scottsburg, 74-72, in the title game).

"Jan is phenomenal. She knows how to build a program and I learned a lot when I was 22, 23, of what to do when you take over a program."

From Lawrence North, Sharon went to Benton Central, which obviously was familiar with her promising coaching skills. She was there three years as the Bison's basketball, volleyball and softball coach.

Then came a critical point in Sharon's professional life. She was making around $45,000 teaching and coaching at Benton Central when she had an offer to be an assistant coach at the University of Louisville.

"You have to choose where you want to go very carefully, because you need to go to a program that's pretty successful, and at the time Louisville was very successful," Sharon said.

"I decided to leave my job at Benton Central to go to Louisville for $8,000 and no benefits. My parents thought I was crazy."

Sharon was at Louisville nine months, then went with coach Bud Childers to James Madison University at Harrisonburg, Va., as the top assistant. She was at James Madison three years before going to the University of Maine at Orono as head coach.

"Maine has been the best five years of my life thus far," Sharon said with a huge smile. "The beauty, the people are simple, and, oh yes, I'm a lobster fan. I had just lost my mother and I got the Maine job, so I threw myself into my work. You lose your last parent and you don't know what to do. The people, the culture, the simplicity of Maine made me feel right at home."

Sharon fell in love with Acadia National Park in Bar Harbor, Maine, along the Atlantic Ocean.

"I'd go there all the time," she said. "I'd hike, I'd bike. I also did snowmobiling and ice fishing."

Late in the 2004-05 season, the Indiana University job became open and a call was made by I.U. officials to the Maine athletic director for permission to talk to Sharon. She interviewed with I.U. after the season, was offered the job and accepted.

"I thought it was great to get back in the Big Ten," Sharon said. "The Big Ten stands for all the right things, championships on and off the field, not just championships athletically."

She says she heard nothing negative from I.U. fans because she was a Purdue graduate.

"At the time everybody was excited," Sharon stated. "I was excited. If Purdue hadn't come after me, I wouldn't have left Bloomington. I'm known as a loyal person. They (I.U. officials) gave me an opportunity to come back to the Big Ten.

"Our one year there we were very successful (19-14). We ended up going to the WNIT. It was a great place to work. I can't say anything but positive things about my experience there. I got hired April 9, 2006, then April 9, 2007, I ended up back at Purdue. A year to the date. It's kinda scary."

Sharon insists it wasn't easy leaving Bloomington for West Lafayette, but she remains a Boilermaker, through and through.

"I helped build the Purdue foundation, I believe in what it stands for, so you want to go back to your alma mater if you possibly can, because you lived it, you love it, you have passion for it," Sharon said.

"Purdue's women's basketball is one of the top 10 winningest programs in the country. It's a top 22 public academic institution and it's top 10 in attendance over the last 15 years, but over the past five we've been top five in the country. So when you have those three it's hard to say no to something like that."

In her first four years at Purdue, Sharon led the Boilermakers to two Big Ten Tournament championships and two NCAA Tournament Elite Eight appearances. She had a 91-49 record in that time.

Sharon says she has a great relationship with Matt Painter, the Purdue men's coach. "Both teams are always cheering for one another. We work together on a daily basis. Matt will talk to our recruits. He'll do anything to help anybody. He wants everybody to be successful.

"Our relationship is very important and I think that's been a big key to both of our successes. Both staffs really care for each other and we spend time together."

Both the Boilermaker women's and men's teams are aiming high.

"We're doing some great things at Purdue," Sharon said. "Some people never get to the Sweet Sixteen or win one game in the NCAA tournament. Our mission is to win championships, whether it's a Big Ten championship or a national championship."

JAN CONNER

Jan Conner could talk basketball 24/7. She almost did when we met at the Indiana High School Athletic Association office in Indianapolis a few days after the coach of Martinsville's successive girls' state championship teams in 1997 and '98 missed an interview session at Lafayette Jeff High School.

"I apologize totally for forgetting our time to talk at Lafayette Jeff," said Jan, who had a 434-71 record in coaching 26 years at Indianapolis' Warren Central (two years), Benton Central in Oxford (15 years), Martinsville (six years) and Lafayette Jeff (three years), after driving to the IHSAA headquarters from her home in Otterbein northwest of Lafayette.

"A friend of my mom passed away and mom was really upset. I live with mom and take care of her (Jan's father is deceased)."

Jan says people were shocked that she didn't try for 500 victories.

"But that's just a number," the 58-year-old go-getter explained. "The number 71 (losses) to me is far greater than 434 (victories)."

Although Jan did not get to play basketball at Benton Central in the late 1960s because girls' sports at that time were run by the Girls Athletic Association (GAA) and Benton Central had no girls' basketball team, basketball was always her first love.

"From the time I was a little girl playing against my brother Mike, who was three years older, basketball was absolutely the most wonderful game in the world," Jan said. "Mike never gave me any slack. Whenever he started letting me have it back, I'd cry, like all girls.

"He'd say, 'She can dish it out, but she can't take it.' That was just to get him upset. I would play with all the guys. Our place was the place to play basketball. When I was 12 we moved from the farm to town (Otterbein).

"We lived on Main Street and we had a basketball goal with a light. We played 'til 2 o'clock in the morning. When I went off to college (Indiana State University), the neighbor who lived across the street came over to my mother and said, 'Finally some peace and quiet.' "

Holiday gatherings at the Conner home were special, and basketball was a main course. Mike Conner coached high school basketball at Seeger and Lakeville and Jan's four uncles coached high school basketball at such places as Otterbein, Rensselaer, Zionsville, Morocco, Kentland and Hammond.

"They were everywhere," she said proudly. "You can't imagine what it was like around our table at family dinners at Thanksgiving and Christmas. All the guys would get their pens out and diagram plays on the table cloth.

"My grandmother would have to boil the table cloth to get the plays out. I heard stories about Red Grange, "The Galloping Ghost," (famed running back, University of Illinois, 1923-1925; Chicago Bears, 1925, 1929-1934) and about going to a game that Knute Rockne coached. Everything was sports in our family, everything. Here I was a little girl and I listened to all the stories. I didn't play with dolls. I just listened to my uncles tell all those great stories."

The "picket fence" play made famous by the character played by the late Dennis Hopper in the movie *Hoosiers* wasn't diagrammed by any of Jan's uncles, but she does remember well another play put on the table cloth.

"I learned a valuable lesson early on in those days," she said. "Everybody is looking for great plays. My brother said, 'I had this old coach who gave me this play. It'll work, it'll work.' Everybody said it wouldn't work. I ran it for 26 years and nobody ever beat it. It came from a guy who was like 90 years old and played basketball years and years ago."

Jan didn't play competitive basketball until her sophomore season at Indiana State.

"They had some high school teams up in Gary and Lowell and places like that," she stated, "and we knew there were some teams in the south, places like Terre Haute and Scottsburg.

"We asked our GAA sponsor, Claudia Zuege, our track coach and volleyball coach—she did it all, and she had four children; I don't know how she did it—if we could have a basketball team. She said no. 'Basketball is a contact sport,' she said. To her generation it probably was. We wanted to play and boy, we had a great team. We all played whenever we could. I would shoot around with the guys if I could and sometimes they'd let me."

Although basketball wasn't offered for girls at Benton Central in GAA days, track, volleyball, badminton and swimming were offered, and Jan was outstanding as a hurdler, high jumper and shot putter.

"We won the state in track four straight years," she said. "I won, I believe, 13 different state titles, including a relay race. The thing that gets me is they didn't put my picture up in the high school because it was GAA. It's up there now because of my basketball coaching days. But it wasn't up there for my track. I told 'em, 'I'm gonna come back some day and you're gonna have to put my picture on this wall (Jan says she never could get pictures of girl basketball players at Lafayette Jeff put up)."

Jan's prowess in track took her to Terre Haute and Indiana State on an athletic scholarship. That would eventually enable her to play college basketball.

"I was the first girl on athletic scholarship in anything in Indiana, they told me," Jan said. "At the time they were playing six-player basketball, like in Iowa. You played either offense or defense, and they had one rover that got to go both ways. In gym class I was always the rover."

It didn't take Jan long to discover in her collegiate track efforts that she was "pretty slow." So the coaches made her into a javelin and discus thrower. "I was second in the country in the javelin for a while and had some Olympic hopes."

Then in 1971, the year before the Olympics in Germany, Jan's life was changed forever. Edith Godleski, who had become the ISU women's varsity basketball coach, saw Jan play intramural basketball one night and she said to Jan, 'I want you to play basketball for me next year."

At the time women's college sports were run by the Association for Intercollegiate Athletics for Women (AIAW), and they had a rule that if you had a scholarship in one sport you could not play in another sport.

"Unbeknownst to me, the powers at Indiana State got together and they took away my track scholarship and gave me a P.E. scholarship that matched my track scholarship," Jan said. "I became a basketball player and I was thrilled, because I always wanted to be a basketball coach, always, forever."

Jan lettered three years for the Lady Sycamores, earning Most Valuable Player (MVP) honors while leading the team in rebounding, field goal percentage and free throw percentage.

After graduating from ISU in 1974, Jan became the head basketball coach and head track coach at Warren Central. It was a bittersweet experience.

"They let me go after two years," she said. "I'm not exactly sure why I was let go. I was pretty green and thought everybody liked me. We were very successful. We won the sectional in basketball and won the sectional in track.

"It was one of those deals where somebody with a bigger name than I had wanted my job. But it was the best thing that ever happened to me, because I went back to Benton Central."

How Jan got the job says a lot about her standing in the Otterbein community.

"I was sitting at a softball game in Otterbein," she recalled. "I had applied at five or six schools and no place would hire me. This lady, whose daughter was playing softball, came up to me. I taught all the girls softball for years.

"She said, 'What are you doing now?' I was pretty much legend in my little community being an athlete. I said, 'Well, I'm looking for a job.' She said, 'Benton Central needs a basketball coach. Would you come to Benton Central?' I said, 'Sure.' "

On the day Jan got fired at Warren Central, the coach taking her place was already in the building.

"The principal said, 'Jan, I think one of these days we're going to regret that we did this.' I just said, 'You can take that to the bank. You will regret this someday.' "

Shortly after that day at the softball field, Jan got a phone call from a junior basketball player she had coached in softball

"I hear you might be our basketball coach," the player said. "A bunch of us get together to play basketball at this girl's house. Why don't you come and watch?' "

Jan picked up the player and played with those girls.

"They were awesome," she said. "I was taking the player home and she said, 'What do you think?' I said, 'I think we won't lose a game.' "

Jan said she didn't care if the school had a teaching job or not (none was available for the 1977-78 season), she wanted to coach those girls. And she did, well.

"The people in Benton County fell in love with our basketball team," Jan said. "And they have followed girls' basketball ever since. The semi-state was held at Benton Central that season and the stands were packed. The four teams were Warsaw, East Chicago Roosevelt, Michigan City Rogers and us.

"We went from practicing in elementary school gyms and having about 10 people watch our first game to losing in double overtime to Michigan City Rogers in the first game of the semi-state. I got paid $400. That's it to coach the girls' varsity team that made it to the semi-state. That was our only loss."

In 1988 and '89 Benton Central made it to the state finals.

"We got beat in the first game in '88 by Noblesville," Jan said. "Courtney Cox made the call that cost us the game. We were up one point and the ball went out of bounds, off her, and she pointed back toward their goal and the ref just pointed to their goal. It would have been our ball and we would have run the clock out. They got it and Courtney went down and scored."

Jan has a fond memory of current Purdue coach Sharon Versyp, who played for the Boilermakers.

"You know how I knew she was gonna be good?" Jan recalled. "She came out to Benton Central her first year out of Purdue and was my assistant coach. I just asked her to help out. She was finishing up her degree and she did not miss one practice, one meeting.

"She came in the morning and worked the girls individually, for no pay. I didn't have anything to pay her with. I promised her I would write her recommendations. By the way she worked with those kids I just knew she was going to be phenomenal."

When Jan turned 40, she had another bittersweet coaching experience. The assistant athletic director at Northeast Missouri State University (located in Kirksville and now known as Truman University after President Harry Truman, a native of Missouri), who was from Indiana, called Jan and said, "We need a basketball coach. Somebody told me you said you might be ready to go to a college job."

Jan went to Kirksville and learned the women's coach had been fired and the school needed a coach immediately. After looking over the school, which she said had "a great academic record," she added, "I don't think I'm interested."

The school officials quickly countered, "How much money would it take?"

"I gave 'em a number and they said okay," Jan said. "I should have said more. I just felt if I didn't do it I'd regret I didn't do it. I took the job and my kids at Benton Central were very unhappy with me."

It didn't take Jan long to realize it wasn't a good move.

"I didn't like it at Northeast Missouri State at all," she declared. "I spent all my time raising money and recruiting and hardly any time at basketball. I liked building the kids' self-esteem, but at a college you don't have much to say about that."

Benton Central had gotten a new principal before Jan went to Kirksville and she had expressed concern about the new position to him.

"Let's do this," he said. "Let's give you a year's leave of absence and let you try this. And if you don't like it, you can come back."

Jan did try it, but her record the first year was 2-24.

"I had a girl on my team and she had never played five-player basketball," she said. "She was from Iowa and she played six-player basketball. She had never played offense, just defense. I said, 'Who recruits a defensive player?' She couldn't catch a ball if her life depended on it. We called her Oven Mitts, because she looked like she had on oven mitts."

Jan called the Benton Central principal and said, "I'm gonna come back." He said, "Well, we don't really want you back." Jan said, "The principal's wife had told me, 'He doesn't like his school known for its girls' basketball program. He wants it to be known as his school, not your school.' "

After recruiting 10 freshmen, five from Indiana, her second year, Jan's Northeast Missouri State team won seven games.

April Traylor (Photo courtesy of Jan Conner)

"My third year we won 12 games," she said. "We had a lot of injuries and it was exasperating. Then my dad passed away unexpectedly. I just thought I had to go home and be closer to mom. I came back and got the job at Martinsville."

Jan's start with the Lady Artesians in the 1995-96 season was rocky.

"Like the second game of the season we play Eminence," she said. "Everybody says, 'Oh, it's a small school.' But they had these two sisters, Danielle and April Traylor. They were really good. Danielle had like 30 points and April like 25. They not only beat us, they killed us."

What did the Martinsville fans think of Jan Conner after that thrashing?

"Not much," she said, frowning. "Jan Conner stood there on the sideline and looked at those sisters and said, 'You live just a little over five miles from us.' "

Jan did have Mackenzie Curless that first season at Martinsville and the 6-1 senior averaged 23.7 points and 11.2 rebounds per game while shooting 56 percent from the field. She became Martinsville's first Indiana All-Star and played her college basketball at Purdue, where she helped the Lady Boilermakers win the 1999 NCAA championship.

How Curless got to Purdue is an interesting story that reveals Conner's concern for her players.

"Mackenzie was one of the best players I ever saw," Jan said. "But she didn't know she was very good. She had no desire whatsoever to show it. I said to her, 'Do you want to play college basketball?' "

Curless said yes without a lot of enthusiasm, and Jan replied, "At Purdue?" When Mackenzie agreed, Jan said, "I'll tell you what, if I can get Lin Dunn (the Purdue coach at the time) in these stands to watch you play, will you step it up a little bit and play harder?' "

Mackenzie said, "Yeah," so Jan, who had known Dunn from her days at Benton Central, called Lin and said, "I need you to come down here and whether you like this girl or not, just please come and watch her play." Lin said okay.

"We were playing Indianapolis Arlington at our place," Jan related, "and I said to Mackenzie, 'You told me that if I got Lin Dunn in the stands you'd put out the effort. Mackenzie had 45 points and 24 rebounds, and only played three quarters. She was unbelievable and Lin offered her a scholarship on the spot.

"You have to show the kids you care about them. And that's what I tried to tell Mackenzie. You work for me and I'll go to the ends of the earth for you. The

Kristen Bodine
(Photo courtesy of Jan Conner)

thing was I never really saw that person again, even when she got the scholarship. Mackenzie averaged over 20 points that season and could have averaged 40. I don't know if I ever had a kid as good as her. Well, I did, April Traylor."

Danielle Traylor graduated from Eminence in 1996.

"All I know is one day I was sitting in class teaching and the Martinsville athletic director knocks on my door and he says, 'There's a really mad parent in the guidance office who wants to talk to you.'

"I go in and there's a lady standing there and I say, 'Do you want to see me?' She said, 'I'm Mrs. Traylor and we're enrolling our daughter April here today.' If anybody thinks I did any recruiting, they just showed up."

Jan says Mrs. Traylor was not mad, that the athletic director just wanted to get the coach upset.

"At 5-foot-10, April was the most phenomenal player who could do anything with the basketball," Jan said. "You put that with Kristen Bodine, who was my 5-11 point guard and one of the best leaders I ever saw.

"Kristen, who was a superstar in her own right, could have been mad someone better than her moved in. She came to me and said,

73

'Coach, can I have your keys to the school? I want to show April around before classes start.' She said she'd do it at night when nobody was around. That's the kind of person Kristen was."

Martinsville lost only to Center Grove, the state champion the year before, en route to the school's first girls' state championship with a 66-59 victory over Crown Point. The Lady Artesians were 26-1 that season.

"I'll never forget," Jan said. "Center Grove threw up a last-second prayer and nobody boxed out. This girl grabbed the ball and put it in at the buzzer. I remember the look on April's face walking off the floor. She looked at me and said, 'That will never happen again.' And it didn't. We didn't lose a game the rest of that year or the next. We won 55 straight games."

In 1998 Martinsville (29-0) defeated Lake Central of St. John (26-1), 71-65, in the state championship game and was ranked second in the nation. How did Martinsville treat Jan and her teams?

"They treated us like we were gods," she said. "When we won that first state championship we got taken out to eat I can't tell you how many times. It was just about every night for three weeks. It was absolutely amazing. And believe me our pictures went up on the wall immediately.

"We won the last single-class state title. That was against everybody. Then we won the first 4A title. This is the one (pointing to her ring) from the last single-class state tournament. I tell everybody I'm more proud of that one that I am of the 4A title."

April Traylor was runner-up to Kelly Komara of Lake Central for Miss Basketball in 1998. April set eight school records, including most career points with 1,836. She played college basketball at Florida State and finished her career with the Lady Seminoles ranked second all-time in assists with 387, third in steals with 217 and fifth in scoring with 1,503 points. She hit the winning shot with 1.9 seconds left as a senior in a victory at Indiana University.

Again Conner assisted one of her stellar players in the recruiting process.

"April wanted to go south where the weather was warmer than in the Midwest and I knew the Florida State coach, Sue Semrau, from her days as an assistant coach at Wisconsin," Jan said. "So I called her and that's how April wound up in Tallahassee."

Jan still teaches health and physical education at Lafayette Jeff.

"I still think health is the most important subject in the building," she said. "I talk to the students about who you marry and who you should marry, and how you should take care of your body for the rest of your life. I tell them, 'You may never use your math again, but you will think about your health every day the rest of your life.'

"Since I hurt my knee in college, I've had 16 knee operations. I've had artificial knees for the past 10 years. I've had six operations on my toes. I have a plate in my neck where I have arthritis so badly from being an athlete in my day and not being taken care of too well.'

"A friend of mine introduced me to this healthy chocolate (Xocai, pronounced Show-PSI). "This will help you with your arthritis,' she said. I ate three pieces a day for a week and all my pain was gone and I stopped taking my medication."

Jan has become a distributor for the chocolate and she remains head of the Indiana Basketball Hall of Fame induction banquet committee for women. She's also an associate director of the hall. Jan went into the hall in the first class for women in 2002.

"I couldn't go in as a player and you had to have 25 years as a coach," she said. "I had only 24 years. The guys said I could go in for the things I had done for girls' basketball over the years."

Asked if she had any regrets about her role in the game she treasures, Jan replied, "Not very many. Oh no, I'd do it all over again. The things we did to get girls' basketball notoriety in the state and get it where it was growing and getting big were a pleasure.

"Virgil Sweet, who was executive director of the Indiana Basketball Coaches Association (IBCA), treated us like we were gold. He was the one who said, 'We can no longer let these women sit here and not get them a say-so.' That's when they let us be a voting member. I feel very gratified by the growth of girls' basketball in Indiana and for my effort in helping that growth."

VICKI HALL

If the outdoor basketball courts at Tarkington Park just west of 4000 North Meridian Street in Indianapolis could talk, they could tell an amazing story about a young white female who asked for no slack and gave none when she competed against males of all races in the mid-1980s.

Vicki Hall, who continues a "new chapter" in her life as an assistant coach at the University of New Mexico in Albuquerque after a stellar career as a high school (Indianapolis Brebeuf), college (University of Texas) and professional player (Europe, American Basketball League and Women's National Basketball Association), earned a unique nickname.

"Everybody used to call me Lady Bird," Vicki said. She couldn't help smiling as she recalled those wonderful days at Tarkington.

"When I went to Texas that name was kinda bad. The real Lady Bird (Johnson, wife of former President Lyndon Baines Johnson) was living there. But I was Lady Bird, because they said I played like Larry Bird.

"The guys at Tarkington Park started giving me that name. 'Here comes Lady Bird,' they'd say. I like that name. I loved Larry Bird."

Vicki's journey to the collegiate coaching ranks began at a young age around the Indianapolis neighborhood of 48th Street and Kessler.

"I was one of the only girls in my neighborhood," she recalled. "There was one other girl and she liked to play with dolls. I really didn't like dolls too much.

"For Christmas one year I got a doll and my older brother David got a basketball. David and his friends would always play and I wouldn't get invited to play. They would be out in the sand box, so I would take his ball and lock myself in the bathroom.

"I started to dribble and play in the bathroom by myself, because I knew they eventually would come in to wash their hands and I wouldn't let 'em in. That's where I learned to love basketball."

Vicki Hall was a standout at Indianapolis Brebeuf Jesuit where she played for Coach Alan Vickrey. (Photo courtesy of Brebeuf)

Vicki's parents, David and Lillian, put up a goal for her in the family yard and she continued to improve her skills.

"I went to a private school, Orchard," Vicki said. "In third grade they had intramural basketball. But it was only for boys. Girls had to be cheerleaders.

"I went home upset. I went back the next day and refused to be a cheerleader. I wanted to be a player. The principal called my mom and they had a discussion. I ended up getting to play intramural basketball with the boys."

Vicki did well. But the decision to allow her to play caused some problems. Some of the parents were upset that a girl was beating their boys at the game of basketball. They didn't like that a girl did that and thought she should not be able to play.

The next year Orchard didn't have a fourth-grade girls' basketball team.

"So I started playing in the fourth grade on the eighth-grade girls' basketball team," Vicki said. "I just caught the bug and continued to love to play. I played CYO ball for St. Michael's. When I really got serious was when I went to Brebeuf."

How serious was Vicki about hoops?

Alan Vickrey, who ended his 32-year career as an Indiana girls' high school basketball coach after the 2010-11 season at Indianapolis North Central, was Vicki's coach four years at Brebeuf, from 1984 through 1988 when she became Miss Basketball and was named Naismith National Girls Basketball Player of the Year, Gatorade National Girls Player of the Year and *Parade Magazine* National Player of the Year.

"Vicki Hall maybe is not the best athlete you'll ever see play the game," he said. "But nobody ever worked harder to make herself a good player. She's one of a kind and probably one in a generation. I see a lot of kids who are really good today and if they worked as hard as Vicki did they'd be unbelievable.

"There are a bunch of guys around town who are in their 40s, 50s now who played basketball and found this little blonde—well, not little blonde (Vicki is 6-foot-1)—that would show up where they'd be playing and she became a first pick soon enough. She would prove herself in every venue she would go to."

Of her high school coach, Vicki says, "Mr. Vickrey is still a great coach and an inspiring person, someone who knows how to motivate young ladies and teach the game."

Vicki knew early that to be really good at the game she had to seek out the best competition possible.

"Wherever there was a game, I was gonna be there," she stressed. "I would play at Tarkington Park. Actually, there was a police officer who lived across the street from me that sometimes would make some rounds to make sure I was okay."

She also played at Indianapolis Ben Davis High School, at Butler University and on the outdoor courts at North Central High School.

"At first the guys never wanted to pick me up, a little girl out there," she said. "Once they saw that I could play, I became one of the players they picked in the top. I think I became a player because I played with the boys. A lot of people who watched me play said

In 1988, Vicki Hall became Miss Basketball.
(Photo courtesy of Brebeuf)

I have a man's game, I guess, because I'm very physical. I guess that's a compliment. I think so."

As Vicki's reputation began to grow she was able to play against some really fine male competition—Scott Skiles, Reggie Miller and Clark Kellogg.

"I was lucky enough that Bob Hill, when he was coach of the Indiana Pacers, allowed me to do some workouts with them," she stated. "That's when I started to do shooting drills and all their ball-handling drills. Of course, when they started to do one-on-ones and two-on-twos I stepped out, 'cause I couldn't really keep up with them."

Vicki remembers reading about Ann Meyers signing a contract with the Pacers but failing to make the roster (Meyers was a standout for UCLA who later married Los Angeles Dodgers pitcher Don Drysdale).

"The woman's body is just very different from the men's," Vicki remarked. "For us a 6-foot guard is really tall. Well, for a guy that's a small point guard. Not only are we smaller, but definitely we don't have the same physical strength, so it's hard to compete at that level."

Although Vicki never won an Indiana high school state

Lady Bird wasn't the only unusual nickname Vicki Hall received as a young player.

Hall's first AAU team was named Love's Carpet. Her coach was Ernie Brewer.

"We wound up winning the 16-and-under national championship, as far as I know the first championship in AAU competition for girls in Indiana," she said. "We also won the 18-and-under national championship.

"When we went to play Lisa Leslie's AAU team in the 18-and-under national championships in Miami, they turned and looked at us and said, 'Oh, a bunch of cornfed chicks.' They thought they were gonna run right over us. We ended up giving it to 'em."

championship, she put up some awesome individual numbers. Vicki is second on Brebeuf's all-time scoring list for girls with 1,755 points, fifth in career assists with 183, second in career field-goal percentage at 59.5 percent and she holds the single-game point total with 44 against Cardinal Ritter in the 1987-88 season.

"We only made it to the regional finals every year but one, my freshman year," Vicki said. "The other three years we were beaten by the eventual champion. And it was always a barn-burner. The worst one was when we were up by 13 points going into the fourth quarter and ended up losing to Noblesville—Courtney Cox, Krissi Davis, Cami Cass. I still remember 'em all."

Vickrey remembers those years with Vicki as bittersweet.

"We caught that stretch where Noblesville had that great bunch and they beat us four straight years in the regional," he said. "The great game was when we were No. 3 and Noblesville was No. 2.You couldn't get a seat in Warren Central's gym before the game.

"Every major college coach in the country was there, Jody Conradt of Texas, Pat Summitt of Tennessee, Andy Landers of Georgia. That was THE place to be in Indiana basketball that night."

As Vicki recalled, Brebeuf was ahead by 13 points going into the fourth quarter. Noblesville put on a full-court press and cut the deficit to two points in the first two minutes of the final period.

"We tried to hold the ball for the last shot in a tie game with a minute left," Vickrey said. "One of our kids got fouled and she made one of two free throws. Noblesville goes to the other end and Courtney Cox gets a fake on the baseline with six, seven seconds left.

"Vicki fouled out on that play. Courtney made both free throws and we got beat by one point. We've watched (the video) again and again and I can't find that foul. Noblesville went on to win the state championship (beating Anderson Highland, 47-38, in the 1987 title game) and we go home."

Nineteen-eighty-eight was an emotional year for Vicki. Her father David died in March. Shortly thereafter she was named Miss Basketball and her college recruitment thrived.

"I was the No. 1 player in the country," she said. "At the time Texas was No. 1 in the country. Tennessee was a very close two. My three visits were Tennessee, Texas and Iowa. Basically it came down to Tennessee and Texas. I chose Texas.

"I had a good experience (in Austin), a learning experience. When you're young and in college, you think you know a whole lot, and you wind up figuring out you don't. Or you're just a little bit before your time.

"We made it to the Elite Eight twice. We got beat by Maryland one year and Louisiana Tech the next. Unfortunately I wasn't able to get any championships in high school or college. I got my championships at the pro level—five in Europe. That was enough."

In 1990 Vicki played on the U.S. National Team that won the World Championship in Malaysia and also the Goodwill Games.

"The World Championships was pretty special," she said with a smile. "Not too many people get those."

Vicki ran into a personal hurdle the first game of her senior year at Texas.

"I blew out my knee—ACL and MCL," she said. "It was a pretty bad injury."

After rehabbing, Vicki played a fifth season in 1992-93. She performed

Known as Lady Bird when she played on Indianapolis' outdoor courts, Vicki Hall became Miss Basketball in 1988 after an outstanding career at Brebeuf Jesuit High School. She also was outstanding at the University of Texas and professionally in Europe. (Photo courtesy of Brebeuf)

well enough in her Austin days to be named to the All-Southwest Conference Decade Team along with Clarissa Davis, Andrea Lloyd, Annette Smith and Sheryl Swoops.

Then it was on to professional basketball. Vicki began her pro career in Twaltoral, Switzerland in 1993. She was literally at the height of her game. "Twaltoral is a small city at the top of a mountain," she said with another chuckle.

"I started in Switzerland, because they weren't really sure how well I had rehabbed from my knee injury," she added. "So I had to work my way up. And at that time there was no pro league for women in the U.S."

From Switzerland, Vicki moved on to play in Greece, Turkey, Israel, Italy and France.

"Playing in all those places was probably one of the best parts of my life, not only getting paid to do something that was my passion, but I also got to see the world. I speak Italian fluently, and I'm okay in French and Greek.

"Israel is kinda like California. Their joke is they call it the 51st state. I was in Tel Aviv. Turkey has a very good and deep culture in basketball."

By the end of the 1990s, Vicki got to play professionally in the U.S. She was drafted by the Colorado Xplosion in the American Basketball League. The Xplosion got to the Western Conference finals. In 2000 Vicki played with the Nashville Noise until December when the league folded.

Vicki had a brief career in the WNBA, playing one year each in Cleveland and Los Angeles early in the new century.

"I always liked the ABL a little better than the WNBA, because it was more of a regular season," she said. "We had six months and we played in the normal time. With the WNBA, especially when I was in my 30s, it was difficult to play all year round.

"By the end I kinda made a decision that I would just play in Europe, because they paid me a lot more and I needed a little bit of a break. My brother David had just had his children and I wanted to see them. I also wanted to have a little bit of a life."

David is Vicki's senior by three years and has a Ph.D. He teaches microbiology at Lawrence University in Appleton, Wis.

In the summer of 2009, Vicki retired from the pro ranks and began looking for a college job.

"Most of the coaching positions were already filled," she recalled. "Luckily a position at Miami University in Oxford, Ohio, in 2009 was open. It was only two hours from my home (Indianapolis) and it had a basketball tradition.

"I felt like it was the logical decision to begin coaching after I had played 16 years professionally and giving 25 years to basketball that now is the time to give back. Basketball has been the most meaningful thing, probably besides my family, in my life, by far. I have a wealth of knowledge from many different and wonderful coaches I've learned from. Now I have an opportunity to teach young players not only how to play the game, but how to succeed in life."

Lisa Hayden, Miami's head coach, said that Vicki's departure at the end of the 2010-2011 season was positive and that "she wanted to go in a different direction."

Vicki ends her telephone answering service at New Mexico this way, "Go Lobos," the team's nickname. (A lobo is a timber wolf native to New Mexico).

JENNIFER JACOBY

While a standout point guard at Purdue University in the 1990s, Jennifer Jacoby would watch the movie *Hoosiers* before every game.

"Wow, I'm not sure I can count how many times I've watched that movie," said the 1991 Indiana Miss Basketball from Rossville. "It's my all-time favorite movie, by far.

"I know I used to watch it before every college game. That was my motivation. I watched basically toward the end when the Hickory Huskers started making their run in the tournament and that final game (when Jimmy Chitwood sank the winning shot for a state championship)."

As a player, coach and administrator, Jacoby says she "has been all over the map." Yet she never dreamed she would wind up as the athletic director at Knightstown High School only a couple of miles from the Hoosier Gym where Gene Hackman, Barbara Hershey and Dennis Hopper starred in Angelo Pizzo's movie *Hoosiers* that put Indiana high school basketball in a wonderful new dimension.

Jacoby knows her way around the Hoosier Gym located at 355 North Washington Street, three blocks north of U.S. 40.

"I think it's only a hundred bucks to rent it out for the day," she said. "Four years ago we had a college coaches clinic there and high school coaches came to listen. How incredible that was. A lot of coaches had never been in the facility."

The Hoosier Gym has become a museum and community center for Knightstown, whose population is a little over 2,000. In 2004 Larry Bird, Magic Johnson, LeBron James and Carmelo Anthony met there for an ESPN special titled "Two on Two," hosted by Jim Gray.

In late 2009, Clark Kellogg, former Ohio State and Indiana Pacers standout and now college basketball analyst for CBS, taped scenes at the Gym for a promotional video for the Athletes in Action sports ministry. The video was presented at the AIA's Legends of the Hardwood Breakfast during the 2010 Final Four weekend in Indianapolis.

After playing four years at Purdue for Coach Lin Dunn, Jennifer Jacoby, now athletic director at Knightstown High School, played two years for the Portland Power (Ore.) in the American Basketball League, calling the experience "incredible." (Photo courtesy of Jennifer Jacoby)

Kellogg couldn't resist shooting at the baskets the Huskers memorialized.

"I can still shoot, I just can't jump," he laughingly said. Clark's pro career lasted only five seasons before bad knee problems forced him to retire.

Jennifer's basketball roots grew deep on her late father Tom's 250-acre farm.

"We milked dairy cows," she recalled. "We did it by machine, thank goodness. We milked about 70 head every morning. I did that until I was about a freshman in high school. Then we got out of the business.

"Every day before school I was up at 5 a.m. and had my chores to do. But you know what? I hated doing it, but it taught me a work ethic. I wouldn't change it for anything. I think it's helped me long-term. You have to work hard to be successful."

Hearing that April McDivitt-Foster, 1999 Indiana Miss Basketball from Connersville, learned to play basketball on a court in a family barn, Jennifer said, "We had about every animal you can imagine, cows, pigs, you name it. It was kind of like the Funny Farm. All my friends spent time out there. It was like one big family.

"We actually had four huge barns. We made the wooden floor in the milk barn into a basketball floor. We had a goal in every one of our barns. We had one barn connected to our garage and one court on the outside of the barn was a full court. My dad would never pave it, because he said, 'If you can dribble on gravel, you can dribble on anything.' We hated it, but he was right."

Jennifer says her dad was instrumental in getting her started in basketball.

"He had an older brother and if you live on a farm, you play basketball," she related. "I think my calling started early. We played all the time and my dad coached me in AAU.

"We went everywhere. The opportunities weren't the same as what the kids have today. But AAU basketball was big for me. That kinda opened the doors to being able to be recruited and go on to play college ball. A lot of kids don't understand how important it is to play in the summer."

Jennifer played for the Rossville Hornets during one-class basketball in Indiana. I said I had mixed emotions about class basketball, which was voted in for the 1997-98 season.

"As do I," she said. "There are pros and cons to everything. I wanted to be the best and I wanted to play the best. That's the way I was brought up. Now you look at it (class basketball), and it is better. It gives more kids opportunities.

"I was at Cathedral High School in Indianapolis as assistant athletic director for two years. Every year they're in state in something. You have to look at it from two different perspectives.

As an athlete, obviously I think I was not real high on a class system. But it's a different perspective now as an administrator. Knightstown is a Class 2A school."

Jennifer says Rossville would have been Class 1A when she played for the Hornets.

"We were in the Frankfort sectional, so we were playing some good-size schools," she said. "My junior year we won the sectional for the first and only time in Rossville history.

"We beat Frankfort in the championship game in Case Arena. It was amazing. Nobody thought we could do it. We got down in the fist quarter something like 17-4, but came back and won. It was like the movie *Hoosiers*, a small school beating a 4A school."

The euphoria Rossville experienced didn't last long. The Hornets went to the Wigwam in Anderson for the regional and "got totally demolished by Anderson High. We were in a whole different league. But just to get out of our sectional was big for us."

Rossville was picked to win the sectional during Jennifer's senior year, but got beat by Clinton Prairie, a team the Hornets had beaten by 14 points during the regular season.

Even so, Jennifer says she had great fun that senior season.

"We got to play in the Hall of Fame Classic (at New Castle)," she remarked. "We played against Bedford North-Lawrence and Edgewood. We got beat by Bedford North-Lawrence (82-66)—that was the year (1991) they won the state championship—and we stayed with 'em. It wasn't as bad as some people thought it would be. Carrie Mount, Amy Walker and Marla Inman (1992 Miss Basketball) were on the team. They were loaded. We beat Edgewood in the consolation game (87-82)."

Bedford North-Lawrence finished 29-0 that year, Rossville 17-4.

On Dec. 28, 1990, in the seventh Hall of Fame Girls Classic, the first time it was held in New Castle, Jennifer had one of the most spectacular performances an Indiana girl has ever had. She scored a record 81 points in the two games, 32 against Bedford North-Lawrence and a record 49 against Edgewood.

Jennifer also holds the record for most three-point field goals in a consolation game—eight. She also shares the record for most field goals made in a consolation game—15—and most three-point goals made in a semifinals game—five.

Those two games went a long way toward Jennifer being chosen Miss Basketball, a rarity for a player from such a small school.

"No, it doesn't happen often," she said. "But I was very fortunate. The media was wonderful in our area. The *Lafayette Journal & Courier* covered a lot of our games. People in the media have been very nice."

Another highlight of the 1990-91 season for Jennifer was playing in the Chicago Dream Games. Rossville won one game and lost a second game, both to Chicago teams.

Indiana, led by Jacoby wearing the No. 1 jersey as Miss Basketball, lost twice to Kentucky in the annual All-Star series between the states in '91. But Jennifer had a big game in the All-Star Classic showcasing the best Indiana boys' and girls' players in a double-header at the end of the season.

Jennifer hit a pull-up jumper in the final five seconds to give the West a 104-102 overtime victory over the East at the Hulman Center in Terre Haute. She led all scorers with 29 points.

For her high school career, Jennifer scored 2,343 points for a 28.9 points per game average. She was a member of *USA Today*'s Top 25 as a senior.

Then it was on to Purdue University, which is 15 miles west of Rossville. Jennifer received her first recruiting letter—from Michigan State—in seventh grade.

"My second letter was from Ohio State," she said. "And then I finally got the one I wanted from Purdue. I did take visits. I went out to USC and I visited Penn State and Purdue. I committed to Purdue, kinda like what Damon Bailey did, very early (to Indiana University), the summer before my junior year. I wanted my parents (Tom and Joan) to be a part of it."

Lin Dunn was Jennifer's Boilermakers coach all four years.

"She was wonderful," Jennifer said, "a great coach, on and off the floor. She knows the game more than anybody I've ever been around. She gets her point across. She makes sure you do what she tells you to do."

As a Purdue freshman, Jennifer tore the ACL in her right knee, something she did as a junior in high school.

"And I've had about nine scopes," she said. "It gave me a whole different perspective. I had to sit and watch, and it made me appreciate being able to play. It was probably the best thing that ever happened to me, because I always was go, go, go. I didn't take a lot of breaks."

Jennifer was back in action as a sophomore, starting 16 games as a 5-foot-7 point guard and leading the team with 47 three-point field goals. She started every game as a junior and senior, earning honorable mention All-Big Ten as a junior and second-team All-Big Ten as a senior. She was team MVP both years.

Purdue went 53-13 in Jennifer's junior and senior seasons and won back-to-back Big Ten co-championships. The Boilermakers made the NCAA Final Four in Jennifer's junior year, winning, 82-65, at Stanford in a regional game she cherishes.

"Oh, wow!" she declared. "That game was amazing. We didn't have a senior on the team. I think we were so young and had no idea what we were about to do. It was the regional final for the right to go to the Final Four. They picked us to be a one seed and they picked them to be a two seed. We were hated before we even got out there."

The Boilermakers played out of their minds, according to Jennifer.

"Coach brought me in before that game started. She said, 'Listen, you're the point guard. If you turn it over, everybody else is going to turn it over. You have to make sure you handle the ball well.'

"The crowd was something else. We were warming up and the floor was actually bouncing. Everything was enhanced three hundred times. They had that tree that was running all over the court, their mascot, that stupid palm tree. The students, the people, it was amazing. The gym was full."

And it got ugly with the Stanford fans, Jennifer said.

"They weren't nice at all. Some of the names I don't want to say at all. We were ahead the whole game. Every game when we went into halftime ahead we were undefeated all year long. It gave us more confidence when we were ahead at halftime. We were ahead four or five points at the half. Stanford tied us fairly early in the second half, but we knuckled down and ended up beating them 17 points."

The Final Four in 1994 was at Richmond, Va., and the Boilermakers drew North Carolina in the semifinal contest. The Tar Heels went on to win the national championship.

For Jennifer it meant guarding Marion Jones, a 6-foot freshman who went on to become known as the fastest woman in the world (100 and 200 meters) after earning five medals (three gold) in the 2000 Summer Olympics in Sydney, Australia.

"Guarding Marion Jones was an experience," said Jennifer, smiling. "She became known as fastest female in the world, and there was a reason. I got to see every bit of it. She was amazing and so athletic. North Carolina was dunking in warm-ups.

"We ended up getting beat, 89-74 (North Carolina defeated Louisiana Tech, 60-59, in the title game). But it was a great run. I wouldn't change any of that. We had a great, great team. We got along so well (it was the first time the Purdue women had made the Final Four).

"We were hoping to get back to the Final Four our senior year, but Stanford beat us in the Elite Eight at UCLA."

Jones played 36 minutes against Purdue in '94 and scored 19 points on 8-of-11 from the field (1-of-2 from three-point range) and 2-of-7 from the foul line. She had five assists, six steals and four turnovers. Jacoby had eight points on 2-of-9 from the field (2-of-5 on three-pointers and 2-of-3 free throws), nine assists, two rebounds, two steals and seven turnovers. Jennifer played 39-plus minutes, fouling out with 31.1 seconds left.

Jones later admitted to taking steroids before the 2000 Olympics. She had to give up her medals and served six months in prison, but signed to play in the WNBA in 2010.

After leaving Purdue, Jennifer traveled far west and played two seasons (1996-98) with the Portland, Ore., Power of the American Basketball League before it folded.

"It was incredible," she said. "I wouldn't trade it for anything. I met all kind of wonderful people and I got to play against some of the best players in the world. To get paid for something that you like to do, that's always a good thing. And it gave me a chance to travel a little."

Jennifer wasn't sure if her playing days ended with the closing of the ABL, but when she got back home in Indiana she decided to try college coaching and took an assistant's position at Indiana University.

"I took a lot of flack, obviously, from being a Purdue grad," Jennifer said. She was in Bloomington two seasons, then spent one season as an assistant at Miami University in Oxford, Ohio, then two years at the University of Illinois (2001-03).

At that time Jennifer took stock of her future and decided that she might land a head coaching job in college in another 10 years, but wasn't sure she could be that patient.

"So I decided to take another route," she said. From 2003-05 she was head coach at Benton Central High School in Oxford. Then came the opportunity to join the administrative staff at Cathedral. She was assistant athletic director two years.

"(Athletic director) Terry Fox was my boss, a great guy," Jennifer said. "Maureen Sullivan was the new athletic secretary and I was the new assistant athletic director. We became quite good friends, because it was new to all of us.

"I had a wonderful experience. To have that many different sports, just to see things from a whole different perspective. I grew up in a small town and Lafayette Central Catholic was one of our big rivals. Everybody always wants to beat the private schools. Just to be a part of all that was so good. It's just such a family atmosphere. Football coaches were going to girls' events. It was amazing the support everybody gave each other. I had never experienced that anywhere."

Jennifer left Cathedral for personal reasons.

"In December of '06 my father passed away," she said. "After 43 years of side-by-side with my father, my mother needed some help. She wanted somebody around and was struggling a little bit. I hated leaving Cathedral, because I loved the people there and it was a great job. But it was something I knew I needed to do for family."

The following summer Jennifer returned to coaching, at Clinton Prairie in Frankfort. In the summer of 2009 she saw on the Board of Education Web site that the athletic director's position at Knightstown was open.

"I guess I got lucky to be in the right place at the right time," she said. "I knew I didn't want to go back to a school the size of Cathedral. I loved it there and it was a great experience. But when you grow up in a small town and a small school, that's what I was comfortable with. I thought I could relate better with those type of kids. I didn't want to apply anywhere else; I wanted it to be at a small school."

Jennifer says she faces a big challenge, but is looking forward to it.

"There are great coaches and great kids at Knightstown," she added. "A goal might be to get a few more kids involved."

Could she coach again? Jennifer emphatically said, "No. I'm 36 years old and I've been about everywhere. This is what I want to do. It's a great school and a great community. I want to make it a better place for everybody.

"My job is to be there for the coaches and to keep kids interested and to keep them out of trouble. There are so many kids that want attention and need attention. Sports is such a great avenue. You build life skills and you're team building. There is so much you can learn from being involved in sports. I want to make sure the kids understand that."

STEPHANIE WHITE

When Stephanie White was growing up in West Lebanon—a town with a population of a little over 800 citizens located seven miles from the Illinois border some 56 miles north of Terre Haute—her father Kevin would put up inspirational quotes in her room or throughout the house.

The one that got the Seeger High School sensation's engine purring was: "Don't wait for your ship to come in, swim out and meet it."

"When I think about that saying, you can't sit back and wait for your dream to come true, because that's not going to happen," said White, 1995 Indiana Miss Basketball who led Purdue to the 1999 NCAA Women's National Championship and is now a women's college basketball analyst for the Big Ten TV Network.

"You have to find a way to envision your dream and then go get it. So many times, especially nowadays, kids think that the things they want are actually going to happen, and they don't understand that you have to make them happen—through your hard work, through your dedication, through your desire, through your vision.

"To me, that quote has always kinda rung true, and always striving for success. Success is a relative term, in my opinion, but you always have to be striving for a goal to accomplish."

The 33-year-old White, who played four years with the Indiana Fever of the WNBA before retiring in 2004 (she rejoined the team as an assistant coach for the 2011 season), has been swimming out to meet her ship all of her life.

At age 10 she asked her grandfather to teach her to play euchre, because her family was always playing sports or cards. She wasn't into sitting and watching TV.

"I wanted to be involved and play something," Stephanie said. "I'm a competitor, so, of course, I wanted to win and I wanted to learn to play the right way. I'd like to think I'm pretty good. I don't like to lose, so I try to strategize the best I can."

As a fourth-grader, Stephanie played basketball at the Y in Danville, Ill., with the boys, because there weren't leagues for girls.

"It wasn't the girly thing to do to play sports," she said. "I played soccer with the boys, because there wasn't a girls' league, and I played baseball as well. Once I got into softball when I got older I played with the girls.

"There is such a sense of pride to understand that it is okay to be a female and okay to be an athlete, and that it is actually not only embraced, but encouraged."

When Stephanie went to Purdue, she enrolled in the school's renowned flying school, again swimming out to meet her ship.

"It's interesting," she remarked, "because in my first semester I was doing solo cross-country flights. I remember the first time I went up on my own, I was like, 'I can't believe I'm a freshman in college and they're letting me fly a plane by myself.'

"I did all right. I wasn't really scared, because they prepare you, and I think being an athlete helped me as well, because you're used to pressure situations. I think in anything I do as long as I have prepared myself I feel that I can handle anything. That's where the work ethic and dedication come in."

Stephanie hasn't flown for a long time because she has concentrated on a coaching career she hopes will lead to a head coaching job at an elite NCAA Division I school. She has been an assistant coach at Ball State, Kansas State, Toledo and the Chicago Sky of the WNBA for four years before joining the Indiana Fever.

"Unfortunately, once I finished college I got involved in the professional aspects of playing and coaching," Stephanie said.

"There just wasn't enough time to fit flying in. It's something I would like to go back to at some point. But life kinda got in the way. That kind of hobby wasn't as feasible for me to do anymore."

Even though she has a busy work schedule, Stephanie has found time to do some competitive swimming.

"I actually have done some sprint triathlons, which are shorter versions of the (regulation) triathlons, over the last few years," she said. "It's something that's new to me. I got into biking quite a few years ago after I had my mini surgeries and running wasn't quite as easy on my body anymore. But swimming is something I had really never done. I picked that up three or four years ago. I'm not very good at it, but I can do it now, comfortably and confidently."

About three years ago Stephanie competed in a sprint triathlon in Toledo, Ohio, and finished second in her age division.

"I came out next-to-last in the swim, but I made up everything in the bike and the run," she said. "It was pretty good, but my swimming still has a little ways to go. I still train as if I'm trying to find another sprint triathlon to do. Would I like to do a full triathlon? Absolutely. As an athlete and as a competitor that's what I have to do, present myself with a new challenge. It's in my blood."

Perhaps Stephanie's biggest challenge came when she became a Seeger High Lady Patriot.

"When I got into high school I was almost degraded to an extent and the boys gave me a hard time. Even

Stephanie White contemplates the free throw she made as a Seeger High School senior on Jan. 19, 1995 that broke the state career scoring record. She went on to finish with 2,869 career points, second only to the 3,085 by Shanna Zolman Crossley of Wawasee. (Photo courtesy of Chris Howell)

Want to upset Stephanie White? Just suggest to the former Purdue University and Indiana Fever standout that "nobody wants to watch women's basketball."

White says one of the things she has learned as a Big Ten TV analyst is that some people still claim that "we can't sell the women's game."

Stephanie disagrees with that claim vehemently.

"That claim eats at me and sets a fire in my belly, because we don't have to sell it to the male audience," she says. "Our core audience and our core demographic is not the same people who watch NBA basketball, not the same people who watch the NFL. I'm not trying to get the guy who sits in a bar and watches a game.

"I'm trying to get the people who are passionate about women in sports. I'm trying to get the young kids who are involved and people who have daughters who are involved in sports and the people in the community who want family events and good role models. And there are people who are passionate about women's sports."

White admits that women's sports still has a long way to go, but she is quick to add, "I think the strides we have made in the last 10 to 15

some of the teachers gave me a hard time. To me, it was a rough high school career, from a personal standpoint because of that."

But Stephanie is quick to point out that the West Lebanon community was very supportive of its girls' team and its star player who went on to score 2,869 career points at Seeger High (second only to Wawasee product Shanna Zolman Crossley's record 3,085) and become the 1995 Gatorade National Player of the Year and the USA Today National Player of the Year.

"At some point in my career I felt like our students, especially the boys, were harder to handle in the stands than the opposing team," Stephanie stated. "But it was a learning experience for me.

"Boys would call me names all the time as I walked in the hallways. There was one game in particular we were playing in our gym and there was one boy in the stands—I can't remember specifically what he was saying—and our athletic director came and said, 'Hey, would you like for me to ask him to leave?'

"I said, 'No, because I'm going to face a lot more of that in my career.' I credit my dad for helping me become more mentally tough, because he used to challenge me all the time on a number of levels. While that hurt, I think from an emotional standpoint it certainly helped me toughen up. It also helped me understand that there is life after high school and one of these days my career is going to take me farther than what I'm experiencing right now."

It was as a high school freshman that Stephanie's dad used a most unusual motivational ploy to help her improve her free throw shooting.

"I shot like 59 percent from the foul line at that time," she said, "and I wasn't a good shooter much at all. My dad would take me out and while I was shooting free throws he'd shoot his shotgun in the background.

"I never knew when it was going to happen, so I had to be focused. It didn't happen frequently, but there were a few instances. I think that helped me create a sense of tunnel vision, so to speak, and try to block out everything that was happening in the background and not be spooked."

Stephanie says there was a game at Wisconsin when she was a Purdue freshman where the shotgun experience paid huge dividends.

"The game went into double overtime and I stepped to the foul line," she said. "As a freshman playing on the road, that was tough. I understood at that point what my dad had been trying to do by shooting his shotgun in the background, because at that time at

years since I've been out of school are amazing.

"Like I've said, going down the street and seeing girls playing basketball on a hoop or out playing soccer to me is not only inspiring, but it was neat to see the USA women's soccer team do so well in the World Cup, seeing the national team winning gold medals.

"We didn't see that when I was growing up. We saw the (men's) Dream Team winning gold medals. We saw Michael Jordan on TV. We didn't see Lisa Leslie on TV. We didn't see Tamika Catchings on TV."

Now, says White, there are female role models such as Leslie and Catchings and it is possible for women to be successful in many fields, not just athletics.

"Not everybody is going to be an athlete, but you can be in media relations, you can be in marketing, you can be in TV, you can do whatever you want to do," she said.

"You can be a doctor, a lawyer, a business woman or whatever. But to be always told what you can't do as opposed to being told what you can do to me is the difference in the transitioning that is still going on for women. Because it hasn't been done doesn't mean it can't be done. I absolutely believe that."

Wisconsin I could drown out the crowd and step to the line and knock down free throws, because of those kinds of lessons."

White played at Seeger High, enrollment 399 at the time, in one-class basketball, which she cherishes. The Lady Patriots advanced to the semi-state round all four years White was wowing the state media.

As a senior she averaged 36.9 points, 13.1 rebounds, 8.2 assists, 7 steals and 2.2 blocks per game. Also as a senior, Stephanie scored a state-record 66 points in a 108-35 victory over Attica.

Then it was on to West Lafayette and the Lady Boilermakers. Stephanie played for three different coaches at Purdue—Lin Dunn, Nell Fortner and Carolyn Peck—from 1995 to 1999.

"It was not easy," Stephanie offered. "The way things that happened from Lin Dunn's time (she coached the Lady Boilermakers for nine years before being forced out by the Purdue administration for minor sanctions by the NCAA for rules violations) to Nell Fortner—and we obviously can't fault her (Fortner) for leaving to coach the Olympic team and going after a gold medal for your country. Carolyn Peck fortunately was there and able to take over and there wasn't as much transition.

"But it was definitely difficult adjusting to a new voice. At the same time life isn't always what we think it's going to be. I think it taught us to be able to deal with a little bit of adversity and to be able to understand what it means to go to war for a team and with a team.

"You can't pick a university based upon the head coach, because those are ever-changing, like a revolving door. You have to pick the university for the people that are there and what you want to accomplish as a basketball player and as a student."

Purdue was 94-33 in White's four years there. The 5-foot-11 guard/forward started all 127 games in her career and averaged 17.2 points per game and shot .445 from the field, .365 from three-point range and .803 at the foul line, thanks to dad's shotgun blasts.

The Lady Boilermakers team made the NCAA tournament all four years, losing in the first round in '96, the second round in '97, the elite eight in '98 and being national champion in '99 with a 34-1 record.

Purdue tied for the Big Ten title in '97 with a 12-4 record and won the title in '99 with a 16-0 record.

Stephanie's first game as a senior was memorable. It was on Nov. 15, 1998, before a crowd of nearly 12,000 in Mackey Arena against Coach Pat Summitt and her Tennessee Lady Vols with Chamique Holdsclaw and Tamika Catchings. Tennessee entered the game with a 46-game winning streak. Purdue won, 78-68, with White having 24 points, 6 rebounds, 4 assists and 2 steals.

As a college senior, Stephanie received a host of honors: National College Player of the Year, Big Ten Conference Player of the Year and Indiana NCAA Woman of the Year. She says her Purdue days were extremely satisfying.

"Purdue has meant so much to me, more than just the experience of being able to play college basketball at a tremendous university," she said. "But also the people that surrounded our program, from my teammates, to coaches, to administrators, to people in the community.

"I'm often asked the question, 'What was it like winning a national championship?' The reality is while it's great to be able to cut down the nets and put on a ring and say that you're a national champion, what made it even more special was the people that we did it with, with the community involvement in our program and the way that we were able to come back from adversity. To me, those were the biggest memories and the biggest inspiration for our team."

Stephanie is the second of three sisters born to Kevin and Jennie White. They grew up in the country outside West Lebanon. Kevin worked for Quaker Oats for 30 years and is now with a John Deere dealership in Williamsport, five miles east of West Lebanon. Jennie is the Seeger varsity volleyball coach.

Stephanie's oldest sister is Shanda. "She is going back to school to be an X-ray technician and is married to an elementary school principal in our hometown," Stephanie said. "My younger sister Stacey is the basketball coach at Danville (Ill.) Junior College."

On May 30, 1998, just before the start of Stephanie's senior year at Purdue, she married Brent McCarty, who played football at Wabash College. He went to Carroll High School in Flora. Brent's twin cousins played on Stephanie's high school team and she met Brent as a high school freshman when he and his father attended a Seeger game.

"We started a long-distance relationship," Stephanie said. "I think we both thought that the logical next step was to get married, even though we were 20 years old at the time and didn't really understand everything that was going to be involved (they eventually divorced).

"You obviously go through things and understand as you grow older the mistakes that we make in our youth. I think the mistake was that we were young and we tried to do something that we probably should have waited to do later in life.

"When you're a college kid, people are saying, 'Oh, maybe you should wait,' and that probably seals your priorities to probably not wait. We had a lot of great years together and we grew up together. It certainly was an experience and one to learn from."

Stephanie has an agent who handles her TV business.

"The agents don't go out and get you a job," she said. "The agents negotiate contracts once you get jobs. I'm in a good situation now (with the Indiana Fever), so I'm going to be picky. I'm going to wait to find an opportunity that gives me the opportunity to be successful at a place where I want to be for a long time, and an opportunity to win championships.

"So many factors go into that, with the support of the administration, with facilities, with communities, with people you surround yourself with and the area you're in. And the school you pick. In all reality kids are coming to get an education. So I want to put myself in a tremendous situation to be successful. I don't want to take a job just to take a job."

Being a TV analyst has brought Stephanie a new respect for the position.

"I never understood how much work it was to be an analyst," she said. "You have to scout both teams. I get to see the game in a unique way. And I get to learn from every coach when I go watch a practice or a shoot-around, see how they do things and how they communicate and what kind of drills they do.

"My strength in basketball has always been my mind, understanding the game and being able to break down a game. It's never been athleticism and skill. I can't jump the highest or can't run the fastest, but I feel like that strength (her mind) allowed me to ease into the analyst work. It's a different perspective and I've thoroughly enjoyed it."

Officials of the Indiana Basketball Hall of Fame in New Castle believe Stephanie is a pretty good jumper, because she and the fabled Oscar Robertson share an exhibit with height measurements on the wall. Patrons are invited to step inside and "try your jumping ability and attempt to block the shot of two of Indiana's finest basketball players."

Stephanie says she was pleased to have played with the Fever in their formative years.

"Being involved with something from the ground up and seeing now how far they have come is very satisfying," she said. "You cannot be without a WNBA team in Indiana. Indiana is about basketball and hopefully it will continue to be here.

"Their personnel are so inspiring, with Tamika (Catchings) and her Catch the Stars Foundation and Katie (Douglas) being able to be home. It's a great opportunity for all of us and for the community, and it's such an amazing experience to have been a part of that organization."

What does the future hold for White, who gave birth to a son, Landon Fletcher, on Sept. 27, 2011, the same day the Fever lost to the Atlanta Dream in a decisive third game of the WNBA Eastern Division championship series in Conseco Fieldhouse? Catchings, who was voted the league's MVP a few days earlier, played, but was far below100 percent after suffering a right foot injury in a playoff loss to the Dream in Atlanta.

"I'm going to try to avoid the real world as long as possible," she said with a laugh. "I love being able to wear shorts and sneakers to work every day and being able to be involved with the game I'm so passionate about.

"There are very few people who have won a national championship, playing and coaching. That's certainly a goal of mine. Hopefully I'll have an opportunity to one day achieve that goal."

No doubt Stephanie will soon swim out to meet her coaching ship and her dream of double national championships will happen.

STACIE SHEPHERD

On a wall opposite the athletic office in the Tiernan Center at Richmond High School is a large photo of Lisa Shepherd-Stidham wearing the No. 1 Indiana All-Star jersey she received after being named Miss Indiana Basketball in 1997.

Next to Lisa's photo is one of Richmond's Woody Austin, 1988 Indiana Mr. Basketball, outfitted in a No. 1 jersey. He and Lisa are the only Red Devils to be so honored.

Stacie Shepherd, Lisa's older sister, was asked where her photo was and she laughed, which she does easily.

"Right over there," Stacie said, pointing to an opposite wall where her smaller photo as runner-up to Miss Basketball Patricia Babcock of Culver Girls Academy in 1990 hangs among several other outstanding Red Devil athletes.

Richmond High officials retired Lisa's No. 20 after her illustrious career ended.

"I wore No. 20, too," Stacie said, smiling. She quickly added that she might warrant a share of that retirement, chuckling at the thought.

Richmond, of course, has the distinction of having female and male siblings who brought the Wayne County city rare individual honors in high school basketball. Chad Austin, Woody's younger brother, helped the Red

Devils win their only state championship by scoring 19 points in a 77-73 victory over Lafayette Jeff in 1992 as a junior.

Chad was selected to the 1993 Indiana All-Star team as the third highest vote getter.

"I went to school with both of the Austins," said Stacie, who had a career-record 1,926 points for the Lady Red Devils before Lisa surpassed the total with 2,140 points, the highest amount for girls or boys at Richmond High. Stacie's total ranks third best—male or female—at Richmond.

"Woody was a couple of years older than me, and Chad was younger. I don't keep in touch with them and I don't know what they're up to. But they are very different, just like Lisa and me. It's pretty interesting to see siblings as different people."

Stacie says she and Lisa were yelled at—and encouraged—frequently by their late father, Glenn Shepherd Jr., before he died unexpectedly of internal bleeding that affected his heart in late 2007.

"As a child, basketball was everything to me," Stacie said. "It brought my family together. Our dad was the driving force behind this. It wasn't always pretty. He made it really tough. I suspect that he didn't get to live out his own dream, and so he did that for Lisa and me.

"I'm a rebel. Lisa is focused. She's organized. It's pretty clear what she wants. She's always been that way. When I graduated in 1995 from St. Joe (St. Joseph's in Rensselaer), in 11 years I moved probably 13 times, Indiana, Florida, Indiana. I didn't know what I wanted. I said one of the biggest things for me was trying to figure out who I was after basketball."

Does Stacie feel cheated in any way by her dad's intensity?

"I've wrestled with some things, because me personally, if you're just looking at sports, I have a wide range of interests. I definitely was kind of channeled in this direction (basketball).

"I graduated from college and it was paid for. I have relationships with friends from my teams that I still have. Basketball taught me probably a million things along the way about life that have carried over. I understand what commitment means, I understand what teamwork means, I understand the ups and downs of life. The good definitely outweighs the bad and as an adult I can say that. I've worked through that (tough love of her father)."

Being yelled at never caused Stacie to consider quitting basketball. On the contrary, it motivated her.

"When my dad yelled at me, it ticked me off, basically," she said. "I just wanted to show him I could do this. I think it's what he wanted it to do, and it did. I'm sure that was part of what continued to drive Lisa and me to seek our dad's approval. He definitely was pleased with us a lot. He was displeased with us a lot, too, but he did give us credit and a lot of love."

Stacie's basketball education began early. She chuckled while recalling her first experience at a basketball camp. She was only five when she attended camp at Taylor University in Upland, Ind.

"I was terrible," Stacie said. "But I learned to shoot a layup and I'm sure I learned a lot of other things. The last day of camp all the campers had to do an exhibition for the parents, what we had learned.

"That was a big deal for my confidence. I feel like that was kinda the, 'Hey, I do want to do this' moment. It was fun and after that I continued to go to camps."

The camp routine elevated Stacie's urge to excel, so she began to haunt Richmond's YMCA.

"I played with the boys every day," she said. "I wasn't the last person chosen. I felt like one of the guys. As I got older and away from Richmond, girls just don't get together and play. I've always had to play with the guys.

"As I've gotten older and I don't play anymore, it's been really hard. I had an ACL surgery in high school and after that it's been cartilage problems. So I've had to kinda hang up the shoes."

Stacie started as a 5-foot-6 guard all four years for Richmond High. She had better success in the state tournament than Lisa, winning the sectional at Connersville as a freshman and senior. Lisa never won a sectional.

"In my freshman year we lost to Greenfield-Central in the regional and my senior year we lost to Rushville in the regional," Stacie said. "We had beaten Rushville in the regular season and we were undefeated when we played Rushville in the regional."

When Stacie finished second in voting for 1990 Miss Basketball, it was an emotional blow.

"When I didn't get Miss Basketball, that may have been the first real blow to my confidence," she said. "I remember my dad spray painting my name, 1990 Miss Basketball, on a garage wall when I was real young. That was a goal of mine for so long. I felt like I had failed."

Then came a disappointing experience in her two All-Star games against Kentucky. Indiana lost twice, 98-76 and 64-58.

"I don't know that the best (Indiana) players were on the floor, and I'm not taking anything from anybody that was out there," Stacie offered. "Kentucky whupped us. But I had a ball with my All-Star experience, meeting so many new people."

Louisiana Tech, an early power in women's collegiate basketball, expressed an interest in Stacie and she had her sights set on going there.

"I wanted to go there hands down," she said. "But I blew my knee out the summer before my junior year. I was in Louisiana for an AAU tournament. In the very first game I drove to the basket, planted my foot, and that was it."

The injury probably cost Stacie a scholarship to Louisiana Tech.

"They didn't write me off right away, but they didn't have confidence to sign me early and I wasn't comfortable with not signing early," she recalled. "I visited Toledo and they were pretty serious about recruiting me. I had narrowed my list down pretty quickly and actually Indiana University wasn't on that list. But I had to expand my horizons a little bit once I blew out my knee."

The sisters through the years . . .
(Photos courtesy of Lisa Shepherd)

Stacie did go to I.U. and "I did play a little bit," she said. But the 1990-91 season had more valleys than hills.

"I had a lot of trouble settling in," she said. "I didn't have great study habits. I found high school fairly easy and when I got to college it was not so easy. And the basketball was really hard, just the demand of the practices. They were so time-consuming and you were sore and tired all the time. I had a lot of trouble balancing all of that.

"And I had trouble with someone in my face yelling. I rebelled against that a little bit and that hindered my playing time."

Stacie severed her ties with the I.U. team just before the start of the 1991-92 season.

"I stayed in school that year, kinda got my head screwed back on and brought my grades up," she said. "Then I decided I needed to be playing basketball."

John Williams, who had been on the Richmond High coaching staff, called Stacie and "kinda hooked me on to Northern Kentucky and St. Joe," she said." The idea was that if I transferred from Division I to Division II I wouldn't have to sit out, that I could play right away. I visited both schools and decided to go to St. Joe."

It proved to be a positive move, although it took Stacie time to regain her confidence.

"St. Joe was a smaller school and I developed better study habits," she said. "Academically I was able to do what I needed to do. But I struggled a little bit with basketball. I had to sit out a year (1991-92) and I think my confidence was blown a little bit after my first year at I.U.

"I went from having a really solid high school career and always being a starter and always being on a good team to not being a starter and just being kind of a number. I struggled with that."

It took Stacie a couple of years at St. Joe to regain her confidence on the basketball court. By her senior season, however, she said, "I feel I was back in the groove. We had a really good year. When everything finally clicked and I understood what I needed to do on the basketball floor, I understood what I needed to do in school, then I graduated and it was over. It was time to do this whole new thing."

That new thing following graduation from St. Joe was life in Florida.

"Richmond has always been my home, but I moved to Florida because I like other places and I like Florida," Stacie said. "I like warm weather."

Stacie (left) visited with Lisa when Penn State played Purdue in Mackey Arena in West Lafayette, Ind. (Photo courtesy of Lisa Shepherd)

Shepherd sisters, Lisa (left) and Stacie, appear at a Richmond High function as Indiana All-Star alums. Lisa was Miss Basketball in 1997. (Photo courtesy of Lisa Shepherd)

She was an assistant high school girls' varsity coach for six years at Winter Haven, Fla.

"The coach I worked with is now at Florida A&M as the head coach," Stacie said. "We did really well at Winter Haven. That was a good experience."

Stacie is divorced from Craig Witty, who coaches basketball in Florida. He is a nephew of Steve Witty, former Indianapolis Ben Davis High School boys' coach who guided the Giants to state championships in 1995 and '96

"Craig and I were together six years maybe, married for a couple of those years," Stacie explained. "Ultimately Craig wanted to stay in Florida and I had this desire to come back to Indiana."

For 13 years Stacie taught English and reading, six years in Florida and seven years in Richmond. She also coached girls' basketball in Richmond off and on for four years, assisting the Lady Red Devils varsity during the 2009-10 season.

Stacie has undergone a big change in her life, a positive one she believes.

"I have moved on from coaching basketball and now have an independent massage therapy business," she said.

Stacie went to the Midwest Academy of Healing Arts in Brownsburg and is certified by the state of Indiana and the United States.

"I am really into alternative medicine," she said. "I'm very fascinated by what's been done for thousands and thousands of years medically for people. Massage school is short and it's helpful to people and it's also more mainstream than it once was. I also teach yoga. I have a few skills or trades to sustain myself."

Even though coaching basketball seems to have ended for Stacie, she still enjoys watching the Lady Red Devils play in season and helping with her sister Lisa's Dream Makers Basketball camp.

"Basketball has been great to me," Stacie said. "I don't know what my life would look like without it. I always shot around with my dad. I followed the Indiana All-Stars and I remember looking up to all those players. They were like the goddesses of basketball. They fueled my dream as well.

"We would get the program for the All-Star game and it would have their information, like how tall they were and where they were from. And sometimes it would have personal information in it. I would just soak that up. I wanted to be like them."

And she was.

LISA SHEPHERD

From basketball dreamer as a youngster growing up in Richmond to Dream Makers Basketball camps founder, owner and director at age 31.

That's the remarkable story of Lisa Shepherd-Stidham, 1997 Indiana Miss Basketball and a member of the 2000 Penn State University women's team that made the school's only NCAA Final Four appearance.

"I was really interested in Purdue my freshman and sophomore years at Richmond," said Lisa, who lives in Fishers with her husband Aaron Stidham, three-year-old daughter Kayla and six-month-old son Braeden.

"Then in my junior year Penn State started recruiting me and I ended up taking an unofficial visit. I verbally committed my junior year when I went out there."

Lisa has become a big Nittany Lions football fan as well as a basketball spectator whenever Penn State plays in Indiana or Columbus, Ohio. She now tailgates with her husband on visits to Happy Valley—"We put the burgers on the grill," she boasted.

The sister of Stacie Shepherd, runner-up in the 1990 Indiana Miss Basketball voting for Richmond, made her mark on Penn State women's basketball.

"I love Penn State, " Lisa said. "I always tell people if I had to do it over I'd go right back there. It's a really neat atmosphere and a fun campus."

She ended her career as three-point leader with 230 and finished No. 5 on the all-time scoring list with 1,663 points.

"My freshman year we won the WNIT (Women's National Invitation Tournament)," Lisa said. "We beat Baylor in the championship game. I think I had 16 points that game. I made two free throws at the end.

"The game was at Baylor and I believe there were about 10,000 people in their arena. It was a fun game, especially being a freshman and getting that experience.

"We went to the NCAA Final Four my junior year in 2000 at Philadelphia. We played Connecticut in the semifinals. It was a tough game. I think we were only down four or six points in the last four to six minutes.

"We only had nine players that year; probably six or seven of us played a lot. Connecticut would just sub five in, and you couldn't tell the difference between their starters and the people coming in off the bench. You feel bad losing, but you couldn't be disappointed. We made history as the first Penn State women's team to go to the Final Four (there was a 10-year reunion for the team in the 2009-10 season)."

The Shepherds of Richmond came within a few votes of becoming the first family to have two girls receive Indiana Miss Basketball honors (there have been two families with two boys be Indiana Mr. Basketballs: twins Dick and Tom VanArsdale of Indianapolis Manual in 1961 and Billy and Dave Shepherd of Carmel in 1968 and 1970, respectively).

"My older sister Stacie was an Indiana All-Star in 1990 and was runner-up to Miss Basketball, Patricia Babcock of Culver Girls Academy," Lisa said. "I think she got beat by four votes. It was one of the closet votes in history.

Lisa Shepherd-Stidham's father painted a motivational sign predicting she would become 1997 Miss Basketball, which she did, in the family garage. (Photo courtesy of Lisa Shepherd)

"Stacie is seven years older. Naturally having an older sister I trailed along right behind her and I followed her everywhere, and I probably annoyed her to no end back then. She always played basketball and I just kinda followed in her footsteps. I'd be out in the driveway nagging her and wanting to rebound for her."

Lisa remembers well the time she knew exactly where she wanted to go with basketball.

"Gosh, I don't even know how old I was," she related. "But I was pretty young, even before I knew what Miss Basketball was. We're out in our garage and my dad started spray-painting on the wall, Stacie Shepherd, 1990 Miss Basketball.

"I said, 'Well, I want my name up there.' So he put, Lisa Shepherd, 1997 Miss Basketball. I was probably six years old and I didn't know what it was. I just wanted my name up there as well.

"So when I got Miss Basketball, they (media) came to our house and filmed the garage, because her name (Stacie's) was still up there."

Lisa played high school basketball when Indiana had one class and she said that inspired her.

"They've gone to class basketball now, but when I was growing up, that (winner take all among IHSAA teams concept) was the excitement," she said. "You dream of winning a state championship and as a little girl becoming Miss Basketball. That definitely was one of my goals growing up. It was something I worked at.

"I picked up a basketball at a very young age. I was about six years old when I started playing on a team. I played at the Richmond YMCA. I was pretty much the only girl that played in a boys' league. I started playing AAU at a very young age and going to camps. I traveled a lot and watched my sister play."

Stacie, who assists Lisa at Dream Makers camps in Richmond, played at Indiana University as a freshman in the 1990-91 season, then transferred to St. Joseph's College in Rensselaer, where she competed from 1992 to 1995.

In the interim, Lisa was making an impact on girls' basketball at Richmond High. She became the first female in Richmond history to have her No. 20 jersey retired. Lisa started all four years for the Lady Red Devils. She is the leading career scorer—male or female—at Richmond with 2,140 points and she shares the school's single-game scoring record of 49 points. As a senior, Lisa averaged 28.5 points a game.

"I was more of a shooting guard," said Lisa, who is 5-foot-10. "I did play every position occasionally."

Not only did Lisa never win a state championship in high school, she never got to help cut down the nets after winning a sectional.

"We always got beat by April McDivitt (1999 Miss Basketball from Connersville)," Lisa said. "She was a couple years younger than me. But we never could get past Connersville, even my freshman and sophomore years before she was in high school, in the sectional. That's who we always got beat by. It was a tough team to beat and we always had to play at their place.

"I remember my freshman year when we went to play at Connersville in the sectional, I think we had five freshmen on varsity. Four or five of them started. I remember going though the tunnel. There were people saying, 'You freshmen, go back home,' and just yelling at us. As a freshman you were very intimidated."

Lisa never got to play professionally, and that remains a huge disappointment.

"I went to the pre-draft workout after my senior year at Penn State and I thought I was going to get drafted in the third round or so," she said. "I ended up not getting drafted. I was very shocked by that. I was kinda angry for a while, didn't touch a basketball for a couple of months.

"I was never the type of player that did well in that type of setting (the pre-draft workout). I needed more of a team setting, where we had plays and could come running off screens and do pick-and-rolls. But when you're in that type of setting it's all one-on-one basketball and take it to the hoop."

The possibility of going overseas to play came up a couple of times for Lisa, but "by the time that happened I was ready to move on in my life. I had my internship in one class to finish for school. I was afraid if I went overseas that when I came back I wouldn't want to finish my degree. That was my No. 1 priority, so I went back for a fifth year and helped out a little bit with the women's team."

Lisa studied therapeutic recreation in college.

"It's funny, you go to college and get a degree in something, then you end up not doing that," she said. "Basically what I did was be an activities director in nursing homes. I did it for a year-and-a-half in Pennsylvania. I enjoyed it, but it wasn't something I could see doing for the rest of my life."

So Lisa decided to move back to Indiana, locating in Indianapolis.

"I wanted to be close enough to home so I could visit, but I also wanted to be in a bigger area for more opportunities," she said. "I was out socially one time and met Aaron. The rest is history."

Aaron played football at Indiana State. He was a guard and center. Aaron is now a national accounts manager for Firestone.

"Most people when they think of Firestone think of tires," Lisa said. "But Aaron is in the building products side. He's been behind me in everything that I've done. I had a career where I had a fulltime job and did that whole eight-to-five thing. When I wanted to leave that and kinda branch out, he was supportive."

How did the name for Lisa's camp—Dream Makers (with the sub-title: Where Dedication Meets Dreams)—come about? She credits Avis Stewart, who played basketball at Marion when the Giants lost two years in a row in the semifinals of the boys' state tournament Final Four (1968 to Indianapolis Shortridge, 58-56, and in 1969 to Indianapolis Washington, 61-60), for the idea. Stewart says it was as much Lisa's idea as it was his.

Stewart played at Earlham College in Richmond under former NBA head coach Del Harris, then made Richmond his home. An Earlham vice president, Avis became a renowned shooting instructor. Lisa credits him for making her "a great shooter."

"We were sitting around and we went back and forth with ideas," Stewart said. "It's the dream of all girls to do well and we settled on Dream Makers."

Stewart says Lisa was an average athlete, but made herself into an outstanding basketball player by maximizing her skills through hard work.

"Lisa worked harder than anybody I've ever been associated with," he said. "She always wanted to get better, and she's a quality person. She is someone for young people to emulate."

November 2007 was a difficult time for Lisa. Her 90-year-old grandfather, Bob Heid, died on Nov. 7, then her father, Glenn Shepherd Jr., passed away unexpectedly on Nov. 15.

"My grandpa was a huge supporter," she said. "He was probably my biggest fan. This man traveled everywhere to watch me play. I remember when I graduated from Penn State and played on an exhibition team that traveled around to play against college teams in their preseason games, he drove down to Alabama and Florida to watch me play. He even got a cell phone in case the car broke down. It was a hard time when he passed."

One of the first things Lisa's mother Linda did after her husband died eight days after the grandfather passed away, was to establish a Shepherd Family Memorial Scholarship Fund "in loving memory" of Glenn. It is awarded annually to a Lady Red Devils senior. Lisa put the scholarship information on her Web site: shepherdhoops.com.

Glenn had not been sick, according to Lisa.

"My mom came in and found him," she said. "Mostly what they said was he had internal bleeding, and because of his weight his heart couldn't take it and stopped. He went peacefully."

Lisa remembers growing up with tough love from her father, which she has learned to appreciate with age.

"My dad was one of those really, really tough parents, mainly with basketball," she said. "He would call me two or three times a day just to bug me. I would always tease him, 'Stop calling me.' I miss those phone calls.

"He had his reasons for being hard on us in basketball. He yelled at me a lot. It was just his way of trying to make me better. That was the only way he knew. Growing up I didn't understand that. Now I do. I loved him very much and I miss him."

APRIL MCDIVITT

Barnyard basketball has paid off handsomely for April McDivitt-Foster, who is back home again in Indiana after a rewarding 10-year collegiate journey through the University of Tennessee and the University of California-Santa Barbara for the 1999 Indiana Miss Basketball from Connersville High School.

"I'm a farm gal, absolutely," confesses April, who has joined fellow Connersville basketball standout Ed Schilling at his Champions Academy whose training facilities are located in Zionsville and Fishers.

April, Champions Academy women's director (Schilling is executive director), grew up on her father Joe's 1,000-acre farm "about 15 miles from any town. A bus came by off a gravel road and took me to school. Those are my roots."

Joe and his wife Cathy helped nourish those roots by building an outdoor court and a court in the barn.

"The court in the barn was cement, nothing real fancy," April said. "It was real cold in the winter, but it gave me a place to play. My grandparents bought me a Shootaway, where they have the rails that rebound your ball through the net and the balls come back to you, so I could get a lot of shots up.

"I would go out more in the morning, because I would play at school in the afternoon and during every recess. It was something I loved. It wasn't something that you've gotta shoot more. It was, 'I want to get better. I want to be the best I can be.' "

In 1979, a year before April was born, Ann Meyers—she later was married to the late Los Angeles Dodgers pitching standout, Don Drysdale—became the only female ever to sign a free-against contract with an NBA team, the Indiana Pacers.

After being released by the Pacers before the regular season began that year, Myers, who played at UCLA, provided color commentary for Pacers broadcasts at a time when women in sports media were rare. She also became an inspiration for April.

"From the first grade on I played with the boys in the Boys and Girls Club in Connersville," April said. "My dad taught me the game and coached me through the sixth grade. We had a film session in the first grade. It wasn't his intent, but it's really neat to see yourself on film when you're that young. We didn't have cable TV when I grew up. I always watched NBA videos—Michael Jordan, Larry Bird, Pistol Pete Maravich. I would watch them over and over and over, then I'd go out to the barn and try to emulate what I just saw."

Those video sessions brought dividends when April was 11. She appeared in the "Hot Shots" section of the September 1992 issue of *SI For Kids* magazine.

"That was a very unique experience because it was the fist time I ever met someone from New York," April stated. "He was the photographer taking pictures for the magazine. I was so young and I wanted to be in the NBA I think I said in the article. I had big dreams."

That photo and story helped put April and Connersville on the national map.

"It was a pretty big story, a local kid getting some publicity," she explained. "My dad went to the post office, like 6 a.m., to get the magazine when it was delivered. He brought it home and they tricked me. They got me up and they said, 'Look outside.' And dad flashed it right in front of the window. My parents supported me so much growing up. They took me all over the nation playing basketball. They invested so much, the time, the financing."

April not only made news in basketball at an early age, she also made news at the Fayette County Fair.

"My dad still farms," she said, "cattle, but no pigs anymore. It's open-field farming. He has corn, soybeans, wheat, vegetables and flowers. And, yes, I did show pigs at the fair."

Did she win any blue ribbons?

"A few," she said, smiling, "showmanship one year. It means you show the pig the best. I guess I was pretty good. I won it one year."

Once April reached varsity status at Connersville High it didn't take long for the 5-foot-7 freshman to show that her barnyard basketball had been excellent training. On Dec. 29, 1995, she was named MVP in the Hall of Fame Classic at New Castle Fieldhouse after leading the Spartans to the championship with victories over Bloomington South (45-39) and Perry Meridian of Indianapolis (65-59).

What does April, who had 17 points in the title game, remember about that day?

"I just remember winning," she stated. "It was a significant win, because we played against Katie Douglas in the championship game (Douglas became an Indiana All-Star in 1997 and helped Purdue win a national title in 1999). She is one of the premiere players in Indiana history and we had a good battle in that championship game."

Douglas, now with the Indiana Fever of the WNBA, had 15 points against the Spartans.

April's high school career continued on an upward spiral after that MVP performance in New Castle. She went on to score a school career-record point total for girls of 1,908,

April McDivitt-Foster, women's director at the Champions Academy in Zionsville and assistant boys coach at Park Tudor High School, plays for the Indiana All-Stars against Kentucky. (Photo courtesy of April McDivitt-Foster)

averaging 17.8 points per game as a freshman, 19.5 as a sophomore, 17.8 as a junior and 22.4 as a senior.

The Spartans were 86-12 in April's four years. They were 19-4, 20-2, 22-4 and 25-2 in that stretch, setting one-season victory totals each season. Unfortunately, April never got to cut down the nets as a state champion.

"Every year we were beaten by the state champs," she said, "so we were, I believe, within one game of winning the state championship. We lost in the regional at Center Grove my freshman year. The next two years it was Martinsville and they went on to win it both years. Martinsville had great, great players I played with in the summer.

"My last year we lost to New Albany, which won state with a 28-0 record (Martinsville was 26-1 and 29-0 in '97 and '98, and Center Grove was 25-2 in '96). Kennitra Johnson of New Albany was an Indiana All-Star my senior year and went to Connecticut for a year and then moved on.

"I have great, great memories of playing in front of the crowds, the environment in Hoosierland. And I was all over the country in recruiting and the world playing."

As a senior, April was a *Parade Magazine* All-American and *Street & Smith's* second-team All-American as well as being selected *The Indianapolis Star*'s Miss Basketball for Indiana's series with Kentucky. She helped Indiana sweep the series, 80-51 and 91-62.

At a very young age April had a goal to become Miss Basketball.

"When I was in the third grade we talked about setting goals," she recalled. "I wrote, '1999 Miss Basketball,' on my poster and put it in my room. So when I woke up every day I could see what I wanted to shoot for. To actually be awarded it was an amazing feeling."

Many colleges tried to land April, and she admits that college recruiting is "really different. What's the way to describe it? Nothing's like Indiana high school basketball. The East Coast, I believe, is really hard-nosed and tough. The South is pretty athletic. The West is really finesse.

"But the Midwest, and especially Indiana, the Mecca, is very skilled. Basketball here is so much better, from coaches to players, and so much more important. I spent a lot of time on the West Coast, coaching (four years as an assistant at California-Santa Barbara) and recruiting high school athletes. Recruiting is just an entirely different ball game."

Of her many college offers, April said it was a no-brainer when Pat Summitt, legendary coach of the Tennessee Vols women's team, offered her a scholarship.

"Tennessee was the top program when I was being recruited," she said. "For me growing up, I wanted to play for the best. I went to their elite camps and kinda met their players and staff, when I was a freshman and sophomore, and even younger in junior high. It was always a dream for me to play for her, to play for one of the best coaches ever to coach the game."

At the end of the 2008-09 season, Summitt's 35-year record at Tennessee was 1005-192. April helped secure nearly 100 of those victories before deciding to transfer to California-Santa Barbara in 2002. She never won a national title, but in her four collegiate seasons, April was the point guard in two Final Fours (Tennessee lost to Connecticut, 71-52, in the 2000 national championship game and lost to eventual champion UConn in the Final Four semifinals in 2002), four Sweet Sixteens (Tennessee lost to Xavier in the 2001 Sweet Sixteen and Santa Barbara lost to Connecticut in the 2004 Sweet Sixteen).

April was Academic All-American all four years.

People ask her, "Why would you leave Tennessee?" She replies, "It's two ends of the spectrum. I knew I wanted to be a coach eventually. I wanted to see how it could be done differently. Santa Barbara was really different. Not to say that either place is perfect.

"But I learned a completely different way of doing things. I think right in the middle is where I stand today. I want to bring the passion and intensity that Pat brings to the game. But I also want to have a perspective where I care about the player on and off the court, because I believe that impacting young women not only for their jumper to be great, but also to be great young ladies. I want both. How to get there, I guess, Pat and I differ in that a little bit."

April says she had a positive experience at Tennessee.

"I wouldn't trade it for anything," she said. "When I see Pat I absolutely go up and talk to her. It's not a strained relationship, in my opinion. I've thanked her so many times for all that she taught me. I was in her office before practice almost every day watching film. So I learned so much from the lady and respect her a ton. She's been a great figure for women's basketball. At that moment in my life I just felt like God led me to move on."

April, 29, was raised Catholic, but now attends Mighty Rivers Church International in Zionsville, where Champions Academy is located, with her husband Brett Foster. "It's an 'I believe in Jesus kind of faith,' " she said.

"My faith is very important to me. When I went to Tennessee, basketball was up on a pedestal. It was everything to me. It's too important, when you look at the big scheme of things. It was a roller coaster ride. Win at all cost was kind of the mentality there. As I grew in my faith and realized what was really important to me in this life, it became not a good fit for me. I know a lot of people don't understand that."

After her one season with the Santa Barbara Gauchos, April spent three years with three different teams in the WNBA. How was her pro career?

"I ran into some injuries," she said. "I had three concussions my first training camp with the New York Liberty. I made it through the entire camp, two-a-days, really, really hard and tough. The general manager said, 'We would love to keep you, but we don't know how fast you're going to recover. You can play in this league, but we can't keep you this year.'

"In the second year I went to the Minnesota Lynx. I coached that winter at Santa Barbara and then was invited to camp. In the final week of training camp I went for a loose ball and my shoulder popped out of place. I had three months of recovery time, which is the entire length of the season.

"My third year I was with the Washington Mystics. That was a shorter camp. They drafted a very different point guard next to me, Nikki Blue, just coming out of UCLA. We brought different things to the table. I coached for three years, so my basketball IQ was pretty good. I was a good shooter, but wasn't athletic, wasn't super flashy. We were different players, so they decided to go the other route; I was cut."

Those three pro seasons gave April valuable insight in how the game is played at the highest level.

"I learned three different styles of play and how they run things," she said. "I learned all their offense and all their drills. I wouldn't trade it for anything. It was great playing against those players for that short of time."

April not only spent four great seasons helping coach the Gauchos, she also met her husband while at Santa Barbara and another basketball legend, Indiana native John Wooden who died in 2010 at age 99.

Brett Foster is a financial planner with Amicus Financial in Indianapolis. He was all-conference in baseball (he was a third baseman and "a big hitter," according to his wife, in college at Southern Arkansas), football (he tried out with the Cincinnati Bengals as a quarterback in 2008, but didn't make the team) and basketball (he was a guard) for Crater High School in Central Point, Ore. He had a 3.87 GPA.

April and Brent were married on Aug. 31, 2007.

"I was just such a fan of Coach Wooden (he won 10 NCAA titles while at UCLA)," she said. "He was an amazing man. He's the one I really look to for my philosophy in how I treat kids and how I coach kids. I met him on several occasions. I went to his apartment in L.A. and my family was with me.

"We went down and had breakfast with Coach Wooden. When my little sister Amada was about eight years old, she met him and he spent time with her, because he cared about people. And you know it by listening to his players speak about him and what Coach Wooden has taught them."

Amanda was a senior in the 2009-10 season for the Spartans and now is playing for Butler's Lady Bulldogs.

Not long after April and Brett were married, they decided to move to Indiana. One of the first things April did on her return home was to call Schilling.

"It is an interesting transition in going from a player to a coach," she said. "I coached four years at Santa Barbara, then moved here, and as I said, this is a dream come true being at Champions Academy, being able to be on the court and teach.

"I called all the people who helped me along the way when I lived here, and my old coaches, and everyone said, 'You need to call Ed Schilling. You're doing the same thing, but on the women's side.' So I called him and we met for a little while. From the very start we agreed on what we need to do.

"Working with Ed is a perfect fit. I do the women's side, he does the men (they also bridge the gender gap; April will work with the men and Ed will work with the women on occasion).

April and Ed became a team in August 2008. Her goal is to make women's basketball even more popular and positive than it has become in the past couple of decades.

"A lot of opportunities have come up for me just working with Ed, from different videos we're going to do to different clinics all over the country, mostly representing Champions Academy," April said.

"Women's basketball has grown so much, and the parity in women's basketball is amazing, because there are so many talented players now in a lot of different places. It is so exciting to be a part of it again, and to come alongside coaches and players and help them to be the best they can be is just a dream come true for me, and to be able to do it in my home state is great."

Schilling, who became the varsity head coach at Park Tudor in Indianapolis in 2009 (he hired April as one of his assistants), says he was quite impressed with April's character and how she carried herself when they first met, but he wondered, "Can she coach? Then she gave me her instructional DVD. It was as good or better than any DVD I'd seen at any level.

"She did it all on her computer. She had different people film for her. It is terrific. We do a coaching academy thing online and we have a Web so people can call in and ask questions from all around the world. There have been people from all over the world who bought the DVD.

"I thought she was going to be really good, but she has far, far exceeded even my high expectations. One, she just has a great passion for the game. But she can also relate it to kids. April is just a home run hitter."

Ed and April have worked together at school assemblies all around the country and they do a ball-handling and dribbling routine to get the kids' attention.

"One of the messages I think that April brings, especially when she's talking to girls at clinics, is that you can do both, be competitive on the court and be a lady off it. You don't have to be hard and tough. She has been a Division I coach for four years. She wants to come back and give back. She wants to be closer to family. I think she's found a niche where she can really help people beyond just as a coach and winning games, but really helping them become the best ladies they can be, the best basketball players, yes, but also the best people, and that's our mission."

Champions Academy, which is not-for-profit, except the pro division, has gone global. Indiana native Del Harris, the former NBA head coach who coached the Chinese Olympic team in 2004, got permission to do a project in China using 2-minute teaching videos created by Ed, Gannon Baker of North Carolina and April that the Chinese can see when they log on free to what is called WOHOOPS.

When Harris approached Schilling about the project, Ed said, "I don't know if you want to go to the women's side, because they're playing, too. I gave him April's DVD and he said, 'Oh, my gosh.' Wherever we go, if there are women coaches or former players and you mention April's name, it's like going out in the guys' world and it's like saying Larry Bird or Oscar Robertson or Rick Mount. That's the respect her name has in this state among female players."

KATIE DOUGLAS

Katie Douglas is back home again in Indiana as a member of the WNBA's Fever, and the former Perry Meridian High School and Purdue University standout couldn't be happier to be reconnected with her roots.

Douglas asked the Connecticut Sun for a trade before the 2008 WNBA season and on Feb. 19 of that year the Sun management sent Katie to the Indiana Fever in exchange for Tamika Whitmore and the Fever's first-round pick in the 2008 WNBA Draft.

Katie and her husband Vasilis Giapalakis, whom she married in 2005 in his native Greece, where she was playing basketball, live in a condo in Indianapolis during the Fever season. They also have a home in Athens, Greece.

Vasilis is a basketball player agent and negotiates his wife's WNBA contract and European contracts.

"I have to pinch myself when I think about how far Indianapolis has come in the development of sports," Katie said of her native city that once was known as Indi-a-no-place.

"I'm blessed. I'm very appreciative and understand how times have changed sports-wise in Indianapolis. I was born in 1979 and I do remember the start of so many good things here and how far this city has come in athletics. I definitely embrace it.

"It's great to be a part of the history and sports legacy in Indianapolis. I'm so fortunate to come back home and have my professional career end here. It's so nice to be home after so many years away."

Katie and Vasilis have no children.

"I have seven nieces and nephews, and I just love being an aunt," said Katie, youngest of four siblings. "I've been an aunt I think since I was 13. It's just a joy being around these kids. I think they love having their Aunt Katie back. Now they're getting older and they come to the games and it's really fun to see them."

Katie Douglas is back home again in Indiana for Fever. (Photo courtesy of Indiana Fever)

Do Katie and her husband plan to have a family?

"Million dollar question," she said. "Aunt Katie definitely would like to have a family of her own with her husband. I think it's definitely something in our future. However, I don't think either one of us is ready at this point.

"I think we love to be the aunt and uncle and spoil the kids. But Vasilis' feelings are extremely respectful and he understands that I want to play and I still have that burn and that desire and mentality. He's not pressing me by any means. I think he ultimately would like me to finish what I've started and feel good about my career. I just turned 32 and I think I've got three or four more years to play."

Katie says Vasilis "was never a player. Definitely I hope that our kids get my athleticism and his intelligence. He's more the intellectual. He's got a great mind, a great brain, a great heart. He's a great guy.

"But his athleticism leaves a lot to be desired. He just is in love with the game. He's been around the game since he was young in Athens and he wanted to find a way to be involved and find his niche."

Katie was only 22 when she arrived in Greece a bit overwhelmed by the size of Athens—6 million people—compared to Indianapolis, less than a million. But Vasilis made her feel welcome.

"He's pretty good at what he does," Katie said. "A lot of people say, 'How did you get that nice contract?' He can pretty much work from anywhere. So I'm definitely very lucky to have him be able to pretty much follow me around.

"Vasilis and I just met and kinda hit it off. But it wasn't love at first sight, because I don't think as a 22-year-old that I was going over there looking for something of that nature. I was looking to have fun, to enjoy a new culture. It just became serious after a few months. He's been with me ever since.

"Again I think it is important, not only for my career, but for my husband and I to just enjoy being married, to enjoy one another, to enjoy the years you and your husband have."

An example of their special togetherness occurred the second week of July 2010, when they watched the ESPYs in their Indianapolis condo. It was an emotional night for Katie, who lost both of her parents to cancer—father Ken to pancreatic cancer in 1997 and mother Karen to breast cancer in 2000.

In 2001, when she was a Purdue senior, Katie received the first Jimmy V Foundation Comeback of the Year Award for Perseverance after a string of tragic personal losses. The Jimmy V Foundation was formed to honor Jim Valvano, who coached North Carolina State to an NCAA title in 1983 before being diagnosed with cancer and delivering his famous, "Don't give up. Don't ever give up," speech on national television during the 1993 ESPYs show just before he passed away.

Denver Nuggets Coach George Karl received the Jimmy V Award for Perseverance at the 2010 ESPYs.

"Obviously Karl has a tremendous network and support system," Katie said. "Having neck and throat cancer, him getting up on the stage and talk, I was just amazed. I was telling my general manager (Kelly Krauskopf), 'Man, it was really powerful that he got up there and won the Jimmy V Perseverance Award."

Katie calls the Jimmy V Award her most special recognition.

The very next night Katie and Vasilis spent a feel-good night at Conseco Fieldhouse, home of the Fever, watching Lady Gaga.

Katie's first sports loves were baseball and softball.

"My dad did not play basketball and I'm not sure he played sports," she said. "He was a huge sports fan. But moreover he was a baseball fan. Everybody asks me my memories. My memories were about Edgewood Ball Park I grew up in Edgewood (on the south side of Indianapolis).

"It's funny. Now my nieces and nephews are playing there. I find myself going back there for their games. I played years and years of softball at Edgewood. Skip Hess was one of my coaches with my dad.

"My dad was a huge Chicago Cubs fan. I've said many times to many different people, the reason I wore No. 23 originally (her number with the Fever) was for Ryne Sandberg (a former Cubs second baseman). I remember my dad taking me to Wrigley Field many times."

Hess is the outdoor writer for *The Indianapolis Star*. He says Katie broke his heart when, after coaching her in softball at Edgewood for some four years, she told him she wanted to play basketball fulltime.

From the time Hess first saw Katie's father shagging fly balls hit by his 6-year-old daughter on a far Edgewood field, he thought she was the best softball prospect he ever saw at that age.

"Boy, that little girl had an arm and she was hitting balls to the wall," Hess remembered. "After they were finished, I went over and introduced myself."

Hess was coach of a team of 8-and-9-year-olds. He made the 6-year-old left-hander a first-round draft choice, a decision that brought laughter from other coaches. Skip is also convinced that had Katie continued to develop her softball skills she would have earned a scholarship to an elite NCAA Division I program.

"My favorite story about Ken, Karen and Katie is about how they reacted in one of our softball games," Hess said. "Karen was in the bleachers on the first base side. Katie was at bat. Ken was coaching at third and said, 'Kate—that's what he called his daughter—'Keep your eye on the ball.' Karen yelled, 'Tuck in your shirt tail, sweetheart.'

Asked to rate Katie Douglas on a scale of 0 to 10 for her imitation of her Indiana Fever coach, Lin Dunn, Lin laughed uproariously.

"Katie is a pretty good actress," Lin said. "She might have missed her calling. Instead of being a professional basketball player, she might should have been a comedian on *Saturday Night Live*. She's pretty close to a 10 on Lin Dunn."

Does it bother Lin that Katie imitates her?

"Of course not," Lin declared emphatically. "We have great fun together.

"The Fever play hard, they work hard and they have fun hard. They love to laugh and that's why you enjoy being around 'em, and I think that's why they enjoy each other."

"Katie played everywhere, shortstop, second base, first base. She hit about .875 to .900. I went to the funerals of her parents, but I haven't seen Katie much recently. But I can't tell you how proud of her I am and what's she done in basketball. It hasn't surprised me at all, having seen how good that little 6-year-old was.

"After she had worked hard on her basketball skills, I went over to Katie's house with my son Matt, who is a year older that Katie, and she wanted to play him in basketball. He at first said he didn't want to play a girl, but they went outside. Matt came in and said, 'Dad, you won't believe this.' He had lost to Katie, 21-0 and 21-0."

Katie says, "I don't know if it was anybody who got me into basketball. I just think it was

Indiana Fever stalwarts Katie Douglas (left), Coach Lin Dunn (center) and Stephanie White, assistant coach. (Photo courtesy of Indiana Fever)

natural. At that young age you played softball in the summer and basketball in the fall. It got to the point there were scheduling conflicts. You can't play both sports, because the travel team wants you for basketball, yet the softball team needs you for regular season. It got to the point where being a kid in Indiana you have to at least try basketball.

"I started about the same time as I played softball, but you get to the grade school level and middle school level, they start to want more commitment. At that time when I needed to make a commitment, I just felt I enjoyed basketball much more than I did softball."

Katie's two older brothers—Brian, six years older, and Scott, four years her senior—did not play basketball at Perry Meridian High School.

"They were recreational players," she said. "I think they just liked to play against me and beat me up a lot. We had a lot of driveway matchups when I was growing up (on Friendship Drive near Perry Meridian High School). My sister (Kim Rastrelli) didn't play anything that I can remember. She was more into her studies and work."

Brian and Scott might have beat up on their younger sister on Friendship Drive, but by the time Katie was 12 she impressed her future high school coach, Mike Armstrong, in a youth game. Katie's team trailed by some 10 points late, then she went to work and led her team to victory.

"The last six or seven minutes of that game, she was the best 12-year-old I've ever seen play," Armstrong said. "That's when I knew this kid could be really good."

In AAU competition, Douglas won a state and national title. She made the Perry Meridian varsity team as a freshman. The team went 9-11, 17-4, 22-4 and 26-1 in Katie's four years as a Lady Falcon.

Perry Meridian lost to eventual state champion Martinsville in the final game of the Indianapolis Southport Semi-state in Katie's senior year before a sellout crowd of over 7,200. Earlier in the day Katie stole the ball, got fouled and hit a free throw for a victory over Center Grove.

"They sold 7,800 tickets to a 7,200-seat arena for that semi-state," Armstrong said. "The fire marshal closed the doors. At our end-of-season banquet, we had something like 240 people. I remember going to the microphone and saying, 'When I started coaching, we couldn't get 240 people to come to the games.' "

Did Katie ever think she was destined for basketball stardom? Not ever, she insisted.

"I was just a kid having fun and loved getting better and loved learning the game," she said. "If I had to pick a point when I knew that maybe I had some kind of talent it was especially in my sophomore year in high school.

"I was getting letter after letter from universities and colleges asking me to take a look at their program and offering me a scholarship. I think at that point I thought, "Hey, that's kinda cool, help my parents out, get a scholarship and get my education paid for.' "

The number of scholarship offers was too great for Katie to know for sure.

"My mom kept an amazing scrapbook," she stated. "She put in all the letters and stuff. I still have it and it definitely will stay with me forever as a keepsake. I didn't know she was doing it, because I was a teenager. I didn't notice what she was doing. You look back now and see all the time she devoted to it and how proud she was. Obviously there were a lot of offers. It was kinda crazy when I look back now."

Why was Purdue Katie's choice?

"Obviously they had a great tradition there," she said. "Lin Dunn started it and she recruited me up to my senior year in high school. Then she left the program (after nine years) and Nell Fortner came along and made me really want to go there. And my father was ill. He had been diagnosed with terminally-ill pancreatic cancer. You know what it does to a family as far as fighting and being there."

In Katie's four years at Purdue, the team made the NCAA tournament every year: 1998, 23-10 record and tied for third in the Big Ten at 10-6, Elite Eight in the tournament; 1999, 34-1 record and

16-0 for first in the Big Ten, NCAA champion; 2000, 23-8 record and tied for third in the Big Ten at 11-5, NCAA second round; 2001, 31-7 record and 14-2 for first in the Big Ten, NCAA runner-up.

Katie Douglas, former Indianapolis Perry Meridian High School and Purdue University standout, drives around WNBA defender for Indiana Fever. (Photo courtesy of Indiana Fever)

As a sophomore in '99, Katie helped the Lady Boilermakers win the NCAA championship at the HP Pavilion in San Jose, Calif., with a 62-45 victory over Duke. Two years later, in Katie's senior year, Purdue finished runner-up to Notre Dame, 68-66, in the NCAA title game at Scottrade Center in St. Louis, Mo.

"My sophomore year was special," Katie said, "because prior to that year we went on a European tour, and we also knew that Carolyn Peck, the coach at that time, had taken a job with the Orlando Miracle of the WNBA.

"We knew it was going to be her last year with the team. We were trying to make the most of that season. We only lost one game that season and I think it showed that we played with urgency every game. We had a special group and enjoyed each other so much. It was a very fun year."

The ball was in Katie's hands when the 1999 title game ended. She threw it in the air as high as she could.

"It was an amazing feeling," she said. "The weight of the world kinda came off my shoulders. There was a lot of pressure, a lot of expectations for that team, but again it was a lot of fun. We knew that team wasn't going to be the same the following year. We wanted to finish off on the right note.

133

"After the NCAA championship I lost my mother to cancer. But as a senior it was another great season. It was the last time I'd be a college student-athlete. I had gone through a lot of adversity and transition, but my four years at Purdue were very gratifying."

For her Purdue career, Katie played in 135 games and started 101. She came off the bench in all 33 games as a freshman. She averaged 14.6 points per game, shot .445 from the field, .343 from three-point range and .798 from the free-throw line in four years.

The 6-foot Douglas, who calls Fever teammate Tamika Catchings the best player she has ever faced, has a myriad of honors:

- She ended her high school career as Perry Meridian's scoring leader with 1,406 points, was a 1997 *Parade Magazine* All-American honorable mention and was named to the Indiana All-Star team.

- She was a Kodak All-America in 2000 and 2001 while at Purdue, as well as being named to the 1999 and 2001 NCAA Women's Final Four All-Tournament Team. In 2001, she was named the Big Ten Player of the Year, received the Silver Basketball from the *Chicago Tribune* and also the Big Ten Suzy Favor Award, which is given to the conference's female athlete of the year across all sports.

- She is Purdue's all-time steals leader with 327.

- She was named Most Valuable Player of the 2006 WNBA All-Star Game. She was the three-point shooting winner at the 2010 Team USA-WNBA All-Star Game (as a member of the All-Star team).

As Mike Armstrong, Douglas' high school coach, says: "For the kids who go to middle school and elementary school, they can see that a kid who lived in the same neighborhoods you live in proved you can come from the south side of Indianapolis and west side of Perry Township and be a professional basketball player."

And a very good one.

ELLEN DEVOE

Ellen DeVoe chuckled when she recalled one of the many memories she has of her late father, John DeVoe, who helped start the Indiana Pacers in 1967, a year before he died unexpectedly while attending the American Basketball Association team's game at the Coliseum in his native Indianapolis.

A virus settled in John's heart as he watched his professional team the night of Dec. 14, 1968.

"I hear my dad was disappointed (when Ellen was born on May 6, 1964), because he wanted a basketball team," Ellen recalled as she sat in the Boston University student union while taking a break from her duties as a School of Social Work assistant professor of clinical practice at BU.

"He didn't know what to do with a girl."

John DeVoe did get two-thirds of a male basketball team in sons John and Tom. There was no Indiana High School Athletic Association girls' basketball tournament at the time of Ellen's birth. The first IHSAA girls' tournament was in 1976.

But the first Pacers president and Princeton University basketball and tennis standout would have been proud of the female who blessed him and wife Jane that spring day 47 years ago.

Ellen not only became an Indiana All-Star after leading Indianapolis Brebeuf Jesuit to the Final Four of the 1982 state girls' high school tournament—the Lady

Braves lost to Valparaiso, 41-33, in the semifinals at Market Square Arena—she carried on the DeVoe basketball tradition at Princeton.

The three DeVoe brothers—Chuck, John and Steve—all played basketball and tennis at Princeton after being graduated from Indianapolis Park School (now known as Park Tudor). Chuck and John, who once scored 73 points in a game while at Park, both won the Bunn Trophy as MVPs their senior years at Princeton. Chuck succeeded John as Pacers president and served in that capacity for seven years.

In an email from Kristy McNeil, assistant director of athletic communications at Princeton, she said, "Based on all the records (Ellen) holds, she is clearly one of the best players in program history."

These are Ellen's most significant accomplishments for the Lady Tigers:

- Four-year letter winner (1983, '84, '85, '86).

- First-team All-Ivy in 1985.

- Second-team All-Ivy in 1983, 1986.

- Ranks 7th in career points (1,290), 7th in scoring average (13.3).

- Ranks 1st in points in a game with 38 against Long Island University on Jan. 14, 1985; also had 34 points vs. Yale on March 2, 1984 and 32 against LIU on January 2, 1984.

- Ranks 1st in field goals made and attempted in a game with 17 made and 30 attempted.

- Ranks 2nd in career rebounds (942), 2nd in rebound average (9.7).

- Ranks 4th in rebounds in a game with 23 against LIU on January 7, 1985.

- Ranks 1st in career blocks (157), 1st in blocks in a game with nine, and has the top two marks for blocks in a season—50 and 49.

Shortly after John DeVoe died, his wife Jane married Indianapolis attorney Alan Nolan, a widower with five children and a Civil War buff whose book entitled *Lee Considered: General Robert E. Lee and Civil War History* received a rave review by the *New York Times* in 1991.

The union of Jane and Alan was a godsend for the DeVoe siblings.

John DeVoe holds a birthday cake for his 2-year-old daughter Ellen, who went on to have a standout career at Princeton where her father excelled. (Photo courtesy of Jane Nolan)

"Alan wasn't involved in the sports world like my dad, but he actually was a sports fanatic," Ellen said. "He played high school football at (Indianapolis) Shortridge and then he went to Indiana University.

"The joke was always that he was honorable mention all-state in football. Maybe it was all-county. I don't know. But he loved basketball. We spent hours and hours in the kitchen watching the Big Ten and March Madness. He was very supportive in every way possible, not just relating to basketball."

Alan Nolan passed away in the summer of 2008 after a long illness. The DeVoe kids called him dad. Alan and Jane were married about 14 months after John died.

"It was too soon, as my mother would admit," Ellen said. "My mother says it would have been longer, but it was hard to navigate with eight kids and two separate households.

"And they decided, very deliberately, that the DeVoe kids would keep their name, so we kept our last name. And my mom took Alan's name, because it was easier. Alan was incredible with us DeVoes. My mom is pretty sturdy."

Ellen and husband Donald Wright, a corporate finance man who took a new job with RBS, the Royal Bank of Scotland, in 2010, live in

They were Ivy League buddies. One was a free style swimmer at Dartmouth, the other a basketball and tennis player at Princeton.

Emerson Houck, who twice competed in the NCAA swimming championship meet, and John DeVoe, who received the Bunn Trophy as Princeton's MVP in basketball as a senior, met in Indianapolis after Houck's parents moved from Oak Park, Ill., to the Hoosier capital when he was a college freshman in 1953.

"John and I became fast friends, fast enough that I was an usher at his wedding and he was an usher at ours (Emerson's wife is named Jane, the same first name of John's wife)," said Houck of the first president of the Indiana Pacers who was one of four people to whom Emerson dedicated his book *Hoosiers All: Indiana High School Basketball Teams*.

DeVoe died unexpectedly while attending a Pacers game at the Coliseum on Dec. 14, 1968, when a virus settled in his heart. He was the father of Ellen DeVoe, also a skilled basketball player at Princeton who is profiled in this book.

"Whenever John came up to Dartmouth to play basketball, we would get

Newton, Mass., just west of Boston, with their three children: Ethan, Jake and Abigail.

"I'm a Ms.," Ellen said, "and sometimes I'm a doctor or a professor. I think I would have remained Ellen DeVoe anyway, but mostly because of my dad. That was a huge part of it. He's with me a lot."

Ellen's oldest son, who is 10, is named Ethan DeVoe Wright.

"He's a basketball and soccer freak," she stated. "I coach two of his basketball teams. As a 9-year-old he scored 27 points and made 9-for-10 at the free-throw line in a playoff game. But I was more proud of the way he passed the ball.

"Jake's middle name is Thomas after my little brother. But I didn't give him DeVoe, because my husband wouldn't let him have four names. But now Jakey would like to have DeVoe added. So he's going to be Jacob Thomas DeVoe Wright.

"The youngest is six and her name is Abigail DeVoe Wright. They all know the stories about my dad, how he died, the Pacers and all that stuff. My kids are athletic, but who knows? My main goal for sports for my kids is if it will help them stay out of trouble in high school, then I want them to play and I'll be supportive."

Ethan plays on three different basketball teams, and to help with her coaching of him, Ellen called her high school coach, Alan Vickrey, and asked him to tell her about some of the drills he used at Brebeuf and at Indianapolis North Central, where he won successive Class 4A state championships in 2004 and 2005.

Of her telephone conversation with Vickrey, who retired from his coaching duties at North Central at the end of the 2010-11 season, in regard to coaching Ethan in AAU basketball, Ellen said, " 'All right, Vic, tell me what to do.' He said, 'Ellen, you've accomplished a lot in your life and in your career, but this may well be the hardest thing you ever do, coach fourth-grade boys' basketball.' We're using his motion offense and we're using his exact drills. I remember all the fundamentals from that and from camp."

In response to Vickrey's thought that it might be the hardest thing Ellen has ever done, she replied, "The dads are very serious about it. They think that this means that their kids are going to get into the NBA or not. It's ridiculous. I'm into it, too, and I hate to lose. But you do have to teach them appropriately for their age and teach them fundamentals. And they have to like it and they have to come back next year."

together," Houck, retired from Eli Lilly & Co. after a 35-year career with the Indianapolis pharmaceutical firm, said. "And when I went to Princeton to swim he would come and watch. John always had a sparkle in his eye.

"In the summers we would double-date a lot. We even played squash together. I didn't dare play tennis with him, he was way too good. I spent a lot of time at his house, the way guys do. We shot some hoops in his backyard."

Emerson will never forget the night John passed away. He and his son Joe, who was eight at the time, had been invited to sit next to John and his wife during the second half.

"I had decided to take my son Joe to the Pacers game," Houck said. "I bought two cheap tickets for Joe and I. We went on the spur of the moment. I didn't even tell John we were coming.

"But, of course, he always had these tickets right by courtside, because he was a part owner. He saw us at halftime. He waved up at us and said, 'Come on down. We've got plenty of room, sit with us.'

"So I said, 'Let's do it.' We worked our way down and

by the time we got there, he had gone in and bought this ABA red, white and blue ball. I think it was signed by somebody—Bob Netolicky, Roger Brown or one of 'em. John gave Joe the ball and made some comment like, 'I had to buy this for you, 'cause I knew your old man was too cheap to do it.' "

Emerson said he and his son enjoyed the game, until Jane DeVoe, who was sitting on his left, grabbed him and said, "Em, there's something wrong with John," who was seated next to Jane. There wasn't much time left in the game.

"We just let out a bit of a yell and somebody with medical skills took over," Emerson said. "It was such a stunner, because John was such a superb athlete, and he seemed to be in great shape. I saw no outward signs. I thought the best thing I should do was to get Joe home."

Emerson had been a big fan of Illinois high school basketball and his appreciation of the sport grew immensely through his friendship with John DeVoe, who had been a standout prep player at Park School (now known as Park Tudor).

"When I moved to Indianapolis, I said, 'My

John DeVoe was 6-foot-3. Ellen inherited his size.

"I think I'm 6-feet," she said. "My brothers would say I'm 5-foot-11. I went to Orchard Country Day School in Indianapolis. I was the tallest girl in the school. I did all the sports that were available, and that included basketball. In seventh and eighth grade we were coached by eighth grade and ninth grade boys, which was not such a great arrangement."

When Ellen was a freshman at Brebeuf, former Pacers standout Billy Keller was the varsity coach.

"Billy Keller was trying to build the girls program and he approached me my freshman year," Ellen said. "He said, 'Ellen, everybody in your family played basketball and you're the tallest girl in the school. You need to come and play basketball.' He sort of convinced me that I should try, so I did.

"Billy Keller is a really nice guy. He actually never coached me. I played on the freshman team and then he left (to join the Purdue coaching staff). By the time I was on the varsity as a sophomore, Alan Vickrey was the coach."

Early in her first varsity season, Ellen broke two fingers on her right hand. It proved to be a blessing.

"I did learn to shoot pretty well with my left hand, so that was great (Ellen is right-handed; her father was left-handed)," she said.

Ellen's work ethic impressed Vickrey.

"Every day she'd come to practice and we'd work on that left hand," he said. "She would dribble with her left hand and work on a little left-handed jump hook shot. And I'll be darned by mid-season she had become our primary offensive weapon and started scoring points and bringing down rebounds. About mid-season she started every game and then two more years and became the leading scorer in the school's history at that point (922 career points) and an Indiana All-Star."

Ellen is now ninth on the school's career scoring list and ranks sixth in career scoring average with 13.3 points per game. She is fourth in career rebounds with 742 and is tied with Ta'Shia Phillips for the single-game rebounding record with 27 vs. Warren Central in the 1980-81 season.

A year later Brebeuf was good enough to challenge for a girls' state championship. Vickrey talked with Ellen about what he expected of his senior co-captain (Melissa Barney was other captain).

goodness, I'm gonna learn about Indiana basketball and I'm gonna see how they do.' I watched all I could and when Jane and I got married and moved here full-time, we would go to high school games. We went to all the sectional tournaments, regionals, semi-states. I was able to buy tickets several times for the state finals at Hinkle Fieldhouse.

"I didn't really have time to do a lot with it until after I retired. Lilly is a pretty all-consuming job. When I retired, the first thing Jane and I wanted to do was to see the country. We'd seen the world, we lived in Australia, we had traveled in Europe and we'd been in 55 countries. But we really hadn't seen the United States.

"Let's see the U.S. by car and do it on the back roads. You can't see America on the interstate highways. You go to the little towns and you see, particularly in the Midwest, it says on the outskirts 'Home of the Wildcats, or the Home of the Braves, or the Home of the Tigers.' And you know that's the hometown basketball team."

Emerson also noted how important the team mascots were to the social fabric of the community, particularly to the communities that had only one school.

"We noticed that some of those mascots were kind of interesting," he said, "like the Centralia (Ill.) Orphans and the Teutopolis (Ill.) Wooden Shoes. So I wrote a book on unique mascots all over the country, and there are about a thousand of 'em."

Roger Dickinson, former executive director of the Indiana Basketball Hall of Fame, said to Emerson, "Why don't you write a book and do for Indiana and our mascots what you did for the United States?"

Emerson picked up the ball and expanded on Dickinson's idea a little bit.

"I said I'll not only get the 400 schools that still exist, but I want to get the 800 we've lost through consolidation," Emerson said. "And I want to get the glory years of all the schools I can. For Muncie Central that's a lot different than it is for Freelandville or Oden.

"Maybe some of the schools had one glory year. Maybe they won one sectional, finally beat the Kokomo Kats or the New Castle Trojans. I wanted to capture that. They still talk about it in those towns: Remember in 1938 when we

"The one thing I loved about Ellen was that it was never about her," Vickrey said. "It was always about other people. She was always committed to finding out how she could help other people.

"When she was a captain her senior year, I talked to her a lot about, 'Yes, you're going to be the focal point of this team. Every team is going to come out and try to stop you after the junior year you had. You're going to have to be willing to accept the fact that you're not going to score as much as you did last year.

"But you're going to play a bigger role, because if we can get people to double team you, that will be to our benefit. She accepted that well. In fact, she cherished that role. It was just the nature of that young lady to be always thinking what talents do I have, what is it about me that can be contributory to the success of the venture we're all involved in now."

In 1982 Brebeuf defeated Bloomington South, 64-50, and Indianapolis Decatur Central, 58-46, in the semi-state at Indianapolis Ben Davis. The Lady Braves went to the state finals at Market Square Arena with a 25-2 record. They were the only team in the finals to be ranked (12th).

So what happened in the upset to Valparaiso in the first round of the finals when Ellen scored eight points on 4-of-13 shooting (she didn't shoot a free throw)?

"Well, we lost in the state finals my senior year, but otherwise we did very well," Ellen said. "But I will never like Valparaiso. You can't blame it all on the coach, but we basically froze, 'cause Valparaiso was not ranked. We were in the top 20 most of the season and had a higher ranking as the season wore on. Valparaiso's whole team was about 5-foot-8 and they were strong. And they just shut us down. They shut me down. We all remember it very well. I'm still bitter about that."

Vickrey agrees with Ellen's assessment.

"I don't think we were totally prepared," he said. "I don't think I was prepared. I was a third-year coach and didn't know what I was walking into, I don't think.

"We thought we had a really good chance of winning it, and probably should have, because Heritage (of Monroeville) ends up winning it that night (52-45 over Valparaiso). Heritage played without its point guard, because she had gotten a concussion (in her team's 66-55 victory over Sullivan) in the

finally beat the Vincennes Alices?

"I wanted to get it in one place so if anybody ever wanted to look it up they could find every school that ever was in Indiana. Now I know I didn't get every single one. But I got a lot of 'em. And I do have over 1,200."

Girls' basketball in Indiana joined the parade in 1976 with the first high school tournament and the girls' game is alive and well in Hoosierland today, right up there with the boys' game.

Ellen DeVoe's late father, John DeVoe, shoots for Princeton, where Ellen played collegiately and well. (Photo courtesy of Jane Nolan)

143

afternoon. But Jody Beerman was a pretty good player and she had a great game that night (23 points)."

Beerman became Miss Basketball in 1983.

Despite the disappointment of the state finals, Ellen has mostly fond memories of her high school career.

"It was before they had the class system in Indiana high school ball, so we played against all the big teams and we were winning, and that was a blast," she says proudly.

"We were playing against schools with 3,000 students and Brebeuf had 500. Our team was great. It was just a group of smart girls. We were doing well in school and the basketball was fun. I was the center, the tallest girl in school. I was a forward in college."

Ellen recalls having "a sort of" 15 minutes of fame

"I made the *Street & Smith* All-America list," she said. "I think it was honorable mention. Once you get on one of those lists you get bombarded with letters. I still have my box of recruitment letters. So that was a lot of fun.

"I had a lot of offers. I figured I might as well go to a school where I'd get an education, because at that point I didn't think women's basketball was going to take me very far or get me rich, so I applied to Princeton. I didn't think I'd get in, but I was accepted. You get into a school like Princeton, you should go. And there was all the family history."

Ellen's first two years at Princeton were rough, she says.

"Coming from Indiana, where basketball is sort of a religion to an Ivy League school, it was a tougher experience. The women's program was very under resourced. We didn't have very good coaching the first two years. We had losing records the first two years, which I wasn't used to. And it's an academically-challenging school. It kept me busy."

Although Ellen never got to play in the NCAA tournament (Princeton made it to the tournament for the first time in 2010), she calls her college basketball career personally satisfying.

"I was a four-year starter and the leading scorer and rebounder for four years. So, yeah, I did have a good career personally, but you want to win, too. The last two years were good."

At the end of Ellen's junior year, she tore the ACL in her left knee.

"The two guards had split and I caught the ball and I crashed," she said. "I remember exactly had it sounded. The same thing happened to my dad (a torn ACL at Princeton), which I think is very bizarre. Jane and Alan happened to be there on parents' night."

Ellen was only five points from 1,000 in her career when she tore her knee.

"I wasn't supposed to do this, but I played for a few minutes in one of the games before I had surgery and got to 999 points," she stated. "Then I got scared because the knee wobbled and I went out of the game, and that was it. Then I confessed to my doctor (that she played on a bad knee)."

Ellen underwent surgery at Methodist Hospital in Indianapolis and rehabbed all that summer. She surpassed the 1,000-point total in her first game as a senior.

"I still have that ball," she said. "That was kind of fun. Princeton game me an orange (a Princeton color) golf cart to get around in when I had my ACL repaired. I think I was also the first woman allowed in the PU training center where they had the knee machine I needed to be tested on."

Ellen has three degrees: bachelor's, master's and Ph.D.

"I have a master's degree in social work from the University of Denver," she said. "I ran away from the East Coast after college and went to Denver. I work with kids around trauma. Then I got a Ph.D. from Michigan in social work and psychology.

"I decided to get the Ph.D. because it was too hard to work directly with kids all the time, so I wanted to have some other things I could do. Now I teach and do research. It's just a little more diverse."

Ellen is in her sixth year at BU after several years at Columbia University in New York City.

"I teach students who are going to be therapists, basically," she said. "Right now I'm working a big project with the military population. I'm working with vets who are coming back from Iraq and Afghanistan—parents of little kids. We are trying to help the families reconnect and get to know each other again."

Asked how life is for Ms DeVoe, Donald and their three kids, Ellen smiled and said, "pretty good. It's never occurred to me to do something sport-minded or athletic-minded (professionally)."

But she quickly added, "Basketball was rewarding for me. I think I root for a lot of women in the game. It teaches you a lot that you can't get anyplace else, about dealing with men and power, about getting along in the world. I think I learned a lot about that from basketball.

"I watch friends of mine from college who are women and they don't have that experience, so they don't handle it as well, or as easily, I guess."

John DeVoe's buttons would pop if he were able to see what kind of a student-athlete and human being his daughter became. Extraordinary.

Jenny Young

Patty Broderick was just beginning to referee college basketball games when she received an assignment to work a Butler University women's contest at Hinkle Fieldhouse in the early 1980s.

The Lady Bulldogs had a rarity at point guard, 4-foot-11 Jenny Young, an accomplished four-sport athlete from Speedway High School, which is just a couple of hundred yards west of the Indianapolis Motor Speedway.

Broderick, one of only two Hoosiers in the Women's Basketball Hall of Fame in Knoxville, Tenn., and currently the coordinator of the Women's Basketball Officiating Consortium which includes eight different college conferences, remembers that Butler game vividly and with great appreciation for what that pint-sized point guard accomplished.

"The smaller the package the bigger the heart, you know that, don't you?" said Broderick, a Cardinal Ritter High School graduate, of Young.

Barbara Greenburg coached Young in softball and tennis at Butler before retiring. She, too, remembers Jenny as an incredibly talented athlete for being so little.

"I gave her credit for being 5-feet," said Greenburg, smiling. "She is one of my favorite people and one of the greatest athletes ever at Butler. Jenny not only was a point guard in basketball, she was a catcher and shortstop in softball and was No.1 in singles and doubles in tennis."

Speedway High School is the home of the Sparkplugs. It is a nickname that fits Young, a 1979 graduate, to a T. Not only did she earn High School All-American honors in basketball, she also received letters in volleyball, tennis and track and field, with a total of 12. Then she went on to win 12 letters in basketball, softball and tennis at Butler where she was inducted into the school's Athletic Hall of Fame in 2000.

Jenny was not voted an Indiana All-Star after her senior year of basketball at Speedway, but Amy Metheny, who helped Indianapolis Southport win the girls' state tournament championship in 1980, says Young deserved the honor.

"Jenny was better than some of the girls voted to that team," Metheny, who played with Young in the Indianapolis-Scarborough Peace Games, said.

Of her sports career, Jenny, who is a supervisor at Allison Transmission in Indianapolis where her late father, Charles, worked, says, "Because I was little and fast, people thought I was pretty good and that I was kinda like a sparkplug."

In notes to Butler officials prior to her induction into the school's Athletic Hall of Fame, Jenny wrote, "If not on the courts, I could be found delivering newspapers or peddling my dad's tomatoes or grandma's sweet corn door-to-door throughout the community, As a result, my recognition was twofold: the athlete and the entrepreneur.

"My quest to become a successful business woman led me seven miles east of Speedway to Butler University where I majored in business administration. I graduated cum laude, was a member of the Blue Key Honorary, was selected as an Academic All-American, and was voted one of Butler's top students.

"I was a member of the Delta Gamma sorority, was a homecoming queen nominee, and I participated in events campus-wide like a normal college co-ed. However, unlike the students who had part-time jobs, I was able to fund my education through my love of sports and earn 12 intercollegiate varsity letters in the process."

From a very young age, Jenny became a sports enthusiast.

"I always had that urge to play baseball and other sports," she said.

Jenny has a picture of her dad throwing a Whiffle ball to her in the backyard when she was about three and Jenny hitting it back to him.

Rosie Young, Jenny's mother, says she thought her husband Charles "was one of the biggest sports nuts I've ever seen. But he wasn't anything compared to her. One day Jenny was watching a baseball game on TV and I was in the kitchen. She came into the kitchen and said, 'I don't know why I had to be a girl. I can't even play ball.' "

Jenny admits to being a tomboy, "but I took organ lessons and I took tap dance lessons. I was supposed to learn how to do everything. I would sit down and do my organ lesson for 30 minutes, but I couldn't wait until the timer went off, because then I could go out and shoot baskets or throw the baseball or whatever, ride my bike, stuff like that. I was an active person.

Although only 4-foot-11, Jenny Young played basketball, softball and tennis with tenacity and soul at Speedway High School and Butler University, where she earned 12 letters and is in the school's athletic hall of fame. (Photo courtesy of Butler University)

"Back then it was always with the boys. Girls didn't play that much."

Dave Garlick wrote an article in *The Indianapolis Star* after Jenny was voted MVP in a basketball tournament in which Butler played. Garlick, who married a tennis teammate of Jenny's, interviewed Charlie Young along with Jenny.

"My dad told Garlick that he couldn't be any more happy having a boy or watching a boy play, because I basically played everything other than football. We even had a chance to do that. We played in the NIKE/NFL Air It Out flag football competition and we won that for the state of Indiana, myself and four other women."

As a tike Jenny would sit on the back step of her parents' house with her glove and ball waiting for Charlie to get home so they could play catch.

"I know a lot of days he didn't feel like playing with me, but he never said no," she said. Father and daughter would go over to the Speedway High grounds and people would stop to watch them.

"He could hit 'em a mile in the air with a fungo bat," she explained. "I'd catch the ball, then I'd have to run a little to throw it back to him. It was pretty amazing to see somebody that little doing that, I think."

Jenny began her competitive sports career at the Northwest Youth Athletic Association at 38th Street and High School Road.

"We drove by and my dad saw that girls were playing softball," she said. "That was the first time we had seen girls playing. There were four diamonds and boys and girls were playing. I was 13 and in eighth grade. It was the first time I got to play. In the fall I got the opportunity to play basketball for the same organization."

Gary Hill of Brownsburg, who has become close friends of the Young family, coached a basketball team and drafted Jenny as his first-round pick. She taught herself to play tennis.

"Jenny ran track at Speedway and when I went to her track meet, I had to go by the tennis court," Rosie said. "I thought this looks like a lot more fun than running track. I told Jenny about it and she said she didn't know how to play tennis. I said, 'Will you at least try out for me?' She said she would.

"A neighbor lady said her daughter was going to try out for tennis that day. So I called Jenny at school and I had never done that. I said, 'You promised me you would try out for tennis.' She said, 'Mom, I'm not that good and I didn't bring my racket.'

"I said, 'I'll bring it to you,' The coach told me that she came out dragging this racket on the ground behind her. Jenny said, 'My mom made me do this.' She started playing and every day she would move up. She finally was No. 1 at Speedway."

Jenny developed her basketball skills in AAU competition and the Indianapolis-Scarborough Peace Games.

"My first year in the Peace Games was when I was in the eighth grade, the year I started playing basketball," she said. "We got picked for the all-star team and there were an awful lot of good players on that team. I played on that team one year and the next year I had to move up because I was in high school.

"I was 14 and I played in the division from 14 to 22. I went to Canada with all these people 20, 21, 22. We didn't have a lot in common, like I was excited for the games and they were excited for after the games. I was going up there to beat Canada. The first year we went up there Canada scored just two points in the whole game (Indianapolis won, 50-2). We beat 'em so bad it wasn't fun."

Amy Metheny and Linda Mallender, a teammate of Metheny's at Southport, were on that team that crushed Canada.

Basketball became Jenny's forte as a Sparkplug. She is tied for third in points scored in a single season with 301 in 1978-79. She is third in steals in a single season with 64 as a senior.

Believe it or not, Jenny holds the school's single-game point total with 34 against Indianapolis Washington in the 1978 sectional at Decatur Central.

"It was my junior year when we played Cheryl Cook's team," she said. "We were definitely the underdog, because Cheryl (Miss Basketball in 1981) was a well-publicized player. She was fantastic.

"At that time the *Star-News* started to cover girls' basketball a little bit. That was my highest-scoring high school game (she never scored more than 12 points in a game at Butler). When I look back, I think that's pretty big, because that ball was big back then. That was a boys ball we played with and there were no three-pointers then.

Jenny Young has roller-bladed and ridden her bike around the 2 ½-mile Indianapolis Motor Speedway. What she wishes she could have done is drive a race car around the world's most famous race track, like several other females such as Janet Guthrie, Lyn St. James, Sarah Fisher and Danica Patrick have done.

"We grew up only three blocks from the Indianapolis Motor Speedway," said the multi-sport athlete at Speedway High School and Butler University in the late 1970s and early 1980s.

"Then it was so much safer to go over there and I'd ride my bike and hang on the fence. I wanted to see the race drivers and I wanted to be one of them, too. I wanted to be the Danica Patrick of my era. Oh, my gosh, I wanted to drive a race car."

Young became friends with four-time 500 champion Al Unser Sr.

"One of my friends was dating Unser for quite a while and I introduced him to my mom and dad," Jenny said. "He came and sat in their kitchen. My friend told him, 'Jenny knows a lot

"Those were a lot of points then. We upset Cheryl Cook's team. But we didn't win the sectional. Being such a small school, it was hard."

One of Jenny's biggest disappointments occurred shortly after her senior basketball season ended. She didn't make the Indiana All-Star team.

"I remember sitting on a little wicker stool on a Saturday evening waiting for the sports news to come on about 5:25," she said. "I wasn't smart enough to understand that if I had already made the team I would have been called by the organizers to say, 'You made it. We need you to come and take your photograph to put in the newspaper (*Star*).'

"My name didn't get called. I felt I should have had a good chance of doing that. It wasn't long after that Amy Metheny called me. She told me how sorry she was and don't worry, you should have made it."

Jenny's first college choice was Purdue. Her parents grew up north of West Lafayette.

"Mom asked me what I wanted to do one time and I said I wanted to go to a college football game," she said. "We went in the rain to Ross-Ade Stadium to see Purdue play USC and I watched Mark Herrmann (Boilermaker quarterback who entered the College Football Hall of Fame in December 2010)."

In those days girls had to try out for college basketball teams. Jenny arranged a tryout at Mackey Arena, but it didn't produce an athletic scholarship. Ruth Jones was the Purdue coach at the time and when she saw Jenny she suggested Jenny and her high school coach, the late Doug Mullen, return to Indianapolis without a tryout.

"I said no," Jenny said. "We had driven an hour to get there and I wanted to play. They took me to a hallway in Mackey and they wanted to take a vertical jump test. They had me raise my hand against the wall and measure me down to a line to start with. The coach walked by and said, 'Make sure you put down her height with shoes on, like that mattered that much. I was already so much smaller than anybody else. My little shoe soles weren't going to make that much difference."

Jenny says her vertical leap in inches was higher than anybody on the team, "but I just started a foot or so lower than everybody did." She beat all players in individual suicide lap times; she made 20-of-20 free throws; and she did well in a scrimmage.

"They said at the end of the practice that I was too short to play for them," Jenny said. "Ruth

about racing.' He said, 'Oh yeah, right.' I said, 'I do know a lot about racing. Ask me some questions.'

"He asked me a few questions I could answer, so I said, 'Hey, I've got something I want to show you.' "

Jenny went to her room and pulled an autograph book out of a drawer to show Unser.

"I have autographs of all the drivers of the '60s, Sammy Sessions, Johnny Rutherford, Jim McElreath, A.J. Foyt, Roger McCluskey, and my favorite, Lloyd Ruby," she said. "He knew I wasn't just going off about my knowledge of the 500."

Unser looked through the book and suddenly laughed, Jenny said.

"There was one autograph in there where he started his name and then the pen ran out of ink. It had just an A. I teased him about that. He said, 'But my name's in there quite a few times.' I said, 'That's probably because nobody (else) wanted your autograph.'

"He went to the back of the book and I had an autograph from his mother who used to always do the chili supper. She had signed it, 'Mom Unser.' When he looked at that he had tears in his eyes. He said, 'Oh, my gosh, you have my mom's autograph in that book.'

"I said, 'Yeah, if you want it, I'll razor that page out and you can have it.' He said, 'No, that needs to stay right there with those other drivers. After that he knew that I paid attention to racing and have been really lucky to go over to the track and do a lot of things behind the scenes.'"

Jenny still goes to the race.

"I love it," she said. "One of the things I'm proud about being from Speedway is that the race is what we're famous for. Most people that know sports know my hometown."

Jones told me that I played a good game. All she wanted was a 6-foot point guard that could dribble, be fast and quick and shoot. But back then the taller girls weren't as coordinated as they are now. She had a big guard that wasn't very good.

"Then I became a Bulldog. In my freshman season they came to play in Hinkle Fieldhouse and we beat them. It ended up for the best."

Jenny went back to Purdue and tried out for tennis and was told she was okay to play, but there was no scholarship left. She also tried out for softball and was accepted, but again there was no scholarship money, so no deal.

Rosie Young suggested that Jenny should try for scholarship help at Butler.

"Jenny said she wanted to go to college on a basketball scholarship,"

Rosie said. "I said, 'You're not tall enough and we can't do anything about that, so we're gonna have to try for tennis."

Rosie contacted Barbara Greenburg, who offered Jenny a quarter of a scholarship.

"I knew Jenny wasn't going to accept that," Rosie said. "So I said to Mrs. Greenburg, 'Can you at least give her a half scholarship?' She said, 'Well, if I thought she could play softball, I would.' I said, 'You won't be disappointed.' "

Greenburg says today, "I cannot say enough about Jenny's parents. They never were negative to me. They were always positive."

Jenny began her collegiate sports career with three-quarters of a scholarship (a half for tennis and a quarter for softball, for which she wore Little League shin guards as a catcher).

"The basketball coach, Linda Mason, had come to my tennis matches," Jenny said. "She wanted to see if I was interested in playing basketball. But I was focused on tennis. I knew in my mind I was going to try out for basketball, but, you know, play a little mind game: Let me get through this season first, because there's several of us that played a couple of sports. But nobody played three like I did."

The first day of basketball practice Jenny was there as a walk-on.

"I knew I'd be just fine," she said. "The program was only organized two years before I got there. This was Association for Intercollegiate Athletics for Women (AIAW before Butler became a part of the NCAA program).

"I wasn't one of the big recruits that they had brought in, but I walked right into the starting lineup. Beth Piepenbrink from Mooresville was our center and Elza Purvlicis was from North Central (Indianapolis). Barb Skinner was the other guard and she was from Fortville (Mount Vernon). Barb Skinner, Liz Piepenbrink, Beth's sister, and I were freshmen starters.

"Everybody on the team was from a 50-mile radius of Indianapolis. We would play teams that had kids from everywhere. It was amazing, really."

At Speedway, Jenny, who was awarded a quarter scholarship in basketball before her first varsity game at Butler giving her a full ride, was almost always an underdog in basketball.

"Once I got to Butler I didn't feel like one," she said. "The tennis team was very successful. Our softball team was very successful, and in basketball we only lost eight games my whole career. One of the things I loved about being at Butler was, 'Wow, we got to win all the time.' "

Jenny was a tennis MVP three times and in basketball she was fourth all-time in career assists and 10th in assists per game when she was inducted into the Butler athletic hall of fame in 2000.

One of the basketball victories Jenny treasures was at Notre Dame.

"We got to meet Digger Phelps (former Irish coach) and one of the Notre Dame players, Orlando Woolridge," she said. "I think his ankle tape came up to about my knees. We got to see their practice and saw the big spread of food the Notre Dame people had.

"When we went to the basketball arena, we got to go in the room where all the Heisman trophies and national championship trophies were. That room was very dark, but it had spotlights that shone on those most important trophies. We also got to see the equipment room where there were stacks of boxes of adidas shoes and to see an athlete come up and say, 'Hi, I play football and I need a size 12 cleat.' We had never seen the supplies of that type of funding."

Jenny says that when she played tennis there she could stand on one side of the court and see Touchdown Jesus (on the library building).

"When I looked up to serve, there he was," she said. "And to see the Golden Dome, that was part of the fun going to all the colleges we did."

Jenny doesn't remember where the game was played, but she recalls being introduced as a 5-11 guard. There obviously was a misprint of her actual height on the Butler roster.

"The whole crowd laughed," she said with a smile. "That is one of my prize moments."

In 1982 Butler made it to the final eight of the AIAW national tournament. The Lady Bulldogs, who finished 23-3 that season, played William Penn in Oskaloosa, Iowa.

"William Penn was the tallest team we had ever seen," Jenny said. "I guarded a girl that was 6-foot-4. I had never seen a girl that tall before. I think we got beat by four points."

How did Jenny fare against the 6-4 gal?

"I had a hard time getting my shot off, I remember that," she declared. "Yeah, I scored. Mom tells the story that we didn't have tape of the game on TV, but we taped it on the radio. They were broadcasting the game back home and they were excited that I finally scored. I guess I had taken a few shots and finally got one to drop. We really struggled, but it was fun."

Jenny and her mom have season tickets to the Butler men's basketball games and she still plays a lot of tennis.

"Life is good," she said. "You learn so many things and you meet so many neat people. People now always laugh when my mom shows those pictures of my little outfits from my tap dance recitals. In hindsight that probably helped me become a more coordinated person, my footwork and things like that for tennis and basketball."

Jenny has been as versatile in her 13-year stint at Allison's Transmission as she was in sports. She has been an area manager, she has been a materials manager and now she's in the quality department.

Sports are still a passion with the small package with a big heart. Jenny continues to play tennis often and she mentors young gals in tennis and basketball. And she remains a 500-Mile Race fan and friends with Dave Calabro, sports director at WTHR (Channel 13) and Brian Hammonds of the Golf Channel, who attended Butler at the same time Jenny did. Both interviewed her in their TV training years.

Rosie Young says she can sum up her life this way: "I have been so lucky. I got to be one of the 11 James children. I thought my mom and dad were just terrific. I got to be Charlie's wife and I got to be Jenny's mother. I have been blessed. It has been an absolute joy ride raising Jenny."

COURTNEY COX

In January 2008 Courtney Cox Cole and her younger sister, Monica Cox Peck, both of whom played well for Noblesville High School's girls' basketball team a little over two decades ago, purchased the Hare Chevrolet dealership on State Road 37 in Noblesville from their father, David Cox.

The sisters, who are equal partners, are the sixth generation of family owners of the nation's oldest transportation company. In 1847 Wesley Hare opened a shop in Noblesville making and selling wagons. The business grew with the development of the auto industry and David Cox married into the Hare family (Jackie Hare Cox is his wife). David was named owner/operator of Hare Chevrolet in 1996 after the death of his father-in-law, Jack Hare.

"Basketball and golf have prepared me very well for later life," said Courtney, who has a rich sports résumé: the only female and a starter at forward on the Jordan Y Travel fourth and fifth grade basketball team in Indianapolis that "won a ton of tournaments," according to one of the male players; an AAU national championship as an 18-year-old; a state high school basketball championship in 1987; two state high school golf championships (1986 and '87); two Big Ten golf championships at Indiana University (1990 and '92); and two Indianapolis women's city golf championships (1992 and '97).

"Doing business now, there's pretty much nothing that you haven't been through and done that," Courtney, an Indiana All-Star as a high school senior in

1989, continued. "In business you form a team and get everybody to go to their positions and contribute, just like in basketball and golf."

Courtney laughed when she recalled what her father told her when she went to work for him a year after graduating from I.U.

"I just remember my dad saying I'd hate selling cars," she said. "But I really did love it. It's a people business. We have to sell cars. That's what I teach our people. If you make people feel comfortable and treat 'em right, they'll keep coming back, and that's basic no matter what you're selling."

The sisters knew that their father was ready to phase out as owner, and they put together "a nice financial plan and figured out a way to both go in and purchase the dealership."

But the nation's poor economy hit home quickly for the new owners.

"We thought we were getting a really low price," Courtney said. "But then the market had gone backwards. Then it really went backwards like when we purchased it in 2008.

"That year and the next, I thought, 'Oh, my god, we're the dumbest people ever.' But it's cyclical. That's probably the greatest lesson ever. You say that in 2009 we probably had a recession, but in the car business it was really a depression. There were stores lost and everything coming at you. You think on your feet. You cut expenses. It's all a great teaching experience."

The sisters weathered the storm and Hare Chevrolet was selected as the only Chevrolet dealership in

Cox sisters, Monica (left) and Courtney, at their Hare Chevrolet dealership in Noblesville, where they both were outstanding basketball players for the Millers. (Photo courtesy of Courtney Cox)

159

Indiana and one of only 20 in the country to receive the prestigious Nations Premier Chevrolet Dealer Award.

"It's a huge honor to receive this award," Courtney said, "and really, it's a reflection of the great people we have working here. It's an award for them and for our customers, because they are what make this place so special."

Courtney learned early how to be a competitor in male-dominated ventures. She tried out as a fourth grader for the Jordan Y Travel team (based near North Central High School) and made it. Among her male teammates were Todd Leary, who later played for Coach Bob Knight at Indiana University; Todd Geyer, Matt Thompson, Greg Akers, Chris Schwartz and David Schuel.

"Courtney had great fundamentals and skills," said Thompson, a North Central and Indiana State University graduate who is regional director (Indiana and Michigan) of loss prevention for Lowe's Home Improvement.

"She was very intense and very tough. She felt odd, I'm sure, being the only female on the team. But it was no girlie thing with her. She was just part of the team. Courtney scored eight or 10 points a game and we won a ton of tournaments with that team. She was a good person and very quiet."

Of that experience, Courtney says, "That kinda got me started and it kinda took off from there." She added that she was treated fairly by her male teammates.

"It was fine," she said. "You learned to play at that pace and then I played AAU basketball and junior high. I got to travel and I loved it, and I went on from there. I think I was 18 when we won the AAU national championship down in Miami. That was a great team, with Vicki Hall and MaChelle Joseph."

Courtney became a two-sport athlete in high school—basketball and golf—and she believes kids should play more than one sport.

"It's ridiculous what's happened now," she said. "Kids are starting so early, it's crazy, in kindergarten, the first grade. There's a big burnout factor if they're not careful. I switched sports from basketball to golf in college. They're trying to get them to play one sport, which is ludicrous. I think you should play as many sports as you want."

Courtney played four years of varsity basketball at Noblesville High as either a two guard or a three forward. The Lady Millers made it to the state finals in her sophomore, junior and senior years.

"It was a great experience," Courtney said. "It was back when they didn't have class basketball. They really messed the whole deal up. We had a huge following. They don't have that anymore at any level, boys or girls. We packed in Market Square Arena (13,240 for the 1987 championship game and 14,869 for the '88 championship game) for girls, and that was kinda unheard of back then."

In Courtney's freshman season, Noblesville lost in the regional to Warren Central "and Linda Godby, like 6-7 or whatever. Then my sophomore year we won the state (47-38 over Anderson Highland with Courtney scoring 17 points and grabbing 11 rebounds).

"I'm glad they didn't have a three-point line then, 'cause it would have been a little closer if they did. They all shot from the outside. Then we played Fort Wayne Snider in the championship game in 1988. I remember leading early, then we got down, but we came back. I think it was a two-point loss (60-58). But it was just a great experience. I'm very proud (Courtney had 29 points and five rebounds in that game)."

As a senior, Courtney lost to eventual champion Scottsburg, 53-45, in the semifinals of the Final Four.

"That was one of my worst ones," she said. "It was a big disappointment. You never like to lose. But it was what it was."

Courtney and two of her teammates, Krissi Davis and Cami Cass, were named to *The Indianapolis News* all-state team in 1987. Courtney's sister Monica was on the 1990 Noblesville team that went to the state finals, losing to eventual champion Huntington North, 44-42, in the semifinals.

Vicki Hall and her Brebeuf team were very good during this time, but the Lady Braves couldn't beat the Lady Millers.

When Courtney Cox Cole went to Indiana University on one of five recruiting visits following her graduation from Noblesville High School in 1989, she had an unforgettable session with men's basketball coach Bob Knight.

"When I mentioned that Ohio State was on my list of possible schools to attend, he said, 'I went to Ohio State and that's nothing but a God-damn hell-hole,' " she said. "And when I said I went out to Stanford, he said, 'We haven't got that son-of-a-bitch straightened out yet.

" 'You're not from Noblesville, Ohio, or Noblesville, Calif., you're from Noblesville, Ind., so you need to come to I.U.' Word for word, that's what he said."

I mentioned to Courtney that Amy Metheny, who helped Southport win the 1980 girls' high school championship, said she would have played for Knight at I.U. if she could have, but had to compete for the Hoosiers girls' team.

"Knight was very supportive of Indiana University in everything," Courtney, who did chose I.U. as her college

"We beat Brebeuf every time," Courtney said. "Vicki was great, though. She was an outstanding player. Carmel was outstanding back then, too, and we beat them every time."

For her high school career, Courtney scored 1,869 points. She won the Dial Award for the American high school athlete/scholar in 1988 and a year later was named to *USA Today*'s All-USA high school girls' basketball team and to *Parade Magazine*'s All-American team.

Courtney says she had college offers "from everywhere." She narrowed the list to five schools—Stanford, UCLA, Ohio State, I.U. and North Carolina.

"When I chose I.U., everyone said, 'Why?' " Courtney said. "I thought I.U. was a better opportunity."

Courtney majored in finance and accounting.

"Doing all that (studies, basketball and golf) was a lot," she said. "My first year in basketball I played a lot, sophomore year not so much (in two seasons she started in 22 games, getting 301 points and 71 assists).

"I had a real good NIT in basketball, but I really liked golf and I wanted to concentrate on that, so I switched to just golf after my sophomore year."

Courtney excelled under I.U. women's golf coach, Sam Carmichael.

"He was fabulous," she said. "I was a little bit late to the golf scene. Carmichael was a great swing coach and I really needed that badly to get to the next level.

"We had a great team. I wasn't very good my freshman year. My sophomore year I really took off

destination, said. "He did all the stuff you're supposed to do. His points were very good (supporting the library and keeping kids in school), except that temper.

"Everything he stood for was good. He was a bully in the process and that's what got him in trouble. That would be my view. You take that away from him and he would be perfect."

and played No. 2 We won the Big Ten twice and finished fifth in the NCAA in 1993. It was nice to travel to California in golf as opposed to Minnesota in January for basketball."

Carmichael, who retired as the women's golf coach at I.U. seven years ago, says Courtney "was an absolute joy to have playing for the Hoosiers. You can't be down in the dumps when you're around Courtney."

He does have one regret about his association with Courtney.

"I should have redshirted her as a freshman," said Carmichael, who still teaches and works on the Martinsville Country Club course he owns. "I could have used her as a fifth-year player (Courtney played varsity golf four years).

"I helped recruit her and she had the freedom to come out for golf as well as play basketball, which didn't pan out for her. She had some catching up to do in golf. But she was a great competitor and she became an excellent golfer. She also was an extremely bright kid."

Did Courtney have pro golf aspirations?

"For a short amount of time, yes," she stated. "But you had to be really, really good. I took a job in public accounting after graduating and I did play in several golf tournaments from May until August when I went to work."

For her four years of golf at I.U. Courtney averaged 78.94 strokes. More impressively, she earned All-Big Ten honors on three occasions and qualified individually for the NCAA Championship in 1993. She also achieved academically, collecting one Academic All-Big Ten honor in basketball and three in golf.

In 2002 Courtney became the first female to be inducted into the Hamilton County Hall of Fame. She went into the Hamilton County Basketball Hall of Fame in the class of 2003-04, along with Mark Hermann, Billy and David Shepherd and Don Jellison as a contributor.

Courtney and husband Ben Cole, who played football for Bill Mallory at I.U., have two children, Gayla, 8, and Blake, 6. With their parents' genes, they no doubt will be well-schooled athletically.

"Basketball and golf were very positive for me," Courtney said. "What you learn from wins and losses, you can't duplicate. What you learn from that you take to the next endeavor."

KELLY FARIS

A player who makes the team great is better than a great player.
—John Wooden

If the legendary Indiana native who won a record 10 NCAA men's championships at UCLA had ever coached women's basketball, he would have loved to have someone like Kelly Faris on his roster.

All the Plainfield native did in four years at Indianapolis Heritage Christian High School and her first year of college at the University of Connecticut was help make her teams champions.

The 5-foot-11 guard/forward who wears No. 34 because her three siblings did earned five championship rings without gaudy statistics and no great ego.

In 112 games at Heritage Christian from 2005 to 2009, Kelly had 1,426 points (12.7 average), 902 rebounds (8.1 average), 526 assists (4.7 average), 442 steals (3.9 average), 147 blocks (1.3 average) and shot 52 percent from the field and 73 percent from the free throw line.

As a UConn freshman, Kelly scored 158 points (4.1 average) in 39 games. She shot .382 from the field (.270 from three-point range) and .775 from the line. She also had 143 rebounds (3.7 average), 82 assists (2.1 average), 48 steals (1.2 average) and 13 blocks (0.3 average). Kelly averaged 18.9 minutes a game.

Drive by the home of Bob and Connie Faris on Nasten Street in Plainfield, where their youngest of four children has lived all of her 20 years, and you won't see any Heritage Christian or UConn signs in the front windows, in the yard or on vehicles in the driveway where there is a weather-beaten basketball goal.

"I'm not into that showy stuff," Kelly said before returning to Storrs, Conn., in the fall of 2010 for the start of her second season with Coach Geno Auriemma's national champion Huskies, who finished the 2009-10 campaign with a second successive 39-0 record for a 78-game winning streak. "I just keep it low-key."

Kelly was wearing a red, white and blue—UConn colors—T-shirt that said, "No 1 but Connecticut" on the front as she reminisced about her freshman year that included a broken nose suffered in practice in early December; a single chest bump all season, with senior Kalana Greene in a January game against Rutgers; and the time two months later in Cameron Indoor Stadium at Duke when she didn't get on the floor until the last minute of the game.

Renee Montgomery, who graduated after the 2008-09 season and is now with the Connecticut Sun in the WNBA, designed the

Connecticut Coach Gino Auriemma gives Plainfield native Kelly Faris some sage advice. (Photo courtesy of University of Connecticut)

T-shirts that said, "No 1 but Connecticut." It was in response to another team's T-shirt that said, "Anyone but Connecticut."

Faris began her love affair with basketball at an early age tagging along behind sisters Kristi and Kimmi and brother Patrick, and "sitting and watching and learning at their games." All three played for Plainfield High and were pretty good, according to Kelly.

Kelly says the strangest place she ever played basketball was on a hoop in her basement. In Indiana, she stressed, you've got to have a goal, wherever it might be.

"I started playing AAU ball at three or four," she said. "I was on my sister Kristi's 10-and-under team. I was kinda little and I'd only get in the game if they were up by a lot, until I started getting a little older."

In 2003 Kelly and her Indiana's Finest team won the 11-and-under AAU national championship and it finished second a couple of other times.

Bob Faris, who played football and basketball at Speedway High School in Indianapolis, was the family coach.

"He knows what he's talking about and I loved him as coach," Kelly said.

He steered his daughter to Heritage Christian and later to UConn.

"My family had been through Plainfield High School and I didn't feel like it was the best fit for me," she said. "And neither did my parents. So we looked around at a few different high schools and tried to figure out what would work for me. Heritage Christian (a Class 2A private school on the far north side of Indianapolis, approximately 30 miles east of Plainfield) ended up being the right choice."

Did it bother Kelly going to a Class 2A school as opposed to Class 4A Plainfield (4A Indiana schools have the largest enrollment)?

"Honestly not really," she said. "Mainly after our freshman year we tried to change our schedule and tried to get as many of the better teams as we possibly could on the schedule. It kinda started growing before we got there. We had a pretty decent class and a lot of athletes. A couple classes after us were pretty decent, too.

"It was great," she stated. "Rick Risinger is a great guy and a great coach. Our high school team was basically like one big family. All the girls got along and the coaching staff got along. We had fun."

As a junior on Nov. 24, 2007, Kelly had a rare accomplishment, a quadruple-double against Fort Wayne Harding—14 points, 10 rebounds, 10 assists and 10 steals.

"I don't remember that game," she said. "I'm not too big on stats."

Kelly is big into helping her team accumulate victories. In the 155 games during her four years at Heritage Christian and first year at UConn, Kelly lost only eight times, all in high school.

The four games in the 2009 Indiana high school state championships drew a record 21,522 fans. Top-ranked Heritage Christian defeated second-ranked Oak Hill of Converse, 60-58, in overtime on Claire Freeman's basket with three seconds left.

With the victory the Eagles tied Fort Wayne Bishop Luers (1999-2002) as the only teams in tournament history to win four successive championships.

Kelly's senior teammates in 2009 were Freeman; Emily Anderson, who plays at Hillsdale in Michigan; Meredith Martin; and Melissa Berman. Anderson led Heritage Christian in the 2009 title game with 14 points. Faris had 13, Liz Stratman 12 and Freeman 11.

Faris, wearing the No. 2 jersey, helped the Indiana All-Stars defeat Kentucky twice to complete a memorable high school career in which she was named a McDonald's All-American and selected to the *Parade Magazine* All-American first team in 2009.

Indianapolis Ben Davis girls' coach Stan Benge was Kelly's All-Star coach. He said he didn't know her well, but chuckled when he related this story.

"I went up to Kelly after our All-Star games and said how much I enjoyed coaching her," he said. "My brother Curt coaches the Plainfield girls' team and he kept talking about how good Kelly was going to be, but she went to Heritage Christian (instead of Plainfield).

"I told Kelly, 'If you had gone to Plainfield, my brother would have state championships.' Kelly has a total all-round game. She's never going to score 25 points a game, because she's very unselfish and she's a team player. When you've got a team like Connecticut had, you have to know that's the kind of role you're going to have when you go there.

"When I coached Shyra Ely and she ended up going to Tennessee, she said she wanted to go there, 'Because I don't want to be the best player on the team when I walk in the gym. I want to have to earn that right.' I'm sure Kelly was probably on the same line."

In high school, Kelly also competed in volleyball and track, being named to the 2007 AAU Junior National Volleyball Championships All-American team.

"Volleyball is a completely different sport," she said. "It's more upbeat and cheery. That's not really my personality. Once I started playing I had to get used to that. But it was a good experience. Everything in volleyball is quick and we just had fun with it.

"I had a great experience at Heritage Christian, not just the basketball, but the school, the atmosphere. There was a lot of support."

Recruiting was a different story for Kelly.

"I didn't know what to expect when I first started getting recruited," she explained. "At that point Purdue was one of the high ones on my list. I didn't know whether they would look at me or what talent was there or what schools were looking for.

"When it first started, it was fun, getting mail and phone calls. But I'm not a big phone talker. Then it kinda got hectic. It was stressful, but it was a good problem to have."

UConn sent Kelly a formal letter during her junior year at Heritage Christian, but that was "about it," she added. "I was about to be done with the whole recruiting thing and trying to narrow it down. My dad asked if there was anybody else I wanted to talk to. I decided I'd like to go out to UConn."

Kelly's request for a visit to Storrs was granted, but she was a bit apprehensive about meeting Auriemma.

"Going into it I didn't know if I'd like coach or not," she said of Auriemma, who is a no-nonsense guy. "But once I got out there and talked to him and talked to the players I really liked it.

"Our campus is kinda out in the middle of nowhere. The closest McDonald's is maybe a 10-minute drive. We don't have time to go too many places. Usually the weather is worse than in Indianapolis. It gets really cold and the campus feels like it's in a wind tunnel."

Kelly committed at the end of her junior year and became UConn's only freshman recruit in 2009-10.

Asked to rate her college freshman season on a scale of one to 10, Kelly smiled and said, "It was a lot of work, but that's what you're there for. You never know when you pick a college if it's right for you.

"I think I made the right choice. Our program is like a big family. There were moments when it was stressful and painful, but we had fun. I'd say my freshman year was a 10 (UConn lost to Notre Dame, 72-63, in the semifinals of the 2011 Final Four at Conseco Fieldhouse in Indianapolis, ending the Huskies' two-year reign as NCAA champion)."

The pain started early when Kelly suffered a broken nose in practice in December and had to wear a mask for a while.

"My nose is fine," she declared. "Hopefully I won't get it broken again. It's a little crooked, but . . . "

In February Kelly had a positive experience against Big East foe West Virginia and drew praise from the coach. Mountaineer guard Liz Repella was hot in the first half in a game that was close at the half. Auriemma started Faris along with regular starters Maya Moore, Tina Charles, Kalana Greene and Tiffany Hayes.

Kelly held Repella to just two field goals in the second half and had a steal and added a free throw for a three-point play soon after the break to help spark the Huskies to an 80-47 victory.

"She's not a freshman in a lot of ways," the coach said of Kelly afterward. "She's also such a much better athlete than people think. When she gets on you defensively, it's not easy to get the shot you want."

Said Kelly, "That's probably one of the best games I've played. Defense is probably one of the things I take the most pride in. I work hard on it."

On March 4, 2010, there was an article published in Hartford, Conn., written by Graham Hays of ESPN.com with the headline, "Don't be fooled by Faris' poker face." A subhead said, "UConn's only freshman is all business—and gets the job done for Huskies."

Did it bother Kelly to be called poker face?

"No," she replied, " 'cause that's kinda how I've been. And we joke about it all the time. I don't really show emotion when I'm playing, not that I think, 'Oh, I can't show emotion.' That's my personality and I'm into the game."

In a game against Rutgers in late January Kelly did show emotion when she chest-bumped with Greene after the senior completed a three-point play.

"Chest-bumping is not me," she said. "I don't pump my fist or anything like that. But it just happened to be in the heat of the moment and my teammate had made a really good play, so I just thought, 'Well, this is one bump that will make her happy and get her excited.'

"I didn't think anybody would notice, and people did because that was so out-of-character for me. It was funny and kinda something dumb. Would I do it again? The heat of the moment kinda brings up things. But that's not really me and that's not really what our program's about."

Kelly Faris, who helped Heritage Christian (Indianapolis) win four Class 2A state championships, registered a big assist in the University of Connecticut's 2010 NCAA Division 1 championship as a freshman. (Photo courtesy of University of Connecticut)

The defining moment in Kelly's freshman season at UConn came a week before she chest-bumped with Greene. She didn't get off the bench until very late in a game at Duke's Cameron Indoor Stadium.

"I stepped on the floor for like a minute or less," Kelly said. "Coach was trying to make a point and he got his point through. It's never fun sitting the bench. I've never missed that much time unless I was hurt.

"I knew what he was trying to do and it was frustrating. But I knew it was my fault, because I knew I hadn't been playing the way

Numbers never have told the real value of Kelly Faris in basketball.

In her first start at the University of Connecticut in the Huskies' 2010-11 season opener, a 117-37 thrashing of Holy Cross, the sophomore guard/forward from Indianapolis Heritage Christian High School had a breakout game offensively.

Kelly scored 15 points on 6-of-10 shooting from the field, including 1-of-3 from three-point territory and 2-of-2 from the free-throw line. She also had nine rebounds, seven assists, one turnover and three blocked shots in 30 minutes, the most of any UConn player.

In UConn's second game, which pitted the No. 1 Huskies against the No. 2 Baylor Bears at Hartford, Conn., Kelly missed her only shot from the field, a three-pointer, but sank both of her free throws for a total of two points in a 65-64 victory that extended UConn's winning streak to 80 games.

Kelly had four rebounds, one assist, no turnovers, no blocked shots and four steals in 32 minutes. She did make possibly the most critical play for the Huskies, who had to rally late to win.

I needed to play. I was thinking too much. I went in to talk to him to see what was going on with him and what he expected from me. It's definitely what a coach is supposed to do."

Kelly's respect for Auriemma increased mightily from that experience.

"Coach is his own person," she said. "He will say whatever he wants to say. He'll leave it out there; that's good, though. He's not going to sugar-coat anything. He doesn't want to make anything seem like it's something that it's not.

"But he's a great guy, on and off the court. He's one of those people that 20 years down the road if you need something, he'll be more than happy to help you out. Everybody kinda sees the hard part of it, but . . . "

Auriemma told Hayes of ESPN. com, "I knew just by her (Faris') body language that something was up. I would just go up to her and say, 'What happened to you? Where did you go? You're not the same player that was here a month ago.'

"And she made an interesting point. She said, 'I'm trying to get everything done in the four minutes I'm in there.' And I said, 'Well, I know; you're going 100 miles an hour. You're going to get your minutes regardless.'

"Then I didn't play her in the Duke game and I said, 'Now, how was that? You like that?' And she said, 'No.' I said, 'So when you get out there, are you gonna just enjoy being out there and have fun and play the way you can play instead of worrying about everything? Because the alternative is (the bench). So she's been different ever since.' "

In the 2010 Final Four in San Antonio, UConn defeated Baylor, 70-50, in a semifinal game. But in the championship game against Stanford, which UConn rallied to win, 53-47, the Huskies fell behind, 20-12, at halftime. The 12 first-half points were the worst total in school history. UConn shot 17.2 percent from the field (5-for-29) and had seven turnovers. Kelly had the team's only assist.

What did the coach say at the half?

With 2:12 left and the score tied, 60-60, Kelly grabbed an offensive rebound and quickly passed out to Bria Hartley, who sank a three-point shot with 2:09 remaining to put UConn ahead, 63-60. The Huskies held on to their lead before a crowd of 12,629 in the XL Center.

Before a crowd of 16,421 at Conseco Fieldhouse on April 3, 2011, UConn saw its two-year NCAA championship reign end in a 72-63 loss to Notre Dame in the semifinals of the women's Final Four. The Huskies finished 36-2.

Faris's numbers were not gaudy, but she did lead her team in assists with five. She was 2-of-6 from the field (0-of-2 from three-point territory) and had four points. She did not shoot a free throw.

"Everybody seems to ask that question," Kelly said. "Honestly he didn't have much to say. He raised his voice a little bit. For him it wasn't much of anything. He said a few things and walked off.

"We were sitting there and weren't too worried. We knew we had probably played the worst we had played the entire season and for some their entire career. We knew what we had to do and what we were capable of doing. It was that kind of feeling. We just knew, dang, we played really bad and we just had to go out and play our game."

The Huskies went on a 30-6 run in the second half to claim Auriemma's seventh national championship, four of which were with unbeaten records—1994-95, 35-0; 2001-02, 39-0; 2008-09, 39-0; and 2009-10, 39-0. Faris didn't score a point in the Final Four.

"I don't really care about that," she said. "As I've said, I'm not into stats."

Kelly did impress Carolyn Peck, former Purdue coach who did color commentary on the Final Four telecast.

"Kelly Faris, a freshman, was huge (in the second half against Stanford)." Peck said. "Her stats didn't show it, but she was outstanding on defense against Stanford's guards."

As Kelly looked ahead to her sophomore season in Storrs, she said, "I would rather pass than shoot. That can turn into a bad thing at times. If coach wants me to shoot, I'll have to work on that more. I've been working on my shooting.

"And I consider myself a thinking player. You can't think too much; that will kinda get you into trouble. That's what happened to me this year. I watched my siblings play and I watched a lot of games, and I recognized things, things I knew shouldn't have happened and put 'em in the back of my head. I like to see the floor and I think that's one of the aspects about how I play that benefits me. I've been taught that way."

Does Kelly ever pinch herself when she considers she became a champion five straight years—four at Heritage Christian and once at UConn?

"I don't know that it's hit me yet," she said. "I remember after every time we won in high school our coaches would keep telling us that 20 years down the road is when it's going to hit you. Right now it just seems all fun and games. It's exciting. Twenty years down the road you're gonna look back and think, wow, we won four state championships.

"And I felt like I contributed to our national championship at UConn. I think everybody on our team contributed, even the ones that didn't play a whole lot. If we didn't have everybody in practice, we wouldn't have been where we were at.

"It's a little bit storybook. Hopefully it will keep going."

John Wooden couldn't have said it better.

Rick Risinger

Heritage Christian girls' basketball coach Rick Risinger didn't know Kelly Faris until she stepped on the court at the far north side Indianapolis high school for her first practice as a freshman in 2005.

"I don't think Kelly enrolled at Heritage until two or three weeks before school started," said Risinger, who guided the Lady Eagles to four successive Class 2A state championships with Faris as a quiet but extremely efficient leader.

"I do know Kelly was very close to the Freeman family. Claire Freeman and Kelly played together on AAU teams through their younger years and I think that was some influence."

Risinger says he had heard there was a girl coming into the program with great talent.

"But I didn't even know the name Kelly Faris," he stated. "I knew Claire Freeman, because I had helped with Cathy Freeman, older sister of Claire. I knew the Freeman family, but I didn't know about Kelly until she came to practice with Claire the first time."

It didn't take long for Risinger to realize what a find the Plainfield native was for Heritage Christian.

"My first impression of Kelly?" he said. "I guess from a coaching standpoint probably the ultimate basketball player. Her focus was to do well on a personal level, but more importantly to make sure that the team did well.

"She would do whatever it took to

make sure the team had success, whether it be rebounding, assists, defense, motivating the team in a kind of non-verbal way. She could care less about stats. In fact, I really encouraged her to take more shots and try to have a higher scoring average."

Risinger then related an interesting story about that challenge.

"We were playing in summer leagues over at Butler," he said. "It was before her senior year and in the second half of a game I asked her to take five shots. She ended up taking four shots and I asked, 'Why didn't you get that fifth shot?' She easily could have done that. She said, 'Well, I would be ball-hogging if I took five shots.'

"That was just an example that she was not at all interested in stats. She was interested in success of the team, and that's why we had the success we had, because of her drive to stay focused."

Kelly wound up as the only freshman recruited by University of Connecticut coach Geno Auriemma. Risinger related a conversation he had with Auriemma when he visited Heritage Christian.

"When coach came in to recruit her, I remember sitting and talking with him, and what he was saying was he was looking basically for a guard who could play defense, rebound, move the ball—'I don't need a lot of scoring out of that position,' " Risinger said.

"Well, that fit exactly what Kelly was about. I think that's one reason she's up at Connecticut. If you watched her play as a freshman, that was exactly her role on that team. He did not need points from that position. He had plenty of points on the floor. But he did need someone who could do all aspects of the game: Defense, rebound, pass, set other players up, run the floor.

"Kelly fit into that, especially in the second half of the season. And in tournament time you really saw what her strengths were, and it goes back to my original comments about her team play versus maybe trying to be a scorer (UConn won a second successive national championship with Kelly contributing)."

ADMINISTRATIVE LEADERSHIP

PAT ROY

When Pat Roy was a student at Harlan High School six miles northeast of Fort Wayne in the early 1950s, she did not play basketball.

"Are you kidding me?" said the retired assistant commissioner for girls' sports at the Indiana High School Athletic Association (IHSAA). "There were no sports programs, none."

So at age 15, Roy became a professional baseball player. She has the Fort Wayne Daisies baseball card to prove it.

"When I was 15, I got involved in a league in Fort Wayne called the All-American Junior Girls Baseball League, which was a feeder system to the Fort Wayne Daisies," Pat said. "And I played for the Daisies in 1954."

The Daisies played in the All-American Girls Professional Baseball League from 1945 to 1954. They played their home games at North Side High School (1945-46) and Memorial Park (1946-1954).

Fort Wayne made it to the playoffs every year from 1947 to 1954, ending in first place from 1951 to 1954. But the Daisies never won the league championship.

Roy played first base for the Daisies for $60 a week. Was she pretty good?

"Well, I only played for about a month," she said. "I was 15 and there was another girl on the team that was 16. She slid into second base and tore an ankle up pretty good.

"They turned it into the insurance company and the insurance company wouldn't pay for it because they considered her to be a minor. Immediately everybody realized you had to be 18 in order to play. So they released us both very quickly. That ended my professional baseball career."

Roy says she didn't hit very well.

"It was tough," she explained. "Everybody was older than I was. I had very little experience. It took everything I had to keep up with it. When you start playing for money, it takes on a completely different perspective. You've got to produce or you're out. But I enjoyed my time with the Daisies."

The 1992 movie *A League of Their Own* was a fictionalized drama-comedy about the All-American Girls Professional Baseball League. It starred Tom Hanks, Geena Davis, Madonna and Rosie O'Donnell. Much of the movie was filmed in Evansville and Huntingburg.

"It was a great movie and was pretty authentic," Roy said. "We wore those short skirts and anytime you slid into a base, you just took the skin right off. I don't have scars today, but I'd walk around all summer long and my mother would just have a fit, seeing my leg all skinned up. You just ignored it and went on."

There is no more Harlan High School. It was consolidated into Woodlan High School. After graduating from Harlan High, Roy enrolled at Ball State University and got a teaching degree. She did play some basketball while there.

Pat's first teaching job was at Chesterton High School. She was there five years. Then she moved to East Gary, which is now Lake Station High School. Pat was there 12 years, then joined the IHSAA as director of girls' athletics in January 1972.

At that time the Girls Athletic Association (GAA) supervised female sports.

"I was involved in lots of GAA programs extensively," Roy, who retired from the IHSAA in June 1999 after becoming an assistant commissioner under then commissioner Ward Brown, said.

The Indiana girls' high school basketball tournament was just two years old when Indiana High School Athletic Association girls' commissioner Pat Roy sought the help of Jan Conner in publicizing the event in particular and the sport over-all.

"When I was coaching at Benton Central, I think it was 1978, Pat Roy called me and said, 'Jan, we need a poll for girls' basketball,' " Conner recalled. "She wanted me to do it and I said okay."

Roy, who is retired after serving the IHSAA for 27 ½ years, says Conner was the right person to get such a project underway.

"In the role of coach, of being on committees, getting other coaches involved, that kind of thing, Jan was instrumental in helping pave the way for girls' basketball, there's no question about it," Roy said.

"Jan poured her heart and soul into everything that she did for girls' sports."

Getting a girls' basketball poll wasn't an easy task, but Conner, in her indomitable way, got it done, at a huge financial cost to herself.

"What I did was I got 30 coaches throughout the state to vote every week," she

The IHSAA decided to sanction a girls' state basketball tournament at the end of the 1975-76 season. How far has girls' basketball come since then?

"Oh, my, it is unbelievable," Roy said. "I worked for Phil Eskew at the IHSAA. He was the first commissioner that I worked for. He hired me.

"The first state tournament we had was at Hinkle Fieldhouse. Nobody knew quite what to expect, myself included. One day he and I were talking and he said, 'Oh, you're not going to have a very good crowd.' I looked at him and I said, 'I'll bet you we have 5,000 people there (for the Final Four).

"He said, 'No, I don't think you'll have 5,000 people there. In fact, I'm so sure of it, I'll just bet you a steak dinner that you don't have 5,000 people there.' I said, 'I'll take you up on it.' Turned out, we had about 7,000 people there (actual attendance was 7,362). He never gave me my steak dinner."

Of that first Final Four in 1976, Roy said, "It was just like everything fell into place. Warsaw (the first champion) came and we had Judi Warren. She just captured the crowd. She was the little guard that dribbled around everybody and made baskets and fired up the team and fired up the fans.

"Warsaw had no cheerleaders. The team led the cheers that day. It was just one of those days that everything fell into place and the tournament took off."

Roy swells with pride when asked what is so appealing about female basketball now.

"You can follow the girls," she said. "They don't play above the rim. The average fan can sit there and see what's gonna happen usually, and I think that's good. And there's something else, that girls have never been afforded before, and that's college scholarships.

"You look at the NCAA women's finals, it's fantastic. The skill level is out of sight. On top of that, we get to the WNBA. In most places that's still going. There are some places that are having some problems. The tough economy that we're in probably does not help that any. And the Indiana Fever almost won the championship in 2009.

"I guess the only disappointment I might have is that we never sold out Market Square Arena for the finals. We came close a couple of times, but never sold it out."

Roy also does not agree with the IHSAA decision to take the Final Four to Fort Wayne in 2010 and 2011.

"I don't know all the ins-and-outs as to what they were up said. "We had no idea what each other was doing. I would make calls to all these newspapers and I got as many scores as I could.

"I would type them up—and this was before computers—and I would send them to the 30 coaches every week. They would call their rankings to me. I called the Associated Press every week and said, 'We have our Indiana Coaches of Girls Sports Association poll.' They would say, 'No, you're not big enough.' "

UPI would take the poll, according to Conner.

"A woman was head of UPI and she would send the poll out," Conner said., "But you know what? Only two percent of the papers were UPI, maybe five percent."

Conner will never forget the day Steve Herman of the Associated Press called her and said, "Coach, we'd like to take your poll."

"I said, 'Really?' " Conner said. "He said, 'We have two teams from Indianapolis who are a little higher up in the poll and they are going to play each other.' My knee-jerk reaction was they needed a story. But I thought, 'Great.' I said, 'Will you take it every week?' and he said, 'We'll see.' "

The upshot was the AP started taking it every week and the poll took off.

"In the meantime four of us (women) were invited to the Indiana Basketball Coaches Association board meeting—and I sat in every board meeting every month for three years—and they finally decided to let us be a voting member of the IBCA."

Conner also will never forget the night Roy told her, "We've got these problems."

"A group of coaches decided I had too much power in the state and they went to the ICGSA, and they took the poll away from me," Conner said. "I spent thousands of dollars of my own money (in promoting the poll). They gave it to somebody else and the ICGSA paid for it.

"But those are the growing pains when you're first starting out. Somebody has to do that kind of stuff and I didn't mind."

against," she said. "I guess it was a conflict with the women's Big Ten tournament (at Conseco Fieldhouse in Indianapolis).

"I just think somebody needs to sit down and do some compromising, so that tournament can be here in Indianapolis. That's where it belongs. I have nothing against Fort Wayne. They probably did a great job."

Roy spends her winters in Bonita Springs, Fla., between Fort Meyers and Naples. She plays golf there.

Asked if she was born too soon for participating in girls sports at Harlan High, Roy said, "In order to play basketball, yes. But for the job that I got and did, the timing was exactly right.

"It's been a good ride for me. I've had a very satisfying career. I look back on it and I don't think I would have done anything different."

Theresia Wynns

April 25, 2009 was a magical day for Theresia and Joe Wynns.

In the morning they drove from their Indianapolis home to the Indiana Basketball Hall of Fame in New Castle for a reception for the 2009 female inductees into the hall that included Theresia.

The induction ceremony was that night. Theresia, an Indiana High School Athletic Association (IHSAA) assistant commissioner since 1997, received the 2009 St. Vincent Silver Medal for meritorious service.

She is responsible for girls' basketball, boys' and girls' soccer and boys' and girls' tennis, and also oversees the IHSAA's officials department.

Earlier that evening Joe Wynns attended the 40th reunion reception at Marian College (now Marian University) for the Indianapolis Caps team that won the 1969 Continental Football League championship at the old Bush Stadium on West 16th Street.

Joe, a retired Indy Parks director, was a wide receiver on that Caps squad. He didn't stay for the reunion dinner, but hurried to watch Theresia receive her prestigious honor.

"Joe saw me inducted and my daughter Whitley drove up from Bloomington, where she was a junior at Indiana University (she went there on a soccer scholarship after helping North Central win a 2005 state high school basketball championship), and was there, too," Theresia said.

"I am very pleased with what happened that day. As a family we've had some success. I believe my daughter has developed into a young lady and I think sports helped to guide her in her decision-making, to become a team player and be confident in herself and her skills. Sports have served our family very well."

Sports brought Theresia to Indiana from Easley, S.C., in 1971, three years after her husband-to-be was drafted by the NFL's Atlanta Falcons.

"I met Joe at South Carolina State College (in Orangeburg)," she said. "I was a cheerleader and he was a football player. The Falcons wanted to give him some experience by playing with a farm team, so to speak.

"He had the choice of going to Alabama or coming to Indianapolis, so he chose Indianapolis. I came to Indianapolis in the summer of 1971 and got a job teaching at School 36 in IPS. Joe, who is from Summerville, S.C., and I were married in December of 1971 in South Carolina."

Theresia saw Joe play for the Caps a few times at Bush Stadium, but she did not attend the 1969 championship game.

Basketball has been Theresia's game. She has been a player in high school at Easley, a licensed basketball official in Indiana

Before she became an IHSAA assistant commissioner, Theresia Wynns was an outstanding basketball referee, officiating several state tournament games. (Photo courtesy of Theresia Wynns)

for 19 years—she worked six state finals in the girls' high school tournament, including the first in 1976 at Hinkle Fieldhouse and the championship game in 1977, and an administrator for 13 years.

South Carolina had developed a girls' basketball state tournament several years before Indiana had done so when Theresia entered high school at Easley in the mid-1960s.

"I was pretty good," she said. "Back then we played three-and-three. Three played defense and there played offense, much like Iowa. I had graduated when they started the rover player. At one point they had one player going both ways. So basically we played half of the court with six-person teams.

"It worked out really well for us. We had a good time. We didn't have a Jayvee team, so to speak, so we had a varsity girls' team and a varsity boys' team. We traveled together. We had male and female chaperons. We played girl-boy doubleheaders. The girls were always first."

Theresia admits that she wasn't the top player, but adds, "I could score. I remember one game I had scored more by halftime than the other team had scored. I was quick and very fast, so I could get around some of those defenders and get to the basket.

"I played basketball and softball during the summer and ran some track. We were active. They had a state basketball tournament. In fact, there were two divisions of the tournament. My high school, which was small, was in Double A. We never made the state tournament. I was probably 5-8. I haven't grown any since. I've grown outward, but I haven't grown up anymore."

She chuckled at the latter comment.

Theresia did not play varsity basketball at South Carolina State.

"At that time there were no scholarships for women, especially in the South, and I was staying in the South," she said. "When I got to college, we played GAA (Girls Athletic Association sports, forerunner to the NCAA)

"It was more like a social gathering. We would go to different schools and we'd have teams made up of individuals from the different schools. But it gave us an opportunity to play. I had a very good experience in college. I wouldn't change that at all. My freshman year I decided not to do anything other than to try and get acclimated. My sophomore year I decided to try out for the cheerleading squad, and I made it. I cheered for two years. My senior year I decided not to cheer."

Theresia did play intramural sports in college. She graduated with a bachelor's degree in health, physical education and recreation.

Coaching basketball was not an option when Theresia began her professional career in Indiana. She taught general science and physical education and health at Indianapolis Public School 36.

"I coached sports in the middle school," she said. "I had the cheerleaders and I did volleyball and kickball. I never coached basketball, because they hadn't started basketball at the middle schools at that time."

Being pragmatic in her life choices, Theresia decided to pursue a master's degree at Butler University in order to professionalize her teaching license. The decision also led her to become a renowned basketball official.

"Because I was coaching—we had to officiate our own games—I decided to take a class under Barb Greenburg, a Butler professor (who was the Bulldog softball coach at the time)," Theresia said. "She was teaching an officiating class.

Theresia Wynns (left) referees as Warsaw's Judi Warren dribbles down Hinkle Fieldhouse floor in 1976 state tournament. (Photo courtesy of Theresia Wynns)

"She would take us to different schools to observe, and she would get us involved in their lower-level programs. St. Agnes was one of the schools we used to go to. It was at Park Tudor and it was just the girls alone. We'd watch the games and eventually they asked us to come and work the games.

"The girls' high school program was beginning, the officiating was starting with the women, so we were learning, the girls were learning, coaches were learning, so we all learned together. That's how I got started. Barb Greenburg was very instrumental in getting me started and getting us out into the community."

Theresia never swallowed her whistle, but it did take her a while to learn to blow it at the right time.

"Well, to begin with, no, I wasn't a good official," she said, smiling. "I was agile and I could run with the young ladies. But learning how to make the calls, learning what to look for, how to recognize the calls and the signals and all that, that took some time to master."

Still relying on her pragmatism, Theresia joined the all-male Fall Creek Officials Association along with some other pioneering women. The gender gap was beginning to disappear, and Theresia salutes the male members of the FCOA.

"Those men welcomed us and worked with us as far as mechanics in basketball were concerned," she said. "They gave us tips about where to move, where to be. They set up scrimmages with the different high schools. It could be a girls' team, it could be a boys' team. I can remember going over to Shortridge and Attucks many a time.

"The men, who had been officiating for years, would work with us. As you ran the floor, they'd tell you, 'Here's where you need to stand, here's where you need to move, this is what you're looking for, make the call, be confident. They taught us how to blow the whistle and they taught us how to practice making the calls."

Theresia recalls one official, Jesse Lynch, telling her, "When you're in the house, walk around with your whistle and blow it. And look at yourself in the mirror and see where you arm is. If your arm is crooked, it's not in the right place. If it's straight up, it's where it needs to be.

"They worked with us on little key things about how to become the best official that you can be. We evolved, because, one, Barb Greenburg worked with us, but, two, the Fall Creek officials took us in and they didn't just put us aside and say, 'Okay, you go work basketball.' They worked with us so that we developed."

When the first Indiana girls' state basketball tournament was scheduled in 1976—65 years after the boys' state tournament started—Theresia was surprised she was chosen to officiate in the state finals at Hinkle Fieldhouse.

"I was surprised all the way," she said. "We had to apply to be a part of the process. I figured I would work sectionals, and I did, at the Indiana Deaf School."

Theresia was again surprised when she was assigned a regional.

"There were some of my friends who said, 'You probably will get a semi-state,' and I did," Theresia said. "I worked in Fort Wayne. It was hosted by Northrop. I worked a Warsaw game and the Tigers won both games (over Norwell of Ossian and over Wes-Del of Gaston). I do remember that the gym was packed for the game I worked with Warsaw. People were right up to the edges of the floor.

"Afterward someone said, 'Theresia, you'll probably go to state.' I'm thinking, 'Naw, I've been blessed to have gone this far.' Then when I got the call that I was gong to state, I was overwhelmed. I thought I had worked hard, but I knew there were other ladies who had been involved in the sport in Indiana trying to get it off the ground and maybe they were a little more deserving.

"But I was chosen to go and I was pleased. I worked the first game in the state finals. It was East Chicago Roosevelt against Warsaw (Warsaw won, 62-44; the Tigers then defeated Bloomfield, 57-52, to become the first state champion).

"I had seen Judi Warren of Warsaw the week before bounce around and take that ball up and down the floor. That was her senior year and she was the first Miss Basketball. LaTaunya Pollard was a freshman for East Chicago that year and she played that morning. East Chicago was a good team. They were athletic and able to get up and down the floor. But Warsaw had a little more momentum going at that particular point. They played really well that morning and were able to pull out a victory."

In 1977 Theresia officiated her first of three state championship games (she also worked the 1981 final when Evansville Reitz defeated Rushville, 74-47, and the 1986 final when Fort Wayne Northrop beat Scottsburg, 58-55)

"I worked with Lowell Smith (in the '77 title game)," she said. "We had East Chicago and Mount Vernon out of Fortville. That's when Mount Vernon had a strong women's team with the Skinner sisters who were very impressive. That community followed their girls' program better than they followed their boys' program. You'd go to the girls' games and people came out of the woodwork. They packed the gym."

Mount Vernon defeated Norwell, 59-47, and East Chicago downed Bloomfield, 66-42, in the semifinals. It was no contest in the championship game, East Chicago winning its first of two state titles within three years, 66-35, over Mount Vernon (Coach Bobbie DeKemper's squad won again in 1979, beating Anderson Madison Heights, 48-23).

"LaTaunya Pollard was out of sight," Theresia recalled. "She was so far advanced in her skills. Her jump shot was just perfect. You didn't see many girls with a true jump shot at that particular point. Many shot a set shot.

"LaTaunya was truly ahead of her time. You could tell that she had spent some time on the playground playing with the boys. Liz Skinner always had a joke that she was the one guarding LaTaunya and LaTaunya scored more points than her team did (36-35) for the whole game. That's how phenomenal she was, just give her the ball and get out of her way."

Fast forward to March 7, 2009 when the four games of the girls' state basketball tournament were decided by a total of 13 points at Lucas Oil Stadium. Fort Wayne Canterbury defeated Vincennes Rivet, 72-66, for the Class A championship; Heritage Christian of Indianapolis beat Oak Hill, 60-58, in overtime for the Class 2A title;

Fort Wayne Elmhurst downed Owen Valley of Spencer, 62-59, for the Class 3A crown; and Ben Davis of Indianapolis topped South Bend Washington, 71-69, for the Class 4A championship.

The four games drew a state-finals class basketball record attendance of 21,522. Theresia Wynns never smiled so much as she did that memorable day in the home of the Indianapolis Colts.

In December 2011 Wynns announced she was leaving the IHSAA as an assistant commisioner to join the National Federation of State High School Associations in downtown Indianapolis adjacent to the NCAA headquarters.

Patty Broderick

Patty Broderick, one of only two people from Indiana in the Women's Basketball Hall of Fame in Knoxville, Tenn. (the other is LaTaunya Pollard-Romanazzi), got her start in the game at Cardinal Ritter High School on the west side of Indianapolis.

"Back in the day we didn't really play that many basketball teams," said Patty, whose official title is Coordinator of Women's Basketball Officials Consortium, which consists of eight conferences, including the Big Ten and Horizon League. "We played Scecina, we played Chartrand, which is now Roncalli, and Chatard.

"The Catholic schools played each other and that's how my basketball career began. We only played three or four games. I graduated from Cardinal Ritter in 1971. I didn't go to college. I went to work. I had a pretty good job offer and I took it."

How good was Patty, who says she is about 5-2, as a basketball player? "I think I probably was a better softball player than I was a basketball player. At the time I thought I could play basketball and referee."

Patty knows Jenny Young, who was a 4-11 basketball dynamo at Speedway High School and Butler University.

"The smaller the package, the bigger the heart, you know that, don't you?" Patty, who refereed a Butler game when Young was a starter at point guard, said. "And the drive. You've gotta do a whole

Patty Broderick, a Cardinal Ritter High School graduate, has refereed an Indiana high school girls' state championship (1982), seven NCAA Women's Final Fours, the 1988 Olympics in Seoul, Korea, against Shaquille O'Neal when he was a freshman at LSU and the first WNBA All-Star Game. She is now head of the Women's Basketball Officials Consortium, which includes the Big 10 Conference and Horizon League. (Photo courtesy of Patty Broderick)

lot more work when you don't have the athletic body to go with it. So you have to fall back on heart, spirit, soul, and Jenny had soul."

Patty was a point guard, too. She played five-on-five at Municipal Gardens. "I started down there when I was about nine-years-old. We did play six-on-six then, and that was with the rovers. I was a rover. I got to go up and down. Back in the day it was called NAGWS, National Association of Girls and Women's Sports."

Patty officiated in the 1982 IHSAA state championship game won by Heritage of Monroeville over Valparaiso, 52-45. She refereed a semifinal game in the Final Four of 1983 when Bedford North Lawrence beat Indianapolis Howe, 47-46.

She went to work out of high school at Indiana Health and Hospital Corp. and got with Blue Cross and Blue Shield insurance.

"I didn't stay with it because I got really involved in basketball and officiating. I fell in love with officiating. I started officiating in CYO for Don Nester. He assigned all officials for CYO basketball, boys' and girls'. I went to St. Michael's and Cardinal Ritter and Monsignor Cavanaugh at St. Michael's asked me to coach the little girls' basketball team. We had to referee our games, so you refereed before or after your game, and that's how we got the little girls' program started. The next year we all took the Indiana high school officiating test, because we wanted to make sure we knew what we were talking about, and I stopped coaching and started officiating."

That was around 1972. The CYO girls' program started in the early '70s, the CYO boys' program much earlier.

Patty started officiating about the same time as Theresia Wynns. She has three brothers. "My brothers probably helped me the most, because they did a little bit of officiating when they were in college to pick up some money, baseball, football, that kind of thing. When I was younger, my brothers were all older and they loved to play basketball. They had to watch me, so to keep me out of their hair they let me referee their games so I'd be quiet and not run home and say they weren't watching me. I would tell 'em whether it was a foul or out of bounds. My brothers are Bill, Bob and Mike. They had an influence on me. I learned to love officiating."

Patty has refereed all around the world. She officiated at the Seoul, Korea, Olympics in 1988. "We couldn't do a whole lot of things. The DMZ Zone was still there. There was a big riff between North Korea and South Korea. We had to be real careful and we all stayed together. They were very protective of us. They wanted us to stay in the Olympic Village. We won double gold in Seoul in 1988. In the Olympics you don't do your own country and you can't do a team that would probably be in the pool with the U.S. I did Korea, I did China, I did Australia. I just did the women's games. That was a highlight. Everything's a highlight. But some of the biggest highlights were just starting out, doing CYO basketball. You do the Olympics, you do the Final Four, you do the WNBA, but it's really not about those kind of things for me. It's just being involved in assisting athletes and the players and the game of basketball. It's pretty cool."

How was Patty as an official? "I think I was a common-sense official. I knew coaches could get pretty crazy. I was pretty successful. I could talk to 'em and I could take 'em down when they were crazy and throwing coats and jackets. Something like, 'If that coat hits the floor, it's gonna be a technical foul,' so they really run over and try to catch it before it hits the floor."

Does Patty think she could have handled The General, former I.U. coach Bob Knight? "I could have handled The General. Matter of fact, I did do a men's game. I reffed Shaquille O'Neal in his freshman year at LSU. Three women officiated that game. They played Australia (in a preseason game). Shaquille was 18 or 19, but obviously he looked like he was 35 or 40. He was just a man child. Dale Brown, the LSU coach then, wanted to be the first to have three women call a game. Dale wanted to be the first to do all kinds of things. Of course I'm 5-2 and I don't think Shaquille was 7-2 at the time but he was probably 7-foot. He towered over us. We weren't used to calling basket interference. Well, he was knocking the ball left and right. He went in to dunk the ball one time and he hung on the rim. That was back when they had the standards and the little chains to hold the base of the backboard . Well, chains just started popping, because he was pulling the basketball standard out of the floor. I'm thinking, 'Please let go, just please let go or you're gonna rip the floor out of this place.' Finally he let go and he flew back. It took us about 20 minutes to get the game started again because he tore up the equipment. He was amazing at 18 years old. He's still doing all kinds of things."

Did Shaquille have any comments to Patty? "He told me one time when I went by him, 'Ref, they're pulling on my shirt, they're pulling on my shirt.' I said, 'If you tuck it in, you won't have a problem.' He says, 'Okay, whatever.' I said, 'It shouldn't be hanging out down around your knees. It's supposed to tucked in and they won't pull on it.' It was a great experience. They were appreciative, they were very, very polite, they were gentlemen-like. They let us do our thing and us being females wasn't a big deal to them, because they were playing basketball. Dale Brown was very kind to us. We can say we were the first."

Patty did the first WNBA All-Star game. "It was at Madison Square Garden amid all that nostalgia. That's where Larry Bird played. It was a great experience. The place was packed and sometimes it's neat to be the first. I have many firsts."

She did seven NCAA women's Final Fours. The last one was in 1992. "The reason I stopped doing Final Fours was because I also was coordinator of training women's officials in the Big Ten and the commissioner decided I had to be either the coordinator or a referee," Patty said. "I chose to come off the floor and be a coordinator. My officiating career actually ended in my 40s. A lot of people go into their 50s or 60s. I chose to do the administrative part of it instead of actually blowing the whistle. I'm kinda glad I did. This is what I do today. I travel all over and it's actually my fulltime job.

"The conferences I oversee are the Big Ten, Big 12, Conference USA, Horizon League, the Summit League, the Mid-America Conference, the Missouri Valley, and the Division II Great Lakes Valley, which has the University of Indianapolis, like 95 schools total. I'm very busy."

Patty says in the months of November, December, January and February "I don't want to really be a VIP because I'm in charge of officials and coaches get kinda upset and unhappy sometimes and they want to yell and place their concerns, and I'm the one that has to do that, too. Sometimes I get those late-night phone calls or a phone call after a game with a coach upset with the officiating. Oh, it gets hot. 'They didn't call a foul at the end of the game' or 'they swallowed their whistles.' blah, blah, blah. Of course, you say, 'Coach, I'll take a look at the clips.' I do handle it. Sometimes I want to say, 'How many turnovers did you have? And what was your free throw percentage? And what was your shooting percentage?' It's usually down in the 20s and 30s, and I'll say, 'We missed four or five calls. Sounds to me like we're in the 80 percentile and you're in the 20 percentile. I think my team might have had a better day.'."

Did Patty ever swallow her whistle. "I don't think so. I blew it pretty good. Oh, I had techs and threw several college coaches out of the gym. Back in the day, there was an Indiana University coach, Jodie Malchoney, and she had a bit of Bobby Knight's demeanor or bench decorum, so she got tossed. And we had a coach from Oklahoma State, his name was Dick Halderman, and he got tossed from several games. I tossed him once. I called the second technical and he had to leave. You have to take care of business sometimes. You can't let things get crazy or doing cartwheels and things on the sidelines. If they're not going to control themselves, then they have to go bye-bye."

Where is women's basketball right now? "I think the state of women's basketball is in great shape. We've got more exposure, we've got more games on TV, we're giving scholarships to women and we've got women basketball coaches that are making million-dollar salaries just like the men's side."

Is Patty jealous of the million-dollar coaches? "Sometimes I say to myself, if you chose coaching instead of officiating, you might be making millions. But then how many coaches make it to the top. You've got 25, 30, 40 coaches. There's a lot more referees. So my avenues were probably better in officiating. Sometimes I wonder if I had chosen that road would I be a Pat Summitt today. I hope to think so, 'cause I think she's the best coach of women's basketball, bar none. And she's pretty high up there in regard to one-on-one with men's coaches, in my opinion. She's won more games than Bob Knight."

Patty doesn't follow high school basketball that much anymore, because she's so involved with women's college basketball. "I travel a lot. I see five games out of a week (in season), sometimes six. I sit and watch the officials. I'm a frequent flyer. I sit in first class and I'm a million miler and it's all because of basketball. I have a connection with Indiana basketball, Theresia Wynns, back in the day with Mildred Ball and Pat Roy."

> " . . . I did do a men's game. I reffed Shaquille O'Neal in his freshman year at LSU . . . Shaquille was 18 or 19, but obviously he looked like he was 35 or 40. He was just a man child . . . He went in to dunk the ball one time and he hung on the rim . . . back when they had the standards and the little chains to hold the base of the backboard. Well, chains just started popping, because he was pulling the basketball standard out of the floor. I'm thinking, 'Please let go, just please let go or you're gonna rip the floor out of this place.'

Patty says "it's been a great ride. Hopefully I might do this another 10 years and then ride off into the sunset. I hope I've left my stamp on the officiating community and some former players. Sometimes you're at the grocery store or the gas station and they say, 'I remember you and you were one of my favorite refs.' I think that's the biggest compliment. That's more than a Naismith Award or a Final Four. Just to know that you made an impact on a kid's life and a kid's experience through basketball."

Patty says she knows Steve Welmer, a top men's official from Columbus very well. "I call him Hitch 'cause he's always hitching up his pants. He's a great official. He's a common-sense official, which I would say that I was. If you don't have people-person skills and a personality, then you're in the rule book (too much), as far as I'm concerned."

Anything that Patty has missed? "I don't think so. Who would have thought that refereeing CYO basketball would take you all across the country and have the experiences that you've had and meet the people you've met and do your job. They pay you to run up and down the floor. You make a career out of it. Most people have jobs nine to five and sit in front of a desk or a computer or something like that. I use a computer, but officiating has been my livelihood. I'm getting paid very well."

Patty has been married and is divorced. She is Patty Roberts Broderick. Her former husband's name is Mark Roberts. "I have a daughter Jamie, who is refereeing now. Jamie has three children. I'm a grandma now, and it's a great feeling."

Of her fellow women's hall of fame member, Patty says, "I reffed LaTaunya's team. She had the body, she had the height, she had the razzle-dazzle moves, she had quickness, she had speed, she could put it behind her back, she would take it off the board and she was a physical player, an outstanding player."

I said to Patty that it might be far out, but I think she might be described as the female Oscar Robertson. "I would give her that title." Patty said.

COACHING EXPERTISE

JANICE SOYEZ

Being a part of the first and third state championship teams in the Indiana girls' high school basketball tournament sanctioned by the Indiana High School Athletic Association was the ultimate thrill for Janice Soyez, coach of the 1976 and 1978 Warsaw titlists that were 22-0 apiece.

Soyez, pronounced So-YEA, "which is French," she says, has a treasure trove of basketball memorabilia in her lovely one-story home on the northeast side of the capital of Kosciusko County where she resides in retirement from Warsaw High School as a coach and physical education and health teacher.

In a story by sports editor Dale Hubler of the *Warsaw Times-Union* on April 26, 2008, Soyez was quoted as saying:

> *"They (the IHSAA) passed a resolution where teams that went undefeated and won state, the whole team goes into the (Indiana) Hall of Fame. It's quite an honor, and I know the girls are quite thrilled about it. We're going to be first again (1976 was the first girls' state tournament sanctioned by the IHSAA; the Warsaw boys' team didn't win a first state championship until 1984)."*

Prior to the induction, the players from those two teams joined their coach for a ceremony at the Hall of Fame in New Castle.

The players were Judi Warren, Miss Basketball in 1976; Chanda Kline,

1ST STATE CHAMP COACH

Miss Basketball in 1978; Anita Folk, Cindi Ross, Leisa Waggoner, Cathy Folk, Marcia Miller, Kelly Smith, Cheryl Kachlik, Lori Novelle, Lisa Vandermark, Kim Rockey, Leona Bruce, Renee Wildman, Sue Loher, Pam Busenberg, Pam Shively and Claudia Kreicker.

Soyez, Warren and Kline are in the Hall of Fame as individuals.

"I've got to hand it to the girls," Soyez related. "Everybody came. They always come to every event, whatever they're asked to do. That's the kind of girls they were. They felt, I don't want to say obligated, but it was like they needed to be there.

"I wrote every player a personalized letter afterward and said how proud I was that they were there. You know I can't believe they're like 50 now.

"We have excellent sports banquets and Judi was the keynote speaker at one of them. She talked about her success and this and that, and her shortcomings with her son Andy (Judi wasn't married when he was born early in her coaching career). She talked about what athletes should look for in the learning process and what to beware of. It was a really good talk."

In 2009 East Chicago Roosevelt's two state championship teams (1977 and 1979) were inducted into the Hall of Fame. Warsaw beat East Chicago Roosevelt in both of its state championship years.

"Since those years we have seen the East Chicago team members out socially," Soyez said. "They're not our enemies anymore. Those kids were funny and they were just like pals. So time heals or whatever. Before they were our arch-rivals. Now it's just a different story."

Soyez was introduced to "Hoosier Hysteria" in a most unusual way. She was born in Peoria, Ill., but grew up in nearby Pekin, Ill., before moving with her parents, Walter and Virginia, to Bloomington-Normal, Ill.

"I went to high school on the campus of Illinois State Normal University," Janice said. "It was called University High School and was like a laboratory school. In high school we played under Girls Athletic Association jurisdiction. I was on the tennis team and the badminton team, and I played a little bit of basketball, but basketball in Illinois wasn't anything like in Indiana. When I graduated, my parents had moved to Muncie, Ind."

Janice says her dad traveled from Illinois to Muncie on weekends. "He said, 'There's a basketball hoop in every driveway. I just can't believe it.' "

The Muncie Bearcats learned well on those hoops, and Janice will never forget the night she first saw them play in the Fieldhouse.

"One of my good friends went to all of the Bearcat games with her husband," Janice said. "I didn't know what the flavor of basketball was. I didn't know anything. We went to the Fieldhouse, and, oh, it was just packed. The people went wild, and I'm like my dad was when we first got to Muncie, 'I can't believe this.' "

That year the Bearcats went to the state finals in Butler Fieldhouse (it's now known as Hinkle Fieldhouse). Ron Bonham and Bearcat teammates lost for the only time to East Chicago Washington (75-59) in the championship game.

Janice went with her friend to Butler Fieldhouse for the state finals.

"We sat at the very top, the nosebleed section," she said. "I never dreamed that I'd ever be down on the floor with my friend who took me to the games with her husband. When our Warsaw team went to the state finals in 1976, I got her seats down at the end of the floor. She said, 'I've never been this close to the floor.' It was pretty exciting for everybody."

Soyez did play basketball at Ball State University in Muncie. She graduated in 1966, then moved to Albuquerque, N. Mex., where she taught physical education for two years at Rio Grande High School.

"The boys did not have a tennis coach," she said. "No one would coach them. They came to me. 'Okay, I'll coach 'em,' I said. I love tennis. I don't play tennis anymore. I'm into golf.

"I coached the boys' tennis team for two years. We were in a little lower socio-economic school. We didn't have quite the talent, but the kids had the heart."

When she returned to Muncie after her second year in Albuquerque, another fortuitous thing happened. The woman who preceded her at Warsaw High School took a job at Manchester College in North Manchester, Ind.

"I interviewed for the job and got it in 1968," Janice said. "I was familiar with the lakes around Warsaw, because friends in Muncie had a cottage at Wawasee. We'd go up on the weekends. I knew the Warsaw area."

Warsaw Coach Janice Soyez cuts down a net at semi-state en route to winning the first girls' state championship in 1976. (Photo courtesy of Janice Soyez)

Janice became a basketball coach by default. Warsaw had a track and field team, a volleyball team, a basketball team and a badminton team in the GAA days when she arrived, and "I had to coach them all," she said.

"Finally I got some help. I said, 'Would you like to coach?' And everybody took a sport. But nobody took basketball. I go, 'Okay, I'll take basketball.' We had a schedule of playing Goshen, Plymouth, Elkhart.

"Then finally the tournaments came and basketball was one of the last sports sanctioned by the IHSAA, because they were afraid that if it bombed, that was it. They would never be able to sell things and whatever."

Janice says she wasn't shocked when she heard the IHSAA had sanctioned a girls' basketball tournament.

"No, I knew what was coming," she said. "It was forced, really. Phil Eskew (IHSAA commissioner at the time) and the old boys didn't want it to happen. It's like, 'Hey, it's time.' I wasn't shocked or anything like that, because the girls had been waiting for this a long time. Yes, finally it happened and the girls put their hands together. They were very excited."

Compared to today's girls' basketball, coaching techniques were quite primitive during Soyez's tenure.

"I gave the kids enough freedom to play their style," she said. "We had some plays. Like I said, I didn't have a coaching class. We did what we did. It's hard to explain. Today you wouldn't get anywhere that way. I didn't use X's and O's and I didn't have a clipboard."

What did she say during timeouts?

"Well, we were always ahead," Janice said, laughing. "I would say, 'Continue what you're doing or watch this or that, they're cutting in.' It's hard to remember."

Once the tournament began, the Tigers increased their resolve to bring home a state championship.

"Our competition wasn't that stiff in our regular schedule," Janice said. "Then when we started going to sectionals, we were playing teams like Goshen, which we hadn't played for three years.

"And we didn't have scouts. We didn't have any of that, except we were going to play East Chicago Roosevelt in the first game of the state finals and we were able to get a film from friends up in Portage. We had films of our games, but nothing of opponents. We knew nothing, except what we read. Or I'd call GAA officers and they'd tell me this and that."

Soyez says it was like Warsaw was meant to go to the state finals.

"Pat Roy (assistant IHSAA commissioner at the time) was ecstatic that half of Warsaw came to Hinkle Fieldhouse, like 5,000 people.

Small towns made the tournament. Hinkle Fieldhouse was packed, and when we won the afternoon game more people came down. There was a sign out of town. It said, 'The last person out of Warsaw turn out the lights.'

"My sisters came from Illinois, my other one from Anderson, my nephews. I had to get tickets for everybody."

Asked if she had 5-foot-1 Judi Warren put on someone's shoulders like Gene Hackman in the movie *Hoosiers* had the Huskies' student manger lifted up to make sure the basket in the Fieldhouse was 10-foot high like all the other baskets in Indiana, Janice smiled and said: "We didn't have to say anything. We walked into Hinkle and Cindi Ross, our tall gal, said, 'This isn't so big.' There was nothing the players couldn't conquer."

What did friends in The Region (the northwestern corner of Indiana) tell Soyez about LaTaunya Pollard, East Chicago Roosevelt's sensational freshman who would become Miss Basketball in 1979 after leading the Roughriders to a second state championship (they also won in 1977)?

"LaTaunya was good, real good," Janice said. "One gal said, 'You won't beat East Chicago Roosevelt.' I saw her at Hinkle Fieldhouse and she was shocked. She couldn't believe that we beat 'em.

"The whole thing was we were quicker, got 'em confused. There's a picture of four of their players and Judi is weaving in and out, like, 'Where did she go?' I think we were behind in the first part. Then we won by about 20 (62-44). Somebody interviewed me and said, 'How did you feel when you were behind?' I go, 'We were? I didn't know.' I said I didn't even look at the scoreboard. I might have had a heart attack if I had."

After beating Bloomfield, 57-52, in the title game, it was pandemonium on the Hinkle Fieldhouse floor, according to Soyez.

"People I knew were on the side and nobody could get on the floor," she said. "It was interview after interview and I think I lost my voice. I'll always remember this. My parents (Walter and Virginia) were there and my mother wanted to get on the floor. They said,

'Sorry, nobody can get on the floor.' She said, 'But I'm her mother.' They said nobody else on the floor. She was so disappointed.

"But I finally knew something about Hoosier Hysteria. I just loved the part about 'first to be first.' They had this one class, and there we were. There was a lot of good competition, and it kept growing."

Soyez donated much of her memorabilia to the Indiana Basketball Hall of Fame. She still has the letter she received from then-Governor Otis Bowen in 1978 offering congratulations for winning the state championship. She also has the Sagamore of the Wabash honor she received on June 8, 2000 from then-Governor Frank O'Bannon.

How is life now for the Illinois native who found happiness in Hoosierland?

"It's always been wonderful," she stated proudly. "I'm just an optimist. Every day's great. The things that have happened to me, it's like I was in the right place at the right time. Everything just kinda flowed.

"If I had a blueprint, I could have never mapped out anything like that. At Warsaw High School I had other honors in teaching. I had deco awards. Things like that just kept happening."

Janice feels blessed to have gotten involved in Indiana basketball.

"The kids made it rewarding," she said. "I don't know if I would be considered a pioneer of Indiana high school girls' basketball. Maybe. The kids did it. They said they were gonna win and take state, and they did. Being first twice is something I'll always treasure."

LIN DUNN

Lin Dunn, who guided Purdue to its first NCAA women's Final Four in 1994 and is now coach of the WNBA's Indiana Fever, scored a basketball halls of fame double-double in 2010.

On Feb. 19, 2010, Dunn, who was born at Vanderbilt Hospital in Nashville, Tenn., was inducted into the Tennessee Hall of Fame.

"That was amazing," she stated. "I was completely surprised. That's an all-sports hall of fame. It was in Nashville and all of my family was there and many of my friends.

Although from Tennessee, Lin Dunn has grown to love Purdue University and the Indiana Fever. (Photo courtesy of Indiana Fever)

"It was an impressive event. I couldn't believe it, then I turn around and get inducted into the Indiana Basketball Hall of Fame, which to me is THE hall of fame of all basketball halls of fame. I think Indiana may be the only state that has just a basketball hall of fame.

"I was honored and humbled. I was looking at the people in that hall of fame and you've got to be kidding me. It's overwhelming. I guess I'm getting old."

Many of Lin's former Purdue players gathered to toast their coach on the night of

April 24—Jennifer Jacoby, Patricia Collup, Jane Calhoun, Stephanie White, MaChelle Joseph and Terri Moorman—among them.

"Whenever you're going to be inducted into some kind of hall of fame it's nice to have your family there and your fiends, but to have your former players there makes it really special."

Being a native Tennessean and graduate of the University of Tennessee-Martin, Lin says she bleeds orange.

"You can't be a Boilermaker for nine years like I was and bleed red (the color of rival Indiana University)," she said with a laugh.

How did Lin do against I.U.?

"It's funny that you would ask me that," Lin said. "When I was induced into the Indiana Basketball Hall of Fame, I mentioned that one of the things I'm proud of is that in the nine years that I coached at Purdue—I think we (Purdue and Indiana) played 18 times, two times every year—that we never lost to I.U.

"And I knew how special that was to our fans. The Boilermaker-Hoosier rivalry is huge. It's like Alabama and Auburn, Vanderbilt-Tennessee. I just treasure the fact that we were able to do that, and if there's ever been a coach that's worked at Purdue that's never lost to I.U., I'd like to meet 'em."

Because she has spent nearly two decades of her coaching career in Indiana, has Lin become an adopted Hoosier?

"It's hard for me to use the term Hoosier, because when I think of Hoosier I think of I.U.," she said. "I have a tremendous love for the state of Indiana. I love the people, I love their spirit, I love how much they love basketball, because I love it the same way.

"I love the city of Indianapolis. It's a great city; it's a great sports town. There's a part of me now, I guess, you could say bleeds a little Hoosier blood. Black and Gold (Purdue colors) Hoosier blood. I learned real quick when I went to Purdue not red."

Dunn says she was born too soon.

"Absolutely," she said, grinning, "because I loved sports so much. I loved to compete. And I tell the story about how my father was a

Marine. He also ran track at Vanderbilt and he was a competitive person himself.

"He had my brother and I in the backyard competing in every sport there's ever been. We even had a pole-vaulting pit in the backyard. We were that competitive. I was pretty good. It was dangerous, but I think he instilled in me that competitive spirit."

Unfortunately, added Lin, she grew up in Alabama before Title IX.

"It was actually against the law in Alabama for girls to play high school basketball. When we moved back to Tennessee I got to play two years of high school basketball at Dresden, my current home, the old fashioned way, the six-person game. I was a forward. I shot and the ones at the other end were guards. You couldn't run full court."

Lin was 5-7 as a member of the Dresden Lady Lions.

"Black and Gold," she exclaimed. "There's a photo of me in my uniform somewhere, but I'm not going to pull it out. It is hilarious."

How good was Lin in high school?

"I was a really good high school basketball player," she said. "I think my senior year I averaged 42 points. I was all-state. I had a jump shot before girls had jump shots. And I was tough. I was mean. I was physical. I probably fouled out of every game I played, because I was so competitive.

"I could not stand to lose. And I still have that in me, but I have mellowed. There's no doubt that as I've gotten older I've learned how to handle losing better. I'm not as relentless. I think now I've transferred all that to when I play spades or gin; I'm pretty ruthless in cards."

Winning is not everything for Lin Dunn, she insists, although it used to be everything, "so I've got that a little bit under control."

Lin did not get to play college basketball.

"When I went to U.T.-Martin in '65, they were starting teams for girls like volleyball and tennis, but no basketball," she said. "It wasn't until after I graduated that they started a basketball team at U.T.-Martin.

Lin Dunn had the pleasure of meeting UCLA men's basketball coach John Wooden when he returned to Purdue, his alma mater, for a banquet in his recognition. The former Boilermaker women's coach is a great admirer of the late Indiana native.

"John Wooden always was an outspoken supporter of women's basketball," she said. "He loved the women's game for a couple of reasons.

"One, we play under the rim. We don't dunk the ball (a lot). And there's not a lot of one-on-one stuff, more teamwork, more execution. And he liked how hard the women play. For him to publicly express his love of the women's game was great for us. It gave us great credibility."

Dunn has an autographed photo of Wooden that is framed and on display in her home in Dresden, Tenn.

"John Wooden was an inspiration to all coaches, male and female," Lin said. "There's been some great coaches, Red Auerbach, now Phil Jackson and Pat Riley. But I think at the end of the day when the dust settles, it's going to be hard to top John Wooden.

"That first year they started it Pat Summit (University of Tennessee women's coach) was a freshman. I had gone on to Knoxville to get my master's (at U. of Tennessee) and they started the team that year. So I missed the opportunity to play college basketball, missed the opportunity to have a scholarship, the whole shebang."

Dunn has turned that negative into a positive.

"I'm just thrilled that now women have the opportunities that I didn't have," she stated. "Every night when I go to bed I say, 'Thank goodness for Title IX.' I say that to my players. If it weren't for Title IX we wouldn't have the opportunities for women we have now.

"It's been wonderful for me to see the growth, from no teams to see tremendous opportunities for girls and women now, not only at the high school, junior high and elementary levels, all the way through college and now professional.

"I take very seriously my responsibility as a mentor. I try to be available for my former players. I've got some young coaches that are just getting started and I try to stay in touch with them and give them a pat on the back if I can."

Lin's coaching career began in 1970 when she was hired to teach physical education at Austin Peay in Clarksville, Tenn. Not long after taking the job, Lin went to the athletic director and said the school needed to have sports teams for women—basketball, tennis, volleyball.

"You don't have a budget, but if you want a team, go ahead," Lin said the AD told her. "We were basically having teams without official sanction by the university. We just didn't have the resources, but we played and competed.

"We'd get in my car and I'd drive everywhere, then I'd drive back that night, because we didn't have money for lodging. We certainly didn't have money for food. If you had food, you were on your own. It was kind of a rag-tag team. We had one set of uniforms. But every year it got a little bit better."

Those days at Austin Peay were some of Lin's most treasured in four decades of coaching.

"I enjoyed coaching those women because they played for the love of the sport. They weren't there on scholarship and they weren't going to get any publicity. Nobody knew when we had a game. They just loved to play. There's something to be said for coaching those kind of people.

"As the years went by I went on to Ole Miss and we were giving

"And he was a Boilermaker and from Indiana. That makes it even more special. The thing about John is, yes, he was a great coach, yes, he was a great teacher. But he was a great man. He was a wonderful husband, he was a wonderful grandfather, he was the whole package."

Indiana Fever Coach Lin Dunn, a Tennessee native who went into the Indiana Basketball Hall of Fame in 2010, studies game action. (Photo courtesy of Indiana Fever)

211

scholarships. Then I went to Miami (of Florida) and started a program there. We gave scholarships there, too. It was all part of the growing process"—from a beginning under the Association of Intercollegiate Athletics for Women (AIAW) banner to the NCAA.

In 1986 Dunn moved to West Lafayette, Ind., as the Purdue women's coach, and she couldn't have been more excited.

"I thought it was a gold mine," she declared. "You've got this wonderful talent in the Midwest. You've got this fantastic academic institution. You've got the Big Ten conference. The potential at Purdue, to me, was unlimited.

"It was a perfect place to recruit players and there was not a lot going on in West Lafayette, a perfect place for the fans to come out. I remember when I took the job we were going to win Big Ten championships, we were gonna go to the Final Four and we were going to win a national championship."

Dunn, who was 206-68 (.752) as Purdue's winningest coach in history over nine seasons, did win three Big Ten championships, took the Boilermakers to seven NCAA tournaments and four Sweet Sixteen appearances, and one trip to the Final Four (1994). But she never achieved that national championship.

In her first Boilermaker season, Lin led Purdue to the WNIT, finishing second to DePaul. Seven years later Purdue won at Stanford to make the Final Four in Richmond, Va., where the Boilermakers lost to eventual national champion North Carolina in the first game.

"The game at Stanford started at 10 o'clock our time, so it was after midnight before the game was over," Lin said. "We had no seniors. We were a bunch of young overachievers that had really great team chemistry. We had no fear.

"You could just feel the momentum building as the season went along, that this team was going to do something really special. I promised them that if they quit getting tattoos and if they got to the Final Four, I would get a tattoo."

After Purdue beat Stanford, the players hollered "tattoo."

"I'm thinking, 'Whatever it takes to motivate a team.' Let's just say that I have a tattoo. It says Final Four and it's somewhere on my body. I'm not going to say where and I'm not going to point at it, either."

Midway of the Portland (Ore.) Power's first American Basketball League's first season in 1996-97, Dunn was named the new coach. She won her first game that night as a fledging professional coach.

A year later, Lin led the Power on a worst-to-first run that culminated with a 27-17 record and a Western Conference championship. As a result, she was named the ABL Coach of the Year. Portland was in first place with a 9-4 record when the ABL folded two days before Christmas in 1998.

In 1999, Dunn joined the WNBA as head coach and general manager of the Seattle Storm, the city's initial women's pro program. Three years later, in her final year with the Storm, Lin led the team to a 17-15 record and the team's first appearance in the playoffs.

Lin has twice been runner-up as the WNBA's Coach of the Year—2002 with Seattle and 2009 with Indiana, when the Fever lost to Phoenix in the championship series, 3-2.

Dunn keeps an apartment in Indianapolis year-round. At the end of the Fever season she goes back to Dresden to take care of her mother, scout for college talent and attend Grand Ole Opry in Nashville as often as possible—"I love the old country music and Patsy Kline is one of my favorite singers." She also spends a month in Indianapolis doing personal appearances.

Indiana Fever stalwarts Katie Douglas (left), Coach Lin Dunn (center) and Stephanie White, assistant coach. (Photo courtesy of Indiana Fever)

In June 2009, Lin was the keystone speaker at the Indianapolis Whale Hunting Women's meeting in Indianapolis.

"I was introduced by one of my long-time heroes, Lyn St. James, the race car driver," Lin said. "That was a unique experience for me, because I've always respected her from afar. She kinda set the tone for women in auto racing. I've always had great admiration for her, Babe Zaharias, Billie Jean King and Wilma Rudolph, who was from Clarksville, Tenn. Those were some of the women I had as role models."

Dunn is not a member of The Whale Hunters, but adds that she has that mentality. The group uses whale hunting as an example of how to succeed in business and community, Lin stated.

"I think in order to survive in this business and in order to be successful in this business you have to be tough, you have to be smart, you have to be competitive, you have to be flexible, you have to be adaptable, you have to change through the years and adjust to your situation. I think that's where that term whale hunters came from."

Asked if she has the Fever, the nickname of the Indiana WNBA franchise, Lin smiled.

"It's funny," she said. "Here I am in my fourth decade of coaching (in her fourth year of coaching the Fever after serving four years as an assistant), and I still have this tremendous desire to coach and teach. I love to watch as players get better every day. I love to find the button that is going to motivate 'em and help 'em get better.

"I love watching a group come together and work together and stay together and fight through adversity and get to where they're just as smooth and clicking and they're successful and they enjoy each other's company.

"As long as I like all that and feel that—I don't know how you describe it. You can't put your finger on it, you can't see it, but you can feel it. I call it team chemistry. I want to stay involved in the game, whether it's coaching, it's scouting, whether it's mentoring, whatever. I love the game of basketball. I'm in my 60s now. I don't know if I'll coach forever, maybe, maybe not. But as long as I feel like I do now, I want to continue coaching."

Of all the players Dunn has coached, she considers Tamika Catchings of the Fever and MaChelle Joseph, current Georgia Teach coach and Purdue's all-time leading scorer, male or female, at the top of the list.

"In a career you don't often have the opportunity to coach someone like Tamika Catchings," Lin said. "Many people have asked me, 'Have you ever coached anyone similar?'. The closest person I've ever coached that had that intensity, that desire, that competitiveness would be MaChelle Joseph.

'She had that relentless 'I will fight through everything, I will beat you, I'm going to play with 110 percent 'all the time' attitude. To get an opportunity to coach two people like that in my career is amazing. They don't come along very often.

"Catchings is relentless in her desire to win. Her work ethic is second to none. She is a great player, but she is also a great person. For all the effort she puts in on the court, she does the same thing in the community. She's for sure a once-in-a-lifetime player. She defends, she rebounds, she dives on the floor for loose balls, she scores. And she does it at a very, very high level. She's like the Energizer Bunny."

Lin concluded by saying she is very fortunate to work for Pacers Sports & Entertainment.

"It is a first-class organization, both sides of the field (male and female)," she offered. "With Larry (Bird) over on the men's side and Kelly (Krauskopf) as our leader, and with Jim Morris' and Rick Fuson's support, we really have a unique situation with our facilities, with the city, with the fans, with the management.

"It's top of the line, the best of the best."

MIKE ARMSTRONG

Mike Armstrong was a freshman at Indiana State University when Larry Bird was a senior. Bird took the Sycamores on a wonderful ride to the 1979 NCAA men's Final Four in Salt Lake City that many say made college basketball a major sporting attraction.

ISU's only loss that 1978-79 season came in the championship game to Magic Johnson and his Michigan State Spartans.

"That year in '78-'79 was just an amazing year to be on campus," said Armstrong, Indianapolis Perry Meridian High School girls' head basketball coach, head girls' cross country coach and assistant athletic director.

"I was a runner at Indiana State and I think that's when I noticed the power that athletics can have over an entire community, just to see Terre Haute get behind that ISU basketball team, and eventually see a lot of people in Indiana get behind that team. That's when I first thought maybe I'd like to coach or be a part of something like that someday."

While student teaching at Terre Haute South High School, Armstrong became friends with the school's boys' basketball coach, Pat Rady. That friendship became a turning point in Mike's life.

"I told Pat I was interested in coaching," he said. "He wasn't sure that if he were starting a coaching career at the time that girls' basketball wouldn't be the way to go, that he might be a head coach a lot sooner.

"I kinda took that advice. When I came home from school, Bob Kirkhoff, a friend of mine, was a girls' coach at Roncalli High School. I actually started there as a volunteer coach for a couple of years with Bob.

"Then I moved to Cathedral High School as an assistant coach for two years before becoming the head coach at Perry Meridian in 1986."

Mike, who graduated from Perry Meridian in 1978, became assistant cross country coach at his alma mater in 1989. Three years later he moved up to head cross country coach. In 1995 he became assistant athletic director.

"My undergrad major at Indiana State was actually in journalism," Mike said. "I never wrote one day in my life for a newspaper. I went right into coaching and teaching, and I've enjoyed it immensely.

"I've had the pleasure to coach some special kids. I've coached a mental attitude award winner. I've coached a state runner-up team. We've coached a really lot of special kids. Laura Gaybrick won the mental attitude award in Class 4A basketball in 2003. That was the year we finished runner-up. We got beat by Kokomo in the championship game, 44-42.

"Obviously, Katie Douglas is our most accomplished basketball player, from high school to college (Purdue) to the WNBA (Indiana Fever). I'm really proud of what we did when Katie was a player for us.

"But I'm also proud of what we've done since she left. Pretty much when I read a story about Katie in the paper Perry Meridian is usually in there somewhere. She's kind of a gift that keeps on giving. She has an effect on our basketball program even today."

Mike, who was an assistant coach with the USA Basketball team that won the gold medal in the first 17-and-under Girls World Championship in France in 2010, did not attend Katie's wedding in Greece in 2005 to Vasilis Giapalakis. But he did attend a ceremony for the couple several months later.

"Vasilis has taken very good care of Katie's career and he's taken very good care of Katie, too," Mike said. "I think they have a very special relationship. If Katie has kids and any of them are girls, I hope she lives in Perry Township, because I'd love to coach them."

In Armstrong's 2 ½-decade tenure as the Perry Meridian High School's girls' coach, he says the improvement in player quality has been amazing.

"There were a lot of good players in the past," he said, "but the players today have so many more opportunities than the players 20, 25 years ago. They're better trained at a younger age, there are more camps available to players today, there is AAU basketball, they're probably better coached today and I'm not talking just in high school, but from the younger ages all the way up.

"We probably cut kids now that probably would have played a lot on my first few teams at Perry Meridian. Too, the NCAA offers so many scholarships today, and thus the players are a lot better today."

Mike wishes there was more coverage of women's sports in Indianapolis, but he understands that the high schools, the WNBA, the Indianapolis Indians and the Indianapolis 500 and Brickyard 400 are trying to find their deserved spot in the pecking order of Indianapolis sports.

"Women's basketball, a lot like minor league baseball, I think has to find its niche in the community," he said. "We wish it were higher, but I understand that the Indianapolis Colts sell more newspapers, so the Colts are going to dominate coverage right now, especially as good as they have been with a special player like Peyton Manning. And the Pacers are always going to be in there, too."

STAN BENGE

A funny thing happened to Stan Benge, one of the most successful Indiana high school girls' basketball coaches in history, on his way to becoming a head high school boys' basketball coach.

While an assistant boys' coach at Roncalli High School in the late '70s, a bunch of girls at the Indianapolis school went to Benge and asked if he would coach them during the summer.

"There were four sisters, the Sexton girls, in the bunch," said Benge, who had four Class 4A state girls' championship teams at Ben Davis High School in the first decade of the 21st century before resigning in June 2011 to become assistant to IUPUI head women's coach Austin Parkinson. "I did coach them and it was a lot of fun. That's how I got into coaching girls."

Benge says his goal was always to be a head coach at the high school level for boys. He was an assistant boys' coach at Roncalli for two years and an assistant boys' coach at Ben Davis for two years.

After four years as a boys' assistant, Benge's career took another significant turn.

"It's funny," he said. "I had always coached basketball, but I thought at that time I might do something else. And so I got out of coaching basketball for a couple of years. Then I missed it and the head girls' coaching job at Ben Davis became open.

"I applied for it and didn't get it the first year. The second year they came and asked me if I would do it. I thought it might be fun and I'd do it for a couple of years. Twenty-six years later I was still doing it before I decided to become a college coach."

Benge had a 519-126 record with the Lady Giants, leading the team to state championships in 2000, '01, '09 and '10. Ben Davis won a state-record 81 consecutive games from 2008 to 2011, ending with a loss to Carmel in a 2011 regional championship game.

"Walking away from Ben Davis and telling those players was one of the hardest things I've ever had to do," Benge told *The Indianapolis Star.* "I'm going to miss those players big-time."

When Benge gave up the job as assistant boys' coach at Ben Davis, he thought he had probably given up his chances of being a head coach.

Bria Goss, Miss Basketball in 2011, helped Indianapolis Ben Davis High School win Class 4A state championships in 2009 and 2010 with unbeaten records both years. She committed to the University of Kentucky as a Ben Davis undergraduate. (Photo courtesy of Ben Davis High School)

"It wasn't a goal to become a girls' head coach," he said. "I thought I could help more than anything else. It was a lot more enjoyable than I thought it would be."

Stan lost his first two games as the Giants' coach, but he called his six seniors "fabulous girls that enjoyed playing. We kept getting better and we wound up winning the sectional and going to the final game of the regional.

"From that point it sort of built. That first year it was like you're teaching everybody everything. After that they sort of helped each other. We didn't win our first state championship until 2000, so how long did I coach without winning one? Fourteen years. It takes a while."

Of Benge's 496 victories through the 2009-10 season, 113 came during state championship seasons: 28-0 in 2000, 27-2 in 2001, 30-0 in 2009 and 28-0 in 2010. Ben Davis was the first team to win 30 games in a season and the first team—boys' or girls'—to have consecutive unbeaten seasons.

Stan is quick to point out how much the sports tradition that Dick Dullaghan started in Ben Davis football helped the Giants' girls' basketball teams in their quest for success. Dullaghan won seven state championships in his 20 years at Ben Davis that ended in 2003.

"The first state championship always is the toughest, because your players don't know if it can be done," Benge said. "I remember when Dullaghan came in and talked to our girls before they won their first state championship in 2000.

"Dick told our girls, 'You've gotta pound on that door a long time before you finally knock it over.' The tradition Dullaghan started in football and Steve Witte continued in boys basketball, and now girls' basketball, and our track team has won three state championships in a row, all that sort of snowballed."

Ironically, each of Benge's state championships has come in a different venue. The first in 2000 was in Hinkle Fieldhouse, the second in 2001 in Market Square Arena, the third in 2009 at Indianapolis'

Skylar Diggins, 2009 Miss Basketball from South Bend Washington High School, was outstanding for Notre Dame in its runner-up finish in the 2011 NCAA Women's Final Four at Conseco Fieldhouse. (Photo courtesy of South Bend Washington High School)

Lucas Oil Stadium and the fourth in 2010 at Allen County War Memorial Coliseum in Fort Wayne.

IHSAA assistant commissioner Theresia Wynns, director of girls' basketball and former girls' basketball referee, says Lucas Oil Stadium is not the ultimate place to hold the state finals.

"We really want to be at Conseco Fieldhouse, because that's a basketball place," she said. "But it was special that we got to play at Lucas Oil Stadium (home of the Indianapolis Colts).

"The staff and administrators at Lucas worked really hard with us to make sure that the basketball experience was the best it could be. We were concerned about shooting into space, it being such a large venue.

"I think the Lucas Oil employees did an excellent job on cutting down the space and how they hung curtains. I didn't get complaints from coaches or players."

The 2009 state championships in Lucas Oil Stadium were memorable because of the site and the quality of play in all four title games. Ben Davis defeated South Bend Washington, 71-69, in Class 4A; Fort Wayne Elmhurst beat Owen Valley of Spencer, 62-59, in Class 3A; Indianapolis Heritage Christian downed Oak Hill of Converse, 60-58, in overtime in Class 2A (it was Heritage Christian's fourth consecutive championship); and Fort Wayne Canterbury defeated Vincennes Rivet, 72-66, in Class A.

Wynns called the 2009 state finals "the best show I've ever seen. Girls' high school basketball in Indiana has come a long, long way compared to the day I officiated in the second state championship game in 1977.

"We were happy at that point, but when you compare the skills of those individuals to the skills of our young ladies today they are worlds apart. That shows the growth, that shows the dedication in making sure our young ladies have an opportunity to grow and shows the growth in coaches as well."

Wynns and Benge speak highly of one another.

"Oh, gosh, Stan Benge is a class act," Wynns said. "I respect him. He's not looking to advance to a men's program. He dedicated himself to developing that Ben Davis program and the players."

Of Wynns, Benge says, "She was a great official. I hated to see her leave officiating girls' basketball."

Stan will never forget his team's matchup with South Bend Washington at Lucas Oil Stadium, which will forever be remembered as one of the finest games in girls' tournament history.

"To me, it was a completely different atmosphere," he said. "The No. 1 (Ben Davis) and No. 2 (South Bend Washington) teams in the country, both teams undefeated, you're playing in a venue that reminded me more of the NCAA collegiate level would be, the raised floor.

"And the way the game was won. We were in control of the game, then South Bend Washington tied the game and Bria Goss hit a shot with 1.4 seconds to go to win the game.

"We were ahead by 11 points and had the ball with 2 ½ minutes to go. Then we got a couple of bad calls, missed a couple of free throws and Skylar Diggins (2009 Miss Basketball now at Notre Dame) goes nuts on us.

"They tied it up (69-69) with 45 seconds to go. We got the ball in Bria Goss's hands. We didn't take a time out. The reason we didn't was because we had the defensive matchups we wanted. I didn't want Skylar guarding Bria, so we had Bria with the ball and they had someone else on her. So I called a one-four-low (formation) and Bria held the ball (before driving to the basket and banking in a shot). Bria said later, 'Coach, did we have a time out left?' I said, 'Yeah.' She said, 'I almost called it. I was getting awful nervous out there.' "

Stan had only one losing season as the Giants' coach, and it came the season when Bria Goss was a freshman (2007-08). The Giants were 9-12, then went 30-0 the next year to win Benge's third state championship.

Benge has lost count of the number of his players that have played college basketball. But he does say that "we had some great,

Stan Benge remembers watching the first girls' Indiana-Kentucky All-Star basketball game in 1976 at Hinkle Fieldhouse and being surprised by one fundamental aspect of the Indiana squad.

"Half of 'em couldn't shoot a left-handed layup and those were the best players in the state," the former Indianapolis Ben Davis High School girls' coach said.

"Now obviously any varsity player can do that. I said when I started coaching at Ben Davis (the 1985-86 season) that girls' basketball has a long way to go. I don't know if they have a long way to go anymore. There are some awfully good players out there now."

Kentucky won the first all-star game in 1976 at Louisville and the Bluegrass girls captured 13 of the first 16 games in the series. From 1995 through 2000, however, Indiana won 10 of 12 games. By 2003 Indiana led the series, 29-27.

Indiana had stretched that advantage to 39-31 by the end of the 2010 season, winning 28 of 38 games from 1993 through 2010. Benge

great athletes during the time I was at Ben Davis. On our undefeated team in 2009 every single player was being recruited by a Division I school, except for one who went to Division I in track.

"Bria Goss committed to the University of Kentucky as a junior (she was a senior in 2010-11). Shyra Ely (2001 Miss Basketball) didn't play in the WNBA in 2010 because she hurt her knee. She went to the University of Tennessee and did very well. She played in four Final Fours, but never won a national championship. I haven't had anybody who's won a national championship.

"Janese Banks (who led the Giants to the 2001 state championship) played at Wisconsin and did very well, as did Ashley Allen at Ohio State. Alex Bentley right now is playing at Penn State (she was the Giants' leading scorer against South Bend Washington in the 2009 state championship game with 18 points)."

In 2009 Ben Davis was rated mythical national champion in one poll. A year later the Giants were ranked third nationally. Benge is mystified by the difference.

"That difference was sort of strange to me," he said. "When they ranked us No. 3 in 2010, I said, 'How do they do this?' They said,

'Well, these teams from California (ranked ahead of Ben Davis) are good.'

"Maybe they were better than us, but maybe we were better than them. The two teams ranked ahead of us were good, but they beat each other during the season. The only thing that bothered me was the players themselves—if I just could have had an explanation for them."

Looking back, Stan says he has had a lot of fun as the Giants coach, but adds that it takes a lot of work to be as successful as he has been.

"I don't care how many you've won or how much talent you have or anything else, it's never easy," he said. "I remember we lost eight games in a row one year and I said to myself, 'I'll never take for granted winning again.'

"You don't do this by yourself. I don't care what any coach says, there are so many people who contributed to Ben Davis' girls' basketball success. I think I had some of the best assistant coaches around. It takes administrative backing, it takes everything. It takes a good group of girls. What I've found is that when I had good parents, I had good teams. What I mean by good parents, people who are supportive and don't question every move."

was the Indiana coach the year before guiding his 2009 all-stars led by Skylar Diggins of South Bend Washington, Miss Basketball, to a pair of victories.

Ben Davis was 58-0 over the 2008-09 and 2009-10 seasons, winning the Giants' third and fourth state championships in Benge's tenure.

"That's unheard of," he stated. "Who would ever think that in basketball that you would win 58 in a row? Maybe if you were a big school and played a bunch of small schools or whatever you might do that.

"But 58-0 in central Indiana is unbelievable. The best basketball in the country, in my opinion, is played right here in central Indiana. We played Bolingbrook, Ill.; we played Detroit Country Day; and we played the two best teams in Chicago.

"And we've never lost a game to those teams. We had good teams when we played 'em. And they maybe had better players. But the coaching, the team work and the fundamentals, in my opinion, are the best right here in central Indiana."

Benge, who is a Giants alum, never taught at Ben Davis High School. He taught physical education from kindergarten through sixth grade at Rhoades Elementary School in Wayne Township.

"In 2000 or 2001 I was asked to go to the high school, because they were doing renovation there," he said. "We'd just gone through renovation at Rhoades and I didn't want to go through another renovation. I was satisfied at Rhoades. I said if you don't mind I'll stay here and they said that was okay."

Stan played basketball at Marian College (now Marian University) for four years under Coach Ed Schilling Sr., who is in the Butler University Athletic Hall of Fame.

"I had a good career at Marian," Stan said. "We didn't do anything outstanding, but we had good teams. I enjoyed myself."

Benge coached Eddie Schilling, the senior Schilling's son, in the third grade. The younger Schilling went on to become an outstanding play-making guard at Miami of Ohio. Ed Schilling Jr., son-in-law of Dick Dullaghan, is now boys' coach at Indianapolis Park Tudor High School and executive director of the Champions Academy in Zionsville.

Benge prides himself in his on-court demeanor.

"I'm never boisterous," he said. "I'm not a yeller and screamer."

And what is his take on class basketball, which occurred two years before the Giants' first state championship in 2000?

"I liked the state tournament the way it was before class basketball, because of the tradition and everything else," he said. "The only thing I have against class basketball is the way it was implemented. It was always, 'Are we going to have class basketball or are we not going to have class basketball?' It was never, 'Okay, we're going to have class basketball, how is it going to be done? Is four classes the best way or should it be three or two?'

"What I hate is when you're in a state championship game half the crowd is walking out of the gym because their team has just played. That kind of thing hurts the atmosphere. I loved the one class. But our road is almost exactly the same anyway. I just wish they could tweak it a little bit and maybe make it a little better."

Coaching female basketball for over two decades has been a blast, says Benge.

"But each year is a new challenge and as a coach you don't know if you could have done better. Did you say the right things at the right time?"

The Ben Davis superintendent tested Benge before the start of the 2010-11 season. He said. "Fifty-eight in a row. What's next?' " Benge replied, "Fifty-nine (Ben Davis did just that, beating Brownsburg, 66-40, in its opener). You want to go on and keep improving yourself. This is all the better I could get if I wouldn't coach anymore. I still want to be a better coach and I still want my players to be better."

That's the Stan Benge way.

THE TRADITION CONTINUES

Diggin' Diggins

Where does women's basketball in the Hoosier state stand today, just 35 years after the first Indiana High School Athletic Association-sanctioned girls' state tournament was held in 1976?

None of the first seven Indiana Miss Basketballs—Judi Warren (Warsaw), Teri Rosinski (Norwwell of Ossian), Chanda Kline (Warsaw), LaTaunya Pollard (East Chicago Roosevelt), Maria Stack (Columbus East), Cheryl Cook (Indianapolis Washington) and Trena Keys (Marion)—was able to play in an NCAA Division I women's basketball tournament, which didn't start until 1982.

But five Indiana Miss Basketballs competed in the 30th NCAA Division I women's tournament, with the Final Four being contested at Indianapolis' Conseco Fieldhouse.

Amber Harris of Indianapolis North Central (2006 Miss Basketball) and Ta'Shia Phillips of Indianapolis Brebeuf (2007) played for Xavier, while Purdue had two Miss Basketballs—Brittany Rayburn of Attica (2008) and Courtney Moses of Oak Hill in Converse (2010).

The fifth was Skylar Diggins of Notre Dame (2009), a sophomore guard from South Bend Washington High School who once again proved that Indiana turns out classic roundballers.

She didn't get to help cut down the nets as a result of an Irish championship on the night of April 5, 2011—senior Danielle Adams and her Texas A&M teammates had that honor, beating Notre Dame, 76-70, in a battle of No. 2 seeds to give the Rams and their colorful coach, Gary Blair, their first national title. UConn and Stanford, which lost to Texas A&M in the semifinals, 63-62, were the No. 1 seeds.

Diggins was spectacular in the tournament. Skylar, who averaged 14 points in the regular season, had 24 points in a 73-59 victory over perennial power Tennessee that put Notre Dame in the Final Four. She followed that with a career-high 28 points in a 72-63 semifinal triumph that ended Connecticut's two-year championship run.

That game pitted Diggins against UConn's senior sensation, Maya Moore, National Player of the Year. Richard Deitsch, writing in his *Inside College Basketball* column for SI.com, described well the artistry of those two:

"Back and forth they went, Maya Moore of UConn and Notre Dame's Skylar Diggins, each offering magic on the floor of the Conseco Fieldhouse. There was Diggins, with a name that oozes basketball and a game as smooth as her name, driving into the lane, pump-faking her defender off her feet, and sinking a mid-range deuce. There was Moore, the four-time All-America, fronting her man on the baseline, dropping a nasty shoulder shake, and sticking a slick turnaround jumper. The game's rising sophomore star and the game's current queen engaged in a battle of Can You Top This?"

Deitsch went on to say, "The ending proved unexpected, but well-deserved. Moore finished with a game-high 36 points, but it was Diggins who walked away a winner . . . It was Notre Dame's first win over UConn in four games this season and ended an ignominious 12-game losing streak to the Huskies. Diggins finished with a season-high 28 points on 10-of-14 shooting and added six assists and two steals. It was one of the great performances in Final Four history and ended one of the great careers in the sport. Moore led UConn to four consecutive Final Four appearances and two national titles. The stat that defines her above all? Her college record: 150-4."

Two of Indiana's finest, Diggins and Kelly Faris of Connecticut, also a sophomore from Plainfield, were teammates on the 2009 Indiana

All-Star team. Faris was the No. 2 All-Star. She had four points, seven rebounds and five assists against the Irish in only her 10th career loss—eight while winning four Class 2A state championships at Heritage Christian High School and just two at UConn.

Kelly lauded Diggins, who played for a state championship all four years at South Bend Washington, going 1-3. She has averaged 26.5 points in five title games in Indianapolis.

"She's a great player and a very smart player, and she was hitting everything," Faris told *The Indianapolis Star*. "She came out with the mentality this wasn't going to be her last game and she carried her team tonight."

Irish coach Muffet McGraw was equally complimentary of Diggins.

"She really stepped up her game in the NCAA tournament, and particularly as the games went on," she said. "At the regional, being MVP as a sophomore, what an accomplishment. I think she came into the season as somebody people were aware of, obviously, since she was on the Naismith list.

'"She gave her self a big shot of credibility coming into next year as one of the top players in the Big East and one of the top players in the country."

Diggins' stats were again formidable in the championship game—23 points, three rebounds, three assists and four steals. But Danielle Adams was dominant for the Rams with 30 points and nine rebounds. She had 22 points in the second half after the Irish led at the break, 32-26.

Blair said it best in his southern drawl, "In the second half, Danielle Adams said, 'Forget my jump shot, let's take it to the paint, Momma.' " Momma knew best to the pleasure of the thousands of Rams fans in the crowd of 17,473.

A sixth Indiana Miss Basketball, Sharon Versyp of Mishawaka (1984), also participated in the tournament as Purdue coach. The Boilermakers returned to the tournament after missing in 2010. They were a No. 9 seed and lost to UConn after beating No. 8 seed Kansas State.

Purdue is the only Big Ten team to win a national championship, doing so in 1999 with Stephanie White, 1995 Miss Basketball from West Lebanon, and Katie Douglas of Indianapolis Perry Meridian High School, in the lineup.

"We are a young team and have everyone returning," Versyp, a former Boilermaker player, said. "There's nothing but great things to come from this experience."

A seventh Indiana Miss Basketball, Bria Goss of Indianapolis Ben Davis (2011), a University of Kentucky recruit, scored 12 points, grabbed eight rebounds and handed out three assists for the Red team in the Women's Basketball Coaches Association High School All-American Game at Conseco Fieldhouse on April 2 as part of the Women's Final Four weekend. The Red team lost to the White team, 83-73.

Women's basketball in Indiana is alive and well, and it will only get better with talent like Diggins, Faris, Rayburn, Moses and Goss.

SUE DONOHOE

When Sue Donohoe wasn't fly-casting in the Snake River by Jackson Hole, Wyoming, or playing golf on her home course—Gray Eagle—in Fishers, she was a "basketball person" in 12 years at the NCAA, and a very good one.

Donohoe, who grew up in Pineville, La., was the NCAA vice president of Division I women's basketball since Nov. 1, 2003. She is extremely proud of how well received around the country the 30th NCAA Women's Final Four was the weekend of April 1-5, 2011, in Indianapolis.

In late October 2011, Donohoe announced she would be leaving the NCAA before the first of the year for family and personal reasons. She left behind a full and positive legacy for women's basketball.

"When you look at not only the two semifinal games but the national championship game and you look at everything that happened that surrounded the Women's Final Four, it was just a game-changer," Donohoe said as she sat in the lobby of the NCAA headquarters.

"We had two great semifinal games and a national championship game that captured the attention of the country. Folks were talking about Notre Dame basketball and Texas A&M basketball, and they never talked about 'em like that before."

There was a strong Indiana girls' high school basketball flavor to

the tournament. Skylar Diggins of South Bend Washington, Miss Basketball in 2009, and Kelly Faris of Plainfield who played at Indianapolis Heritage Christian and was the No. 2 Indiana All-Star in '09, met in the second semifinal game during the Final Four.

Diggins had an outstanding Final Four for Notre Dame, which beat Faris' Connecticut team, 72-63. The Irish then lost to Texas A&M, 76-70, in the championship game at Conseco Fieldhouse.

Amber Harris of Indianapolis North Central and Ta'Shia Phillips of Indianapolis Brebeuf, both Miss Basketballs (Harris in 2006, Phillips in 2007), competed for Xavier, which lost before the Final Four. In the WNBA Draft held shortly after the Final Four, Harris went to the Minnesota Lynx as the No. 4 pick and Phillips to the Atlanta Dream as the No. 8 selection.

Sue Donohoe (Photo courtesy of Sue Donohoe)

Kayla Pedersen of Stanford, which lost 63-62, to A&M, in a semifinal game at the Final Four, went to the Indiana Fever in the WNBA Draft as a No. 9 choice.

The difference in quality between the championship game of the Men's Final Four between Connecticut and Butler (UConn won, 53-41) televised by CBS on April 4 from Houston and the championship game of the Women's Final Four between Texas A&M and Notre Dame televised by ESPN was stark. Butler shot only 18.8 percent, an all-time low for the tournament. A&M and Notre Dame combined to shoot .505 percent.

Of the men's championship game, Donohoe said, "It's a shame, because you feel bad for both teams when they don't have a good game. It just happened that on that championship night regretfully you had two teams that didn't have great games and you hate it for everybody involved.

"There have been years at the Women's Final Four when you get down to that championship night and the teams just don't play at their best. And it's regretful, because you hope that when they're on a national platform like that, they perform at their utmost level. I think we were very fortunate that that happened in both of our semifinal games and in our championship game."

Donohoe is very positive about the future of women's basketball, but she's also very realistic.

"I think women have proven themselves in basketball, but I also think it's an on-going process, where they have to prove themselves time and time again," she said. "There's nothing wrong with that.

"I realize that women's basketball has its challenges. We are challenged in the sports market, but I also feel very positive that we can continue to carve out our niche in the market place."

Donohoe told about talking with a woman who went to the Final Four.

" 'I've never watched an entire women's game,' the woman said. 'And I watched that Notre Dame-A&M game and I'm now hooked forever.' That's what it takes. It's one fan at a time, one experience at a time."

Even though Sue admits that she wasn't very good as a player at Pineville High School in central Louisiana, basketball became her passion.

"I wasn't much of a defensive stopper, but I could shoot the ball, right- or left-handed, and I worked hard," she said. "I enjoyed every minute of the game and I played early-on in college at Louisiana Tech. Then I realized I had tapped out my skill level. But I stayed really involved in the game in a variety of different ways."

Donohoe graduated summa cum laude from Louisiana Tech in 1981, then earned a master's degree in physiology in 1983 while serving for two seasons as a graduate assistant coach for the Lady Techsters. It was in the latter capacity that Sue developed a strong relationship with Gary Blair, who coached Texas A&M to its first national championship at Conseco Fieldhouse.

"Gary and I coached together at Louisiana Tech," she said. "He was an assistant coach and I was a graduate assistant. We won the first-ever NCAA Women's Final Four in 1982. We beat Cheney State.

"Then I went and coached high school ball in Texas (from 1983 to 1990 she compiled a 124-24 record). In the meantime Gary became head coach at Stephen F. Austin and I was an assistant with him three years. Then Gary took the Arkansas job and I coached with him one year, then I moved into administration.

"It was fun to watch how thrilled Gary was at the Final Four in Indianapolis, with one, just being there, then two, winning the whole thing. It was one of those special times for him."

Donohoe was associate commissioner of the Southland Conference when she interviewed for a position as a director at the NCAA a few days before Thanksgiving 1999.

"They told me I would hear from them in a couple of weeks," she related. "I heard from them in two days. They offered me the job and I accepted it. I moved here in January of 2000, about six months after the NCAA opened in Indianapolis. My first Women's Final Four was in 2000.

Sue Donohoe (right), former NCAA vice president for Division I Women's Basketball, talks basketball with Condoleezza Rice, Secretary of State under President George W. Bush. Rice, a former Stanford professor (political science) and Provost, sat with Donohoe at the 2011 women's Final Four at Conseco Fieldhouse. Stanford lost to eventual champion Texas A&M. (Photo courtesy of Sue Donohoe)

"I was responsible for the operational elements of the championship, transportation and games management. I served in that role through 2003. Then I went over to the men's staff and served as the director of the men's tournament. I think the folks that had oversight for the men's championship felt I brought some good skills and talents, so I directed the men's championship for about 18 months. I loved every minute of it."

Sue says she was treated well while serving as director of the men's championship.

"Certainly the men coaches dealt with me very respectfully. I learned a great deal and some of the things I learned on the men's side I transferred to the women's side. I think those things have made the women's championship a better championship.

"When the opportunity came for me to come back on the women's side, I was elated. This game has been a part of me since I was knee-high. To come back to a leadership role within women's basketball was really important to me. I felt like I could definitely impact the game."

Donohoe didn't take up golf until she started coaching.

"Coach Blair told me, 'Sue, if you're going to be in coaching, you've gotta play golf, because everybody plays golf.' I had been playing about six months and I was horrible. I said, 'This is the hardest game I've ever played in my life,' and I consider myself pretty athletic."

Then a most unusual thing happened. One of the guys Sue was playing with was left-handed. He left a club on the ground and she picked it up.

"I started swinging it left-handed and it was the most natural feeling in the world to me," she said. "I had been playing right-handed, but I do a lot of things left-handed. It's kind of a weird thing, but it works for me. Although I'm right-handed, I play golf left-handed."

In her NCAA office, Donohoe had signed books by Indiana native John Wooden and Byron Nelson. She met Wooden several times in Indianapolis and also in his adopted state of California, and she met Nelson at his Texas golf tournament.

"In my mind, those were two wise gentlemen with gentle souls," she said. "I think their contributions to mankind will be everlasting in many ways."

Wooden always said he enjoyed the way women play basketball, because their game is so fundamentally sound.

"I think coach Wooden was absolutely right," Sue stated. "The women's game is played a little bit different than the men's game. I think our student-athletes play good fundamental ball and they play team ball."

Women's basketball has not had major scandals such as have happened in the men's game.

"I credit our coaches for having been great caretakers of the game," Sue said. "Some of our legendary coaches have understood what it means to be a guardian of the game. I think one of the challenges we have now is that our up-and-coming coaches continue to guard and protect the game with the same care that some of our legendary coaches have done.

"I think that's critical, because the bigger the game gets and the more resources that are applied to the game the more careful and more protective of the game that we have to be."

Why is Jackson Hole and the Snake River so appealing to Donohoe?

"I can stand in the middle of that river and I can see bald eagles flying over the river and see buffalo out in the pastures," she said.

Sue Donohoe was a graduate assistant for the Louisiana Tech team that won the first NCAA Division I women's championship. (Photo courtesy of Sue Donohoe)

"It's just me and the river and the fly rod. That's the one place I can probably get away and let the world pass me by for a little bit.

"I'm pretty good in that river. I like grilled rainbow trout. I'll always take some home to my family. I don't keep 'em all. I catch and release a lot."

Sue taught herself how to make fishing rods. She made a fishing rod for everybody in her family. Her brother-in-law has a casting rod, her nephew a spinning rod.

"I also made one for my mom and my dad, my sister and my nieces and nephews," she said. "It took me about a year-and-a-half to make them all. It was kind of fun."

Jackson Hole is at the south entrance to Yellow Stone Park.

"There are days when I'm at Jackson Hole that I'll drive into Yellow Stone and spend the day," she said. "I've rented a Jeep from the same rental car place for about 10 years, so they know what I want and when I'm coming. I'll get out in the park and walk and have lunch at the lodge. I go by myself and I enjoy it."

Life has indeed been good for the "basketball person," who loves to fish and golf, and she does those well, too.

LEARN FROM THE BEST: INDIANA CAMPS

So you would like to become a girl basketball player with more than a little skill. Here is a sampling of basketball instructional programs in Indiana that might enhance that goal:

Billy Keller Basketball Camps
Phone: (317) 218-3827
Email: learntoshoot@billykellercamps.com
Keller was 1965 Indiana Mr. Basketball after helping Indianapolis Washington High School to a state championship. He was an all-Big Ten guard at Purdue and was a member of the American Basketball Association Indiana Pacers championship teams of 1970, '72 and '73. A 1992 inductee into the Indiana Basketball Hall of Fame, Keller is the Director of Player Development for the Pacers.

Butler Basketball Camps
Address: Hinkle Fieldhouse, 4600 Sunset Ave., Indianapolis (46208)
Phone: (317) 940-9375
Website: MyOnlineCamp.com
Beth Couture is the coach of the Lady Bulldogs.

Champions Academy
Women's Director: April McDivitt-Foster
Address: 8990 Stonewick Way, Zionsville (46077)
Phone: (317) 847-3853
Email: april@fosteringchampions.com
Ed Schilling, former Division I college head coach (Wright-State), National Basketball Association assistant coach (New York Nets) and head high school coach (Logansport and Park Tudor), is founder and CEO. McDivitt-Foster, from Connsersville was Indiana Miss Basketball in 1999.

Crown Point High School Camps
Address: 1500 S. Main St., Crown Point (45307)
Phone: (219) 663-4885
Website: crownpointbasketballcamps.com

Dream Makers Camps, Where Dedication Meets Dreams
Contact: Lisa Shepherd-Stidham
Address: P.O. Box 255, Fishers (46038)
Phone: (317) 292-3099
Website: shepherdhoops.com
Shepherd-Stidham, the 1997 Indiana Miss Basketball from Richmond, is owner and instructor. Stacie Shepherd, an Indiana All-Star in 1990, assists her younger sister at the camps.

Indiana Basketball Academy
Address: 3800 Bauer Drive West, Indianapolis (46280)
Phone: (317) 844-6677
Tom Abernethy, starting forward on Indiana University's 1976 national championship team, the last to win NCAA title with a perfect record (32-0), is founder and owner.

Indiana State Basketball Camps
Address: ISU Arena, Suite 107, Terre Haute (47809)
Phone: (812) 237-8357
Email: melanie.boeglin@indstate.edu
Teri Moren is head coach of the Lady Sycamores.

Indiana University Basketball Camps
Address: Assembly Hall and Cook Hall Practice Facility,
      Bloomington (47405)
Phone: (812) 855-3013
Website: hoosiersportscamps.com
Felisha Legette-Jack is head coach of the Lady Hoosiers.

Notre Dame Basketball Camps
Address: WNDU, 54516 Indiana SR 933, South Bend (46637)
Phone: (574) 631-8788
Email: ndcamps@nd.edu
Muffet McGraw is head coach of the Lady Irish.

Purdue Basketball Camps
Contact: Terry Kix
Address: Mackey Arena, West Lafayette (47907)
Phone: (765) 413-3804
Email: tkix@purdue.edu
Sharon Versyp is the head coach of the Lady Boilermakers.

Rick Mount Shooting School
Address: D-1 Basketball Camps, 209 N. Illinois St., Monticello (47960)
Phone: 1-800-407-DONE
Rick Mount, 1966 Indiana Mr. Basketball from Lebanon High School, was the first high schooler to be on the cover of *Sports Illustrated* magazine as a member of a team sport. He was Big Ten Player of the Year twice and led the Boilermakers to a runner-up finish in the 1969 NCAA tournament. As a professional, Mount played for the Pacers, Kentucky Colonels and Memphis Sounds.

The Fieldhouse in Fishers
Address: 11825 Technology Drive, Fishers (46038)
Phone: (317) 842-2255
Website: thefieldhouse.com

The Monon Center
Address: 1235 Central Park Drive East, Carmel (46032)
Phone: (317) 848-7275
There are three basketball courts among many sports activities operated by Carmel Clay Parks and Recreation.

University of Evansville Basketball Camps
Camp Director: Nicki Motto
Address: 1800 Lincoln Avenue, Evansville (47722)
Phone: (812) 488-2957
Website: gopurpleaces.com
Otis Epps is head coach of the Lady Aces.

Valparaiso High School Camps
Address: 2727 N. Campbell, Valparaiso (46383)
Phone: (219) 531-3080
Website: valpohighsportscamps.com

Valparaiso University Basketball Camps
Contact: Sherry Williams
Address: Athletics-Recreation Center, Valparaiso (46383)
Phone: (219) 464-5146
Email: Sherry.Williams@valpo.edu
Keith Freeman is head coach of the Lady Crusaders.

INDIANA MISS BASKETBALL RECIPIENTS

YEAR	PLAYER	TEAM
1976	Judi Warren	Warsaw Tigers
1977	Teri Rosinki	Norwell Knights of Ossian
1978	Chanda Kline	Warsaw Tigers
1979	LaTaunya Pollard	Roosevelt Rough Riders (East Chicago)
1980	Maria Stack	Columbus East Olympians
1981	Cheryl Cook	Washington Continentals (Indianapolis)
1982	Trena Keys	Marion Giants
1983	Jody Beerman	Heritage Patriots (Monroeville)
1984	Sharon Versyp	Mishawaka Cavemen
1985	Jodie Whitaker	Austin Eagles
1986	Kim Barrier	Jimtown Jimmies (Elkhart)
1987	Lori Meinerding	Northrop Bruins (Fort Wayne)
1988	Vicki Hall	Brebeuf Braves (Indianapolis)
1989	Renee Westmoreland	Scottsburg Warriors
1990	Patricia Babcock	Culver Girls Academy Eagles
1991	Jennifer Jacoby	Rossville Hornets
1992	Marla Inman	Bedford North Lawrence Stars
1993	Abby Conklin	Charlestown Pirates
1994	Tiffany Gooden	Snider Panthers (Fort Wayne)
1995	Stephanie White	Seeger Patriots (West Lebanon)
1996	Lisa Winter	Huntington North Vikings
1997	Lisa Shepherd	Richmond Red Devils
1998	Kelly Komara	Lake Central Indians (St. John)
1999	April McDivitt	Connersville Spartans
2000	Sara Nord	Jeffersonville Red Devils
2001	Shyra Ely	Ben Davis Giants (Indianapolis)

YEAR	PLAYER	TEAM
2002	Shanna Zolman	Wawasee Warriors (Syracuse)
2003	Katie Geralds	Beech Grove Hornets (Indianapolis)
2004	Jaclyn Leininger	Warsaw Tigers
2005	Jodi Howell	Alexandria Monroe Tigers
2006	Amber Harris	North Central Panthers (Indianapolis)
2007	Ta'Shia Phillips	Brebeuf Braves (Indianapolis)
2008	Brittany Rayburn	Attica Red Ramblers
2009	Skylar Diggins	Washington Panthers (South Bend)
2010	Courtney Moses	Oak Hill Golden Eagles of Converse
2011	Bria Goss	Ben Davis Giants (Indianapolis)

INDIANA BASKETBALL HALL OF FAME INDUCTEES

NAME	INDUCTED	TEAM
Cathy Beesley Acton	2010	Western Boone Stars (Thorntown)
Cindy Beesley Aguirre	2011	Western Boone Stars
Bernita Adkins	2004	Mexico Bulldogs (Dubois County)
Linda Kay Rule Barnett	2003	Clinton Central Bulldogs (Michigantown)
Jody Beerman Kelley	2010	Heritage Patriots (Monroeville)
Debbie Benak	2007	Bishop Noll Warriors (Hammond)
Carol Blauvelt	2007	Heritage Patriots
Jean Ann Bowers Walker	2002	Alexandria Tigers
Cindy Rice Brown	2002	New Salem Eagles
Tonya Burns-Cohrs	2010	Leo Lions
Jacqueline Graham Burton	2008	Crawfordsville Athenians
Jeannie Butler	2006	Wiley Red Streaks (Terre Haute)
Ruth Ann Doub Callon	2005	Silver Medalist for Meritorious Service (Whiteland Warriors)
Donna Cheatham	2003	Dupont Hornets
Dale Ciciora	2010	Liberty Center Lions
Betty Lou Clark	2008	Orleans Bulldogs
Ian Conner	2002	Silver Medalist for Meritorious Service (Benton Central, Bison, Oxford)

NAME	INDUCTED	TEAM
Cheryl Cook	2010	Washington Continentals (Indianapolis)
Dru Cox Pearcy	2004	Plainfield Quakers
Cindy Piet Cruz	2004	Scottsburg Warriors
Judy Cummings	2006	Brownsburg Bulldogs
Bobbi DeKemper	2002	Marian Heights Academy Highlanders
Lenore Doering Pletcher	2010	Wakarusa Indians
Claudia Kreicker Dozier	2009	Warsaw Tigers
Carmella Lynn Martin Dunn	2003	Washington Senators (East Chicago)
Lin Dunn	2010	Silver Medalist for Meritorious Service (Dresden, Tenn.; Purdue University Coach; Indiana Fever Coach)
Carla Eades Krebs	2009	Madison Cubs
1977 Team	2009	Roosevelt Rough Riders (East Chicago)
1979 Team	2009	Roosevelt Rough Riders (East Chicago)
Mary Louise Eisenhardt	2006	Madison Cubs
Ruth Heitman Elliott	2005	Huntingburg Happy Hunters
Jane Emke	2011	Seymour Owls
Cheryl Endicott Weatherman	2005	St. Bernice
Fred Fields	2011	Muncie South Rebels
1986 Team	2011	Northrop Bruins (Fort Wayne)
Rita Foster	2008	Jac-Cen-Del Eagles (Osgood)

NAME	INDUCTED	TEAM
Debbie Funkhouser	2008	Zionsville Eagles
Connie Garrett	2004	Marion Giants
Lisa Goodin	2007	Austin Eagles
Barbara Jean Graves	2005	Madison Heights Argylls (Anderson)
Elza Purvlicis Harris	2009	North Central Panthers (Indianapolis)
Margaret Eleanor Kelly	2003	Ladywood St. Agnes Academy (Indianapolis)
Trina Keys	2009	Marion Giants
Chanda Kline	2004	Warsaw Tigers
Wayne Kreiger	2006	Huntington Vikings
Lamar Kilmer	2007	Syracuse Yellow Jackets
Debbie Law Marr	2009	Columbus North Bull Dogs
Dru Lisman	2011	Sullivan Golden Arrows
Florida Lowry	2004	Fontanet Beantowners
Linda Mallender	2010	Southport Cardinals (Indianapolis)
Tom May	2009	Cannelton Bulldogs
Debra McClurg	2007	Wes-Del Warriors (Gaston)
Janice McCracken O'Brien	2011	Vincennes Lincoln Alices
Kyle O'Brien Stevens	2011	North Central Panthers (Indianapolis)
Amy Metheny	2008	Southport Cardinals (Indianapolis)
Cecilia Marie Mimms	2003	Cathedral Irish (Indianapolis)

NAME	INDUCTED	TEAM
Steve Neff	2006	Wakarusa Indians
Laura Newcomb Titus	2011	Rochester Zebras
Rochelle Newell	2004	Rochester Zebras
LaTaunya Pollard-Romanazzi	2005	Roosevelt Rough Riders (East Chicago)
Rita Price Simpson	2004	Bourbon Trojans
Marilyn Ramsey	2005	Union Rockets (Modoc)
Nancy Rehm	2009	Bishop Luers Knights (Fort Wayne)
Teri Lynn Rosinski	2003	Norwell Knights
Patricia Roy	2003	Silver Medalist (Harlan Hawks)
Mary Beth Schueth Cain	2008	Perry Meridian Falcons (Indianapolis)
Barbara Skinner	2005	Mount Vernon Maurauders
Janice Soyez	2002	University High Normal, Ill. (Warsaw's state championship coach, 1976, 1978)
Melinda Sparkman	2010	Scottsburg Warriors
Liz Skinner Spencer	2008	Mount Vernon Maurauders
Maria Stack	2007	Columbus East Olympians
Donna Sullivan	2002	Orleans Bulldogs
Phyllis Tubbs	2007	Silver Medalist for Meritorious Service

NAME	INDUCTED	TEAM
Carol Tumey	2011	Silver Medalist for Meritorious Service (Leavenworth Rivermen & Wyandottes)
Normela Upshaw	2005	Roosevelt Rough Riders (East Chicago)
Sharon Versyp	2010	Mishawaka Cavemen
Jennifer Voreis	2009	North Judson-San Pierre Bluejays
Debra Walker-Augurson	2011	LaSalle Lions (South Bend)
Judi Warren	2002	Warsaw Tigers
1976 Team	2008	Warsaw Tigers
1978 Team	2008	Warsaw Tigers
Cathy Welch-Conrad	2006	Tippecanoe Valley Vikings
Jodie Whitaker	2011	Austin Eagles
Theresia Wynns	2009	Silver Medalist for Meritorious Service (Indiana High School Athletic Association assistant commissioner)
Darlene Zinn	2006	Carroll Cougars (Flora)